The Complete Book of
US PRESIDENTS

The Complete Book of
US PRESIDENTS

Third Edition

Bill Yenne

CRESTLINE

© 2016 Quarto Publishing Group USA Inc.
Text © 2016 and 2020 Bill Yenne

This edition published in 2020 by Crestline,
an imprint of The Quarto Group,
142 West 36th Street, 4th Floor,
New York, NY, 10018
T (212) 779-4972 F (212) 779-6058
www.QuartoKnows.com

First published in 2016 by Zenith Press, an imprint of The Quarto Group,
100 Cummings Center Suite 265D, Beverly, MA 01915.

10 9 8 7 6 5 4 3 2

Crestline titles are also available at discount for retail, wholesale, promotional, and bulk purchase. For details, contact the Special Sales Manager by email at specialsales@quarto.com or by mail at The Quarto Group, Attn: Special Sales Manager, 100 Cummings Center Suite 265D, Beverly, MA 01915, USA.

ISBN: 978-0-7858-3845-6

Project Manager: Sherry Anisi
Art Director and Cover Design: James Kegley
Layout: Bill Yenne

Printed in China EV072020

Contents

George Washington

THE ONLY PRESIDENT UNAFFILIATED WITH A POLITICAL PARTY

The first president of the United States, George Washington was also famously eulogized by Gen. Henry "Light Horse Harry" Lee, who served under Washington during the American Revolution, as "first in war, first in peace, and first in the hearts of his countrymen." He was the only president to be unanimously elected by the Electoral College, the only president who was not a member of a political party, and the only president not to reside at the White House. A charismatic figure, he served as commander in chief of the Continental Army during the American Revolution and went on to serve two terms as president. He

was Episcopalian, but like many of the founding fathers of the United States, he was also a member of the Freemasons.

Washington was born on February 22, 1732, in Westmoreland County, Virginia, the eldest of the six children of Augustine Washington, a modestly successful tobacco planter, and his second wife, Mary Ball Washington. The family had been in Virginia since 1656, when George's great grandfather, John Washington, immigrated from Purleigh, Essex, in England. Four of his siblings, as well as his two half brothers, Augustine's sons from his first marriage to Jane Butler Washington, lived to adulthood.

top: A George Washington portrait by Rembrandt Peale. *National Portrait Gallery*

left: George Washington and his generals as seen in an 1870 engraving by A. H. Ritchie. *National Archives*

When he was eleven, George's father died and he was taken under the wing of his half brother, Lawrence, who was politically well connected in nearby Stafford County. Through Lawrence, he met Lord Fairfax and was hired on to a survey expedition into the wilds of the Shenandoah Mountains in 1748. This was to make a lasting impression on the young Washington. Subsequently, he received an appointment as the official surveyor for Culpeper County. In 1752, when Lawrence died of tuberculosis, George inherited his estate at Mount Vernon. He also was named to a post as a leader in the Virginia Militia in which Lawrence had served. George found his calling as a military man.

In 1753, on the eve of the French and Indian War, Lieutenant Governor Robert Dinwiddie sent a militia unit under Washington's command into the upper Ohio Valley (now western Pennsylvania) to underscore the British claim to the region in the face of French incursions. In a skirmish with a French detachment, the French officer in charge was killed. Washington was captured, but released.

In 1755, Washington returned to the Ohio Country as aide to Gen. Edward Braddock, who led a major British offensive against the French. When Braddock was killed, Washington

-: George Washington at the signing of the US Constitution on September 17, 1787, by Howard Chandler Christy. *Architect of the Capitol*

above: Washington rallying the troops at the Battle of Monmouth on June 28, 1778. *National Archives*

FIRST LADY
MARTHA WASHINGTON

Born on June 13, 1731, in New Kent County, Virginia, Martha Dandridge was the eldest daughter of planter and English immigrant John Dandridge and his wife, Frances Jones. In 1750, she married Daniel Parke Custis, with whom she had two children who lived to young adulthood. Martha "Patsy" Custis died at seventeen, and John "Jacky" Custis died at twenty-seven while serving in the Revolutionary War. Martha inherited substantial agricultural land upon the death of her first husband.

Martha married George Washington, eight months her junior, on January 6, 1759. While George was commuting to New York and Philadelphia for his various prewar activities, she remained at Mount Vernon. However, during the war, she joined him while the Continental Army was in winter quarters. Though she did not attend George's first inauguration in New York, she moved to New York and was with him there and in Philadelphia during his presidency. Like her husband, she lived her final years at Mount Vernon and was interred there. She died on May 22, 1802. On the centennial of her death, in 1902, she became the first woman commemorated on a United States postage stamp.

Martha Washington by Eliphalet Frazer Andrews. *White House*

heroically rallied the troops, turning a chaotic retreat into an organized withdrawal. Dinwiddie, now governor, promoted Washington to colonel and made him commander of the Virginia regiment, the first permanent all-colonial unit led by an American-born commander.

In 1759, after the French and Indian War, Washington married Martha Dandridge Custis, a wealthy widow with two children, and settled down at Mount Vernon. As a gentleman farmer, he diversified away from tobacco and into grain and livestock.

By the 1760s, there was a growing dissatisfaction with British rule in the colonies, especially as exemplified by the Stamp Act of 1765 and the Townshend Acts of 1767, which were decried as "taxation without representation." Washington became outspoken in the protests and was named as a Virginia delegate to the First Continental Congress in 1774. At the Second Continental Congress in 1775, held in the wake of the Battles of Lexington and Concord, the Continental Army was created and Washington was named as its commander in chief. As such, he was responsible for raising the army, training it, and providing it with both supplies and strategic direction.

The British sent a sizable force under Gen. William Howe to defeat Washington and quell the rebellion, but the initial

George Washington and his family, painted by Edward Savage between 1789 and 1796. Pictured from left to right are step-grandson and adopted son George Washington Parke Custis, George Washington himself, Eleanor Parke Custis, and Martha Washington. Eleanor, known as "Nelly," was the granddaughter of Martha Washington and the step-granddaughter of George Washington. *National Gallery of Art*

American victory at Bunker Hill in June 1775 was more costly than anticipated. After initial defeats, Washington's Continental Army achieved a decisive victory at Boston in March 1776 but was defeated on Long Island in August 1776, shortly after the Declaration of Independence was adopted on July 4. Having escaped encirclement in New York City, Washington scored a daring win at Trenton, New Jersey, on Christmas Day 1776 by leading his troops across the icy Delaware River in the dead of night.

In September 1777, after the British captured Philadelphia, the United States capital, unopposed, Washington's troops decisively defeated the British at Saratoga. This victory was a morale booster and the event that convinced the French to intervene as allies of the United States. Washington's Continental Army spent a difficult winter at Valley Forge, Pennsylvania, but survived intact and forced the British to withdraw from Philadelphia in 1778.

In October 1781, with the French fleet opposing the British offshore, Washington achieved a final victory over the British, defeating Gen. Charles Cornwallis at Yorktown, Virginia. In November 1783, after the signing of the Treaty of Paris, the British made their final withdrawal from the United States and Washington disbanded the Continental Army.

George Washington attended the Constitutional Convention in Philadelphia in the summer of 1787 and was elected as its president. Using his powers of persuasion, he ensured that the Constitution was ratified by all thirteen states. In January 1789, he was unanimously elected by the Electoral College to serve as the first person to hold the office of president of the United States. In 1792, he was elected, again unanimously, to a second four-year term, although he had considered not running. Elected as his vice president both times was John Adams of Massachusetts, who would go on to be elected as the second president of the United States.

Washington was sworn in as president at Federal Hall in New York, but while in office, he presided over plans to build a new "federal city." It would be located at a site on the Potomac River that he personally selected. Incorporating land from Maryland and Virginia, this federal enclave was known as the District of Columbia.

While in office, Washington oversaw ratification of the Bill of Rights and worked with Congress to create many institutions that are still an integral part of the United States government. Washington played a key role in the creation of the Supreme Court (then with six members) and the federal district courts. He established the first presidential cabinet, comprising the first executive departments, beginning with

General George Washington and Gilbert du Motier, the Marquis de Lafayette, review the Continental Army at Valley Forge in Pennsylvania, the quarters of the army through the winter of 1777–1778 during the American Revolutionary War. This painting by John Ward Dunsmore was published in 1907. *Library of Congress*

VICE PRESIDENT

JOHN ADAMS

A member of the Continental Congress from Massachusetts and the former ambassador to France and to Great Britain, John Adams was elected as vice president in the Electoral College balloting in 1789. Under rules then in effect, electors cast two ballots, with the higher vote getter being named as president and the runner-up being named vice president. George Washington received sixty-nine votes, which was moot because he was elected president unanimously. Adams was second with thirty-four. In 1792, Washington was again elected unanimously, and Adams again came in second. In 1796, Adams was elected as president of the United States; he is discussed in the following chapter.

Washington's famous crossing of the Delaware River on December 25, 1776, as painted in 1851. *Emanuel Leutze*

State, Treasury, and War, and named the first secretaries of these departments. Also at cabinet level, he appointed an attorney general and a postmaster general.

Political polarization within the Washington presidency revolved mainly around disagreements between those who favored a more prominent role for the individual states and those, calling themselves Federalists, who favored a strong federal government. The former faction was led by secretary of state and future president Thomas Jefferson, while the Federalists were led by Vice President John Adams and Secretary of the Treasury Alexander Hamilton. Indeed, they created the Federalist Party, the first United States political party. As a Federalist and head of the Treasury Department, Hamilton favored creation of a "national bank," the First Bank of the United States, which existed until 1811.

Hamilton favored taxation as a means of paying down the national debt, which led to a tax on distilled spirits, the first on a domestic product, enacted in 1791. Initially seen as minimally invasive, the tax was immensely unpopular among western farmers who distilled corn into whiskey

because, pound for pound, it was cheaper to ship, making them more able to compete for the national market with eastern farmers. When shots were fired and disagreement escalated into the widespread Whiskey Rebellion, it startled Washington, who feared a full-scale revolt. Thus, Washington was compelled to assume direct command of militia troops under his presidential role as commander in chief. This was a clear illustration of the primacy of the federal government over the states and Washington's biggest domestic crisis as president. After his troops prevailed, Washington pardoned those whom he defeated.

On the foreign policy front, Jefferson and Hamilton were at odds over how to react to the French Revolution in 1789 to 1792, during which time France and Britain were at war. Jefferson favored active support for the rebels, while Hamilton favored neutrality, a position supported by Washington. Meanwhile, there was continued trouble between the United States and Britain on the western frontier and on the high seas, but diplomatic efforts by the Washington administration successfully resolved many of the issues, avoided another war,

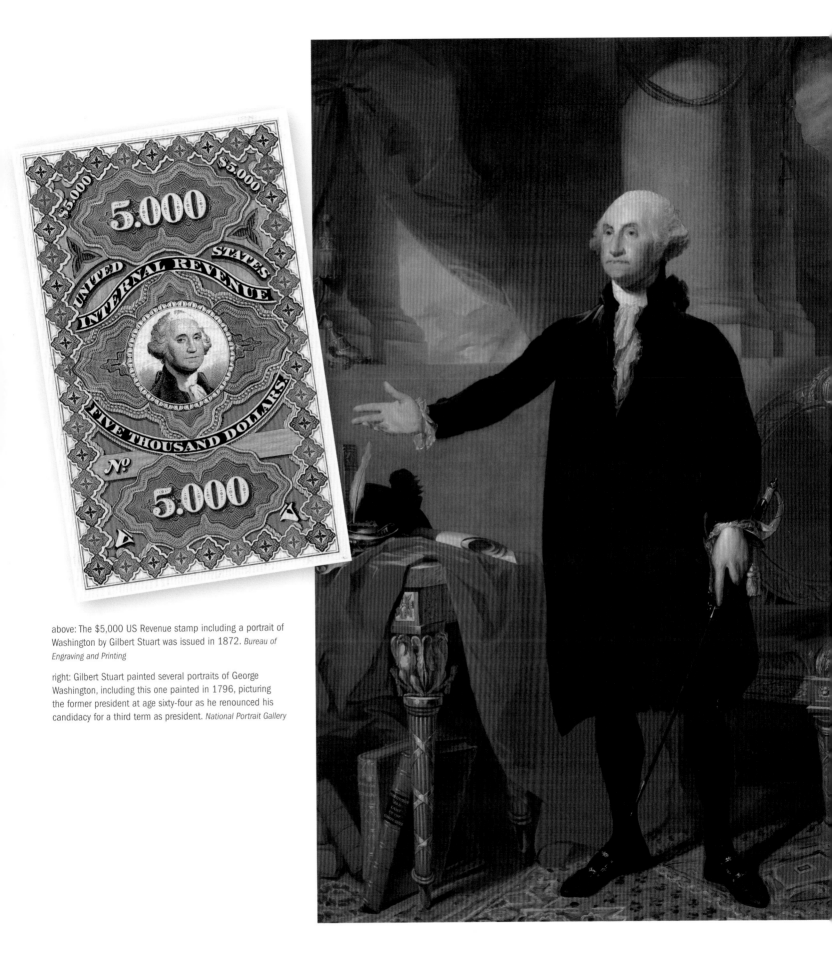

above: The $5,000 US Revenue stamp including a portrait of Washington by Gilbert Stuart was issued in 1872. *Bureau of Engraving and Printing*

right: Gilbert Stuart painted several portraits of George Washington, including this one painted in 1796, picturing the former president at age sixty-four as he renounced his candidacy for a third term as president. *National Portrait Gallery*

George Washington 11

above: By 1795, with the admission of the original thirteen colonies, the United States flag had thirteen stars and thirteen stripes. There were several variants, with the one above being the most famous. Legend holds that it was created by Betsy Ross of Philadelphia. *Author's collection*

below: Some of the dozens of United States stamps featuring the likeness of George Washington have included, from left to right, a three-cent 1861 issue, a three-cent proprietary revenue stamp issued in 1871, and a two-cent postage stamp from 1883. US Postal Service

and resulted in increased trade—although this led to friction with France. Under Washington, the United States was also able to negotiate unrestricted access to the Mississippi River, then controlled by Spain, which improved trading opportunities for Americans on the western frontier.

In 1796, Washington chose not to be a candidate for a third term, although he remained popular and it was likely that he would have been elected. This established an unwritten precedent until Franklin Roosevelt ran for a third term in 1940.

When George Washington assumed office, the United States consisted of thirteen colonies that had become states after their ratification of the Articles of Confederation. However, they are considered to have been "admitted" to the Union on the date that each ratified the United States Constitution, and only twelve had done so when Washington took office. Delaware, Pennsylvania, New Jersey, Georgia, Connecticut, Massachusetts, Maryland, South Carolina, New Hampshire, Virginia, and New York ratified the Constitution in that order in 1787 and 1788. During his presidency, North Carolina became the last of the original thirteen colonies to become a state, joined by Rhode Island, Vermont, Kentucky, and Tennessee.

George Washington retired to Mount Vernon and his long-neglected agricultural pursuits. Ironically, in light of his role in the Whiskey Rebellion, he became one of the leading whiskey distillers in the United States.

In 1789, as relations with France continued to deteriorate, President John Adams asked Washington to assume the role

George Washington's iconic Mount Vernon estate overlooks the Potomac River near Alexandria, Virginia. *Library of Congress*

of commander in chief of the US Army, to which he agreed. He delegated the organizational work for an army that never took the field to Alexander Hamilton.

On December 12, 1799, Washington became ill while inspecting his property during a sleet storm and died two days later at the age of sixty-seven. His actual cause of death is the subject of speculation, although bloodletting, then a common practice, is believed to have contributed greatly, because around half of his blood was drained during a short period of time. As they had no children, Martha Washington was his only heir.

George Washington was interred at Mount Vernon, though the plan was to move his body to a crypt beneath the United States Capitol. After several decades of debate, Washington was reinterred in a new crypt at Mount Vernon in 1831, where he remains. Washington is commemorated in a number of ways, including in the naming of the federal city as "Washington" and the construction of the 555-foot Washington Monument, the obelisk that is the tallest structure in that city and was the tallest in the world when completed in 1884. More than two dozen other cities and a state are named for him, and more than half of the states have a Washington County. His likeness has appeared on numerous coins and postage stamps, as well as on currency, including the current one-dollar bill.

In his famous eulogy, Harry Lee observed that Washington "was second to none in the humble and enduring scenes

GEORGE WASHINGTON'S NATIONAL PROCLAMATION, DECLARING NOVEMBER 26, 1789, AS THANKSGIVING DAY

October 3, 1789

Whereas it is the duty of all Nations to acknowledge the providence of Almighty God, to obey his will, to be grateful for his benefits, and humbly to implore his protection and favor, and whereas both Houses of Congress have by their joint Committee requested me "to recommend to the People of the United States a day of public thanksgiving and prayer to be observed by acknowledging with grateful hearts the many signal favors of Almighty God especially by affording them an opportunity peaceably to establish a form of government for their safety and happiness.

of private life; pious, just, humane, temperate, and sincere; uniform, dignified, and commanding, his example was as edifying to all around him as were the effects of that example lasting. To his equals he was condescending, to his inferiors kind, and to the dear object of his affections exemplarily tender; correct throughout, vice shuddered in his presence, and virtue always felt his fostering hand; the purity of his private character gave effulgence to his public virtues."

John Adams

FEDERALIST PARTY

John Adams was the first president of the United States to run in a contested election and the first to live in the White House, although it was not finished during his presidency. He was the only president for over two hundred years to have a son who also served in the office. Born on October 30, 1735, in Braintree (now Quincy), Massachusetts, he was the son of farmer and cobbler John Adams Sr. and Susanna Boylston Adams.

The Adams family had been in Massachusetts for six generations since Henry Adams emigrated from England in 1638. John Adams graduated from Harvard College in 1758, having considered becoming a Unitarian minister before deciding instead to become a lawyer. In 1764, Adams married Abigail Smith, the daughter of a Congregationalist minister in nearby Weymouth, Massachusetts. They corresponded regularly until her death in 1818, and the letters have been preserved.

By the 1760s, he was a leading proponent of colonial rights, especially in reaction to the 1765 Stamp Act and 1767 Townshend Acts, and joined those who were opposed to the idea of "taxation without representation." Thoughtful and methodical, John Adams was overshadowed by his charismatic and more outspoken second cousin Samuel Adams. After the 1770 Boston Massacre, in which five civilians were killed by British soldiers, Samuel Adams began calling for independence, while John Adams took the controversial step of volunteering to represent the British troops in their murder trial, famously saying that "it is more important that

innocence be protected than it is that guilt be punished." Six of eight British soldiers were acquitted.

John Adams was elected by Massachusetts to the First and Second Continental Congresses in 1774 and 1775 and nominated George Washington to command the Continental Army. He became a leading proponent of independence from Britain and the creation of the United States as a republic. In his 1776 pamphlet "Thoughts on Government," he wrote, "There is no good government but what is republican. That the only valuable part of the British constitution is so; because the very definition of a republic is an empire of laws, and not of men."

On May 15, 1776, he proposed a preamble to a resolution of the Continental Congress to authorize new governments in each of the colonies. Its approval propelled the Congress toward the final break with Great Britain.

During the War of Independence, Adams served first as head of the Board of War, the organization tasked with the administration of personnel and logistical support for the Continental Army, which was commanded by Washington. In 1778 and again in 1779, the Continental Congress sent him to France as the official envoy of the United States in Europe. In 1782, he negotiated the recognition of the United States by Holland and served as the first American ambassador to that country, then one of the few European republics. This also paved the way for substantial loans from banks in Amsterdam.

Adams was one of the signatories of the 1783 Treaty of Paris, which concluded the War of Independence, and in

above: The drafting committee of the Declaration of Independence delivering their final draft to the Continental Congress, as envisioned by John Trumbull. From the left, they are John Adams, Roger Sherman, Robert Livingston, Thomas Jefferson, and Benjamin Franklin. *Architect of the Capitol*

opposite: The official portrait of John Adams by John Trumbull, circa 1792. *White House*

1785, he was named as the first ambassador to Great Britain from the newly independent United States. Though he had written the Massachusetts Constitution largely on his own, his post in London prevented his attending the United States Constitutional Convention. He had already made his opinions on Federalism and republicanism well known when he drafted the 1780 Massachusetts Constitution. Like Thomas Jefferson, who was serving as ambassador to France, Adams communicated regularly with the delegates.

In 1789, Adams was elected as the first vice president of the United States, a post to which he was reelected in 1792. In both instances, he ran as a Federalist, while President George Washington claimed adherence to no political party. During his tenure in office, Adams was rarely consulted by Washington. In a letter to his wife, he expressed a sentiment that was to be shared by many future vice presidents, that the job is "the most insignificant office that ever the invention of man contrived or his imagination conceived." Adams did

JOHN ADAMS'S FIRST ANNUAL MESSAGE AS PRESIDENT

November 22, 1797

We are met together at a most interesting period. The situation of the principal powers of Europe is singular and portentous. Connected with some by treaties and with all by commerce, no important event there can be indifferent to us. Such circumstances call with peculiar importunity not less for a disposition to unite in all those measures on which the honor, safety, and prosperity of our country depend than for all the exertions of wisdom and firmness. In all such measures you may rely on my zealous and hearty concurrence.

serve actively in the vice presidential role as president of the United States Senate. As such, he cast more tie-breaking votes than any other vice president would.

In 1796, running as a Federalist, Adams was elected in the first contested presidential election, defeating his

FIRST LADY
ABIGAIL SMITH ADAMS

Born in Weymouth, Massachusetts, on November 22, 1744, Abigail was the daughter of Reverend William Smith and Elizabeth Quincy Smith, both of whom were from old New England families. Though not formally educated, Abigail and her sisters were home-schooled and exposed to the substantial libraries of their father and grandfather.

After she married John Adams, her third cousin, on October 25, 1764, they resided in Braintree before moving to Boston, where he practiced law. She remained at home, raising the children on her own, during her husband's extensive overseas assignments, though she joined him in Paris in 1784, taking son John Quincy and daughter Nabby with her. She was also with him while he served as ambassador to Britain.

As first lady, she is recalled as having been well read, intellectually sophisticated, and very much in tune with affairs of the day. Unlike Martha Washington, she took an active role in the social and political affairs of the nation's capital.

She died of typhoid on October 28, 1818, and was buried at the United First Parish Church in Quincy, Massachusetts.

The Children of John Adams and Abigail Adams
Abigail "Nabby" Adams Smith (1765–1813)
John Quincy Adams (1767–1848)
Grace Susanna "Suky" Adams (1768–1770)
Charles Adams (1770–1800)
Thomas Boylston Adams (1772–1832)
Elizabeth Adams (1777)

A portrait of Abigail Smith Adams, wife of President John Adams, painted by Gilbert Stuart, circa 1800–1815. *National Gallery of Art*

political rival Thomas Jefferson, who ran as a Democratic-Republican (originally called Republicans). It was a narrow win in the Electoral College, with Adams winning seventy-one votes to Jefferson's sixty-eight and 53.4 percent of the popular vote. Because Jefferson came in second, he was elected as vice president.

Adams was a firm believer in the Federalist principal of a strong central government, with which Jefferson disagreed. He also disagreed with fellow Federalist Alexander Hamilton over the question of becoming involved in the war between Britain and France, which began in 1792 in the wake of the French Revolution of 1789.

The overthrow of the French monarchy, which had been allied with the United States, and the American normalization of relations with Britain put the United States at odds with Republican France. This came to a head in the "XYZ Affair," in which France demanded bribes in exchange for normalization of relations.

When the French began attacking American merchant ships at sea, Adams resisted the call for war, maintaining Washington's policy of not being drawn into European alliances and conflicts. However, he increased the size of the US Navy in order to actively protect the American merchant fleet and added a Department of the Navy to his cabinet. The "Quasi War," as the undeclared naval conflict was called, continued from 1798 to 1800 and resulted in a number of French privateers being sunk or captured. It tapered to an end when Napoleon Bonaparte took power in France as first consul and struck a more conciliatory tone with the United States.

One of the most serious controversies during the Adams administration were the Alien and Sedition Acts, legislation that was favored by the Federalists and opposed by the Democratic-Republicans, which made it easier to imprison or deport aliens considered dangerous. Though they did not originate with Adams, the acts were unpopular, and he was unpopular for having signed them into law.

One of his last, and most lasting, acts as president was to name Federalist John Marshall as Chief Justice of the Supreme Court. Marshall remained in this post for thirty-four years, the formative years of the American legal system, consistently ruling in favor of the supremacy of federal law over state law.

In 1800, Adams stood for reelection against the backdrop of controversy and undeclared war, as well as with a gradual decline and disorganization of the Federalist Party. Adams came in third with sixty-five electoral votes. Thomas Jefferson and Aaron Burr, both Democratic-Republicans, were tied with seventy-three votes, and the election was put into the hands of the House of Representatives, who ultimately elected Thomas Jefferson as the third president.

Adams left Washington before Jefferson's inaugural, depressed by his having lost reelection and by the death of his son Charles. He is recalled as having lived longer as a former president, a quarter of a century, than any other until Herbert Hoover.

It was not until 1812 that he made up with Thomas Jefferson, but thereafter, the two ex-presidents carried on a long, voluminous, and cordial correspondence. He and Jefferson both died on July 4, 1826, the fiftieth anniversary of the signing of the Declaration of Independence. Adams's last words were reportedly, "Jefferson survives." He never learned that Jefferson died earlier the same day.

Adams outlived all but two of his children, Thomas Boylston and John Quincy Adams. The latter was elected as the sixth president of the United States in 1824.

John Adams was interred in a crypt at the United First Parish Church in Quincy, Massachusetts, along with his wife. The church is also the final resting place of John Quincy Adams and his wife.

above left: The residence of John Adams and Abigail Adams at 135 Adams Street in Quincy, Massachusetts. *National Park Service*

above: A painting of President John Adams by Asher B. Durand, courtesy of the Naval Historical Center in Washington, DC. Adams was one of the leading advocates for the creation of a Continental Navy, and he drafted the first set of rules and regulations for the new navy. He was able to convince the Congress to pass an "Act Providing a Naval Armament," which was less than he thought was necessary but at least provided for the equipping of three frigates, the *Constitution*, the *United States*, and the *Constellation*. *US Navy*

VICE PRESIDENT

THOMAS JEFFERSON

A close second place in the 1796 presidential election made Virginian Thomas Jefferson, a political colleague and rival of John Adams, the vice president. As a Democratic-Republican (then called Republicans), Jefferson often disagreed with Federalist Adams, insisting that the federal government did not have the right to exercise powers not specifically granted to it by the states. In 1800, Jefferson again ran against Adams and was elected as president of the United States. He is discussed in the following chapter.

Thomas Jefferson

DEMOCRATIC-REPUBLICAN PARTY

The principal author of the Declaration of Independence, Thomas Jefferson was a lawyer, musician, philosopher, inventor, and the founder of the University of Virginia, and he is credited with being the father of American architecture. During his presidency, he doubled the size of the United States through the Louisiana Purchase and saw Ohio admitted as the seventeenth state.

He learned Greek and Latin as a young man and could speak French, Italian, and Spanish as well. He was a leading figure in the Age of Enlightenment, an era of cultural and intellectual trends in which reason and logic challenged traditional dogma.

Speaking at a dinner honoring Nobel Prize winners, John F. Kennedy famously remarked, "this is the most extraordinary collection of talent, of human knowledge, that has ever been gathered together at the White House, with the possible exception of when Thomas Jefferson dined alone."

Kennedy added that Thomas Jefferson could "calculate an eclipse, survey an estate, tie an artery, plan an edifice, try a cause, break a horse, and dance the minuet."

Jefferson was a die-hard champion of the freedom of speech and of the press, believing that each would contribute to democracy by contributing to an educated populace. He was responsible for many facets of governmental theory and practice that we take for granted, including the basic monetary system, the system for the admission of new states into the Union, and the theory of the public school system.

Thomas Jefferson was born on April 13, 1743, at Shadwell in Goochland (now part of Albemarle) County, Virginia, the son of a surveyor named Peter Jefferson, the cartographer of the first accurate map of Virginia, and his wife, Jane Randolph Jefferson. A precocious child and an avid reader, Jefferson inherited his father's gift for mathematics, and he was already conversant in several languages when he entered the College of William and Mary at the age of sixteen. He graduated in 1762 and worked as a law clerk before becoming a member of the bar in 1767. A practicing attorney, Jefferson also represented Albemarle County in the Virginia House of Burgesses from 1769 to 1775.

In the meantime, in 1768, Jefferson began work on his hilltop estate near Charlottesville in Albemarle County. He named it Monticello, meaning "Small Mountain" in Italian, and designed it himself, based on the works of the Renaissance Italian architect Andrea Palladio.

On the first day of 1772, Jefferson married Martha Wayles, his third cousin and the widow of Bathurst Skelton. They had six children, of whom only two lived to adulthood. Martha never lived to be first lady of the United States, although she was first lady of Virginia when Jefferson was governor. She died in 1782 after the birth of their youngest, who lived only two years. She reportedly asked Jefferson never to remarry, and he did not.

In 1775, Jefferson attended the Second Continental Congress as a delegate from Virginia. It was here that he became a friend of John Adams, with whom he would later have a long and bitter rivalry. In 1776, Jefferson and Adams, along with Benjamin Franklin, Robert Livingston, and Roger Sherman, set to work on the Declaration of Independence, but this committee decided to entrust Jefferson alone with writing the final draft.

above: The Jefferson Memorial on the Tidal Basin in Washington, DC, was designed by John Russell Pope and officially dedicated by President Roosevelt on April 13, 1943, the bicentennial of Jefferson's birth. *Joe Ravi, via Creative Commons, license CC-BY-SA 3.0*

left: In 1803, Thomas Jefferson nearly doubled the area of the United States through the Louisiana Purchase. In 1804, he sent Capt. Meriwether Lewis (his Virginia neighbor) and Lt. William Clark to explore the farthest reaches of this territory and to find a route to the Pacific. They reached the Pacific in 1805 and returned to St. Louis in 1806. *Paintings by Charles Willson Peale, courtesy of the National Park Service*

opposite: Portrait of Thomas Jefferson by Charles Willson Peale. *Department of State*

Later in 1776, Jefferson returned to Albemarle County, where he was elected to the Virginia House of Delegates, the post-independence successor to the House of Burgesses. In 1779, he was elected to the first of two consecutive one-year terms as governor of Virginia. During this time, he officially moved the capital from Williamsburg to Richmond but had to evacuate the government from Richmond to get away from the British advance. He also designed the Virginia State Capitol in Richmond, which opened in 1788.

In 1783, following the Treaty of Paris, Jefferson was elected to the Congress of the Confederation, the interim legislature between the Continental Congress and the present Congress of the United States, which dates to 1789. In 1784, he went overseas to join Benjamin Franklin and John Adams in establishing treaty relationships with leading European powers.

In 1785, Jefferson succeeded Franklin as the United States minister to France. In this post, he was accompanied by his teenage daughter Patsy, who was educated in France. In 1787, Jefferson and Patsy were joined by Polly, Patsy's only surviving sibling. Also arriving in Paris at this time was Sally Hemings, the enslaved servant from Monticello with whom Jefferson is widely believed to have had an affair lasting for many years. While in Paris, Jefferson was sympathetic with many prominent individuals in the French republican movement, which he

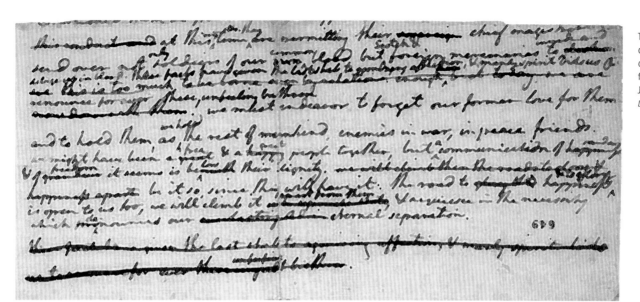

The earliest known draft of the Declaration of Independence, from June 1776, is in Jefferson's handwriting.
Library of Congress

MARTHA WAYLES SKELTON JEFFERSON

The only wife of Thomas Jefferson, Martha Wayles was born on October 30, 1748, in Charles City County, Virginia. She was the only child of British-born planter and attorney John Wayles and his first wife, Martha Eppes, who died six days after the birth of the younger Martha. John later married Mary Cocke, who raised Martha, along with her own three children (a fourth died in infancy). In turn, John married Elizabeth Lomax Skelton, who passed away less than two years later in 1761. Thereafter, John Wayles took a mistress, the mixed-race enslaved servant Elizabeth "Betty" Hemings, with whom he lived until his death in 1773 and with whom he had several children.

In 1766, Martha Wayles married Bathurst Skelton, the brother of the first husband of her father's third wife. Bathurst died in 1768 and their only son died at age four. Martha married Thomas Jefferson on January 1, 1772, and was first lady of Virginia from June 1779 to June 1781.

The couple had six children, three of whom died before Martha. She died on September 6, 1782, from complications arising from the birth of Lucy Elizabeth Jefferson, the second Jefferson daughter to be so named. Lucy herself died two years later. Martha and all of her children with Thomas Jefferson are interred at Monticello.

The Children of Thomas Jefferson and
Martha Wayles Skelton Jefferson

Martha "Patsy" Jefferson (1772-1836)
Jane Jefferson (1774-1775)
Peter Jefferson (1777-1777)
Mary "Maria" (called "Polly" as a child) Jefferson (1778-1804)
Lucy Elizabeth Jefferson (1780-1781)
Lucy Elizabeth Jefferson (2nd) (1782-1785)

supported. Among these was the Marquis de Lafayette, who had commanded French troops aiding the Continental Army in the War of Independence. Jefferson was in Paris at the beginning of the French Revolution but departed in September 1789.

Back in the United States, Jefferson received an invitation from fellow Virginian George Washington to serve as the first secretary of state, a post he accepted. His continued backing of the French republic, even during the extreme violence of the 1793–1794 Reign of Terror, was unpopular.

As a member of the cabinet, Jefferson came into conflict with Secretary of the Treasury Alexander Hamilton over Hamilton's backing a strong central government and locating the permanent capital of the United States in a major northern commercial center such as Philadelphia or New York. In the latter, Jefferson had Washington's support for the eventual location on the Potomac, although Washington leaned toward a robust national government. It was Washington's unhappiness with Jefferson's continued attacks on Hamilton that eventually led to Jefferson's resignation.

In 1796, Thomas Jefferson made his first serious bid for the presidency, running as a Democratic-Republican (then called a Republican) against Federalists John Adams and Thomas Pinckney and several other candidates. Adams was elected with seventy-one votes to sixty-eight for Jefferson and fifty-nine for Pinckney, while fellow Democratic-Republican Aaron Burr received thirty. Having come in second, Jefferson became vice president, marking the only time in United States history that the president and vice president were from opposing parties. It put a great deal of strain on the Adams administration to have a states' rights advocate like Jefferson second-guessing the Federalist president.

Thomas Jefferson (right), Benjamin Franklin (left), and John Adams (center) meeting at Jefferson's apartment on the corner of Seventh and High streets in Philadelphia to review a draft of the Declaration of Independence. *Library of Congress*

SALLY HEMINGS

Sally Hemings, the presumed mistress of Thomas Jefferson, was the much younger half-sister of Martha Wayles, the wife of Thomas Jefferson. She was born in July 1773 in Charles City County, Virginia, the youngest daughter of John Wayles and Elizabeth "Betty" Hemings, his mixed-race enslaved mistress. John Wayles died before Sally's birth, and both she and her mother were inherited as the property of Martha Wayles Skelton Jefferson and Thomas Jefferson.

In 1787, Sally accompanied Jefferson's daughter Polly to Paris, where Jefferson was serving as the United States minister to France, and where Sally's older brother, James Hemings, was being trained as a chef. Though not part of the historical record, it is today widely presumed that widower Jefferson took Sally, who was three decades younger than he was, as his mistress while they were in Paris and she remained as such for the rest of his life.

It is also presumed that they had six children, four of whom reached adulthood. Period accounts note light-skinned servants at Monticello (the children would have been seven-eighths non-African); Jefferson never denied being their father and freed them upon his death. DNA tests indicate a relationship between the Hemings descendants and a male from Jefferson's line. In 2012, the Smithsonian Institution and the Thomas Jefferson Foundation concluded that the various elements of "evidence strongly support the conclusion that Jefferson was the father of Sally Hemings's children."

Sally herself passed away in 1835, nine years after Jefferson, having been informally freed by Jefferson's daughter, Martha Jefferson Randolph, after his death.

The Possible Children of Thomas Jefferson and Sally Hemings
Harriet Hemings (1795–1797)
[William] Beverley Hemings (1798–circa 1873)
Thenia Hemings (1799–1799)
Harriet Hemings (2nd) (1801–1863)
[James] Madison Hemings (1805–1877)
[Thomas] Eston Hemings (1808–1856)

In 1800, Jefferson ran against Adams again. With the popularity of the Federalists on the wane because of the ongoing undeclared naval war with France, Adams came in third with sixty-five Electoral College votes. Jefferson, meanwhile, received seventy-three votes, tying him with Aaron Burr. The tie in the Electoral College resulted in the election being thrown into the House of Representatives. Over the course of seven days in February 1801, the Federalists in the House withheld their support from Jefferson, and in thirty-five ballots, neither Jefferson nor Burr was able to gain a majority. Alexander Hamilton broke the impasse by convincing some of his Federalist allies in the House to support Jefferson, who was then elected on the thirty-sixth ballot. This made him the winner and Burr his vice president.

Jefferson's domestic program initially revolved around a reduction of federal taxes and the size and power of the federal government, while expanding the electorate by eliminating property requirements for suffrage. As for the Alien and Sedition Acts, he repealed them or allowed them to expire and released those imprisoned. He urged Congress to abolish a number of district courts created under his Federalist predecessor, but even the Democratic-Republicans in Congress would not let Jefferson go as far as he wished.

Though Jefferson was himself a slaveholder from a southern state, he advocated and achieved a permanent ban

AARON BURR

Thomas Jefferson's first vice president, Aaron Burr, was born February 6, 1756, in Newark, New Jersey, served in the Continental Army, and held various elective posts in New York before being elected to the US Senate from New York in 1790. In 1800, he came close to beating Jefferson in the presidential election. As vice president, he presided over the Senate, notably during the impeachment trial of Supreme Court Justice Samuel Chase. The justice was acquitted and Burr, known for pushing the limits of civility as a political candidate, earned both praise and surprise for his even-handed impartiality.

Burr is well known for challenging political rival, fellow New Yorker, and former treasury secretary Alexander Hamilton to a duel in 1804 in which Hamilton was fatally wounded.

After losing the confidence of Jefferson and leaving the vice presidency in 1805, Burr traveled west and became involved in a scheme to create an independent country in areas west of the Mississippi River that were then dominions of Spain or parts of the Louisiana Purchase. When the plan mushroomed into one that was rumored to involve the overthrow of the United States, Burr was arrested and tried for treason. Though acquitted in 1807, Burr's reputation was dashed. He lived abroad until 1812 and kept a low profile upon his return. He died on September 14, 1836, two years after suffering a debilitating stroke.

left: A portrait of Aaron Burr from 1802. *John Vanderlyn*

GEORGE CLINTON

George Clinton served twice as governor of New York and as vice president of the United States under two presidents. He is unrelated to President Bill Clinton, whose birth surname was Blythe. Born on July 26, 1739, in Little Britain, New York, George Clinton served in the British Army during the French and Indian War but came to support the colonial cause and was a friend of George Washington. He and his brother James Clinton were both commissioned as generals in the Continental Army, but George was elected as governor of New York in 1777. Having won reelection five times, he served in this post until 1795. He served a final term as governor from 1801 to 1804.

Running for president of the United States as a Democratic-Republican (then called a Republican), Clinton came in third in 1792 and a distant seventh in 1796. He was elected vice president in 1804, the first year that the electors in the Electoral College specified separate roles for president and vice president under the Twelfth Amendment. Though Jefferson left office after their joint term, Clinton ran for reelection in 1808 as James Madison's running mate and won by a wide margin.

Clinton died on April 20, 1812, the first vice president to die in office. He was originally interred in Washington, DC, but moved to Kingston, New York, in 1908.

right: An 1814 portrait of George Clinton. Ezra Ames

on the importation of slaves into the United States. Though the international slave trade was abolished in 1808, it took two generations and a great deal of anguish to formally free the slaves already living in the United States and their descendants.

Internationally, concern over angering the domestic slave-owner constituency prevented Jefferson from recognizing Haiti—the Western Hemisphere's second republic after the United States—after a successful slave rebellion over French rule in 1804. Jefferson did, however, aid the rebels covertly.

Meanwhile, the United States was drawn into a war with the Islamic city-states of the Barbary Coast, the area of North Africa between Morocco and Libya. American merchant ships in the Mediterranean were being captured and held for ransom, and the sultans of the region were actively engaged in piracy themselves or demanding protection money. Jefferson felt compelled to intervene militarily, and the success of these operations, between 1801 and 1805, demonstrated the effectiveness of the new and untested US Navy and US Marine Corps.

Jefferson's greatest accomplishment as president was almost certainly the Louisiana Purchase, which added 828,000 square miles to the area of the United States. At the time, the Louisiana Territory included the watershed of the Mississippi River west of the river, including the drainage of the Missouri River, its largest tributary. Claimed by France, it was ceded to Spain in 1762 but regained by France in 1800.

Three years later, Secretary of State (and future president) James Monroe traveled to Paris to offer to buy the city of New Orleans and the mouth of the Mississippi and the southern tip of Louisiana. Napoleon Bonaparte, fearing that Britain or the United States might simply seize Louisiana, offered to sell it all to the United States. Though there was some domestic opposition to the acquisition, Jefferson deemed it a good deal and bought Louisiana.

In turn, Jefferson commissioned Capt. Meriwether Lewis, a former Virginia neighbor, to lead a military expedition into the vast and largely unexplored region and to find the headwaters of the Missouri River on the Continental Divide. From there, Lewis was ordered to travel west and identify a practical route between the headwaters of the Missouri and the Pacific Ocean. With his "co-captain," William Clark, and a Corps of Discovery consisting of thirty-five military personnel and a small number of civilians, Lewis departed from the mouth of the Missouri near St. Louis in May 1804. The Lewis and Clark Expedition reached the mouth of the Columbia River and the Pacific Ocean in November 1805 and returned to St. Louis in September 1806. The expedition, which suffered only one fatality, from

A portrait of Alexander Hamilton. Founder of the nation's financial system, the founder of the Federalist Party, and secretary of the treasury from 1789 to 1795, he was a political rival of Jefferson and was shot by Aaron Burr in a duel. *John Trumbull*

FROM THOMAS JEFFERSON'S FIRST INAUGURAL ADDRESS
March 4, 1801

A rising nation, spread over a wide and fruitful land, traversing all the seas with the rich productions of their industry, engaged in commerce with nations who feel power and forget right, advancing rapidly to destinies beyond the reach of mortal eye—when I contemplate these transcendent objects, and see the honor, the happiness, and the hopes of this beloved country committed to the issue, and the auspices of this day, I shrink from the contemplation, and humble myself before the magnitude of the undertaking. Utterly, indeed, should I despair did not the presence of many whom I here see remind me that in the other high authorities provided by our Constitution I shall find resources of wisdom, of virtue, and of zeal on which to rely under all difficulties. To you, then, gentlemen, who are charged with the sovereign functions of legislation, and to those associated with you, I look with encouragement for that guidance and support which may enable us to steer with safety the vessel in which we are all embarked amidst the conflicting elements of a troubled world.

appendicitis, was immensely successful from a scientific point of view and provided early, accurate cartography of the breadth of the continent. Jefferson also sent Zebulon Pike on a similar expedition into the Rocky Mountains and the Southwest in 1806 to 1807.

Thomas Jefferson left the presidency after two terms, following the non-binding precedent of George Washington. In retirement, one of his most important accomplishments was his founding of the University of Virginia in 1819. It is visible from his estate at Monticello. In his role as an architect, he designed the campus layout and many of the most important buildings, and he bequeathed his own extensive library to the university.

left: The official presidential portrait of Thomas Jefferson by Rembrandt Peale. *White House*

below: The east and west facades of Monticello, near Charlottesville, Virginia. Designed by Jefferson himself, the estate was his primary residence after 1770, except while he was president. *Bill Yenne*

In later life, he reconciled with his old rival and fellow Declaration of Independence signatory, John Adams, and the two of them both died on July 4, 1826. His final words were said to have been "I have done for my country, and for all mankind, all that I could do, and I now resign my soul, without fear, to my God, my daughter to my country." He then asked whether it was the Fourth of July.

He was interred on the grounds of Monticello beneath an epitaph, written himself, that reads, "Here was buried Thomas Jefferson author of the Declaration of American Independence of the statute of Virginia for religious freedom and father of the University of Virginia." He did not mention his having been president of the United States.

Despite his accomplishments, at the time of his death Jefferson was in debt—some of it debts inherited from his father-in-law—and his assets were sold. Fortunately, Monticello was eventually acquired by Uriah Levy, a great fan of Jefferson, who preserved it. The Levy family sold it in 1923 to the Thomas Jefferson Foundation, which preserves it as a museum.

FROM THOMAS JEFFERSON'S EIGHTH AND FINAL STATE OF THE UNION ADDRESS

November 8, 1808

Availing myself of this the last occasion which will occur of addressing the two Houses of the Legislature at their meeting, I can not omit the expression of my sincere gratitude for the repeated proofs of confidence manifested to me by themselves and their predecessors since my call to the administration and the many indulgences experienced at their hands. These same grateful acknowledgements are due to my fellow citizens generally, whose support has been my great encouragement under all embarrassments. In the transaction of their business I cannot have escaped error. It is incident to our imperfect nature. But I may say with truth my errors have been of the understanding, not of intention, and that the advancement of their rights and interests has been the constant motive for every measure. On these considerations I solicit their indulgence. Looking forward with anxiety to future destinies, I trust that in their steady character, unshaken by difficulties, in their love of liberty, obedience to law, and support of the public authorities, I see a sure guaranty of the permanence of our Republic; and, retiring from the charge of their affairs, I carry with me the consolation of a firm persuasion that Heaven has in store for our beloved country long ages to come of prosperity and happiness.

This statue of Thomas Jefferson by Rudulph Evans was mounted in the Jefferson Memorial in Washington, DC, 1947, four years after the memorial opened. *Library of Congress*

4

1809–1817

James Madison

DEMOCRATIC-REPUBLICAN PARTY

Though he looms large in history as the "father" of the United States Constitution and a leading proponent of the Bill of Rights, James Madison was the smallest president of the United States, weighing less than one hundred pounds and standing only five feet, four inches tall. The third of the first four American presidents from Virginia, he was born at Belle Grove Plantation near Port Conway on March 16, 1751, the eldest of the twelve children of James Madison Sr. and Nelly Conway Madison. He grew up at Mount Pleasant plantation (later called Montpelier) in Orange County, Virginia.

Madison graduated from the College of New Jersey (now Princeton University) in 1771, having learned Greek and Latin as well as Hebrew and having developed an interest in political science. He was in the Virginia legislature during the early years of the War of Independence, became the youngest member of the Continental Congress, and returned to the legislature between 1784 and 1786.

In 1787, Madison went to Philadelphia as a delegate to the convention that sought to create a permanent constitution to supersede the Articles of Confederation. Though a founder of the Democratic-Republican (then called Republican) Party and a follower of Thomas Jefferson, Madison joined the Federalists in supporting a strong federal government and emerged as one of the leading figures in drafting the United States Constitution.

Madison collaborated with prominent Federalists John Jay and Alexander Hamilton in the drafting of the Federalist Papers, a series of essays published in 1787 and 1788 that are

considered to have been the theoretical foundation of the Constitution and a rebuttal to those who opposed the Federalist vision. Madison's finest moment in the process came in his debates with anti-Federalist Patrick Henry when he was able to successfully convince Virginia, the most populous state, to ratify the United States Constitution.

In 1789, Madison was elected to the United States House of Representatives, defeating future president of the United States James Monroe. In a rematch in 1790, Madison won again with nearly 98 percent of the vote.

In Congress, Madison introduced and championed the adoption of the Bill of Rights, guaranteeing such basic freedoms as freedom of religion, freedom of speech, freedom of assembly, freedom of the press, freedom from unreasonable search and seizure, and the right to bear arms. Madison hoped to have these included as articles of the Constitution, but they were adopted as the first ten amendments, ratified in 1791.

As a member of Congress, Madison also joined Jefferson in opposing the Alien and Sedition Acts as unconstitutional.

Public life consumed Madison's early years, and he was forty-three when he married Dolley Payne Todd, a twenty-six-year-old widow, in 1794. They had no children, but Madison adopted her son, John Payne Todd, from her previous marriage. Also on the personal side, Madison inherited the plantation at Montpelier when his father died in 1801, although he had been managing the property since about 1780.

In 1801, as Thomas Jefferson took office as president of the United States, he selected James Madison as his secretary of state, in which post he served for Jefferson's entire term. Among his key international challenges was maintaining the United States' neutrality as the Napoleonic Wars consumed Europe.

In 1803, Madison was a party to the landmark *Marbury v. Madison* case before the United States Supreme Court, which resulted in the far-reaching decision that established the doctrine of judicial review, meaning that the courts have the power to invalidate legislation that conflicts with constitutional provisions.

In 1808, James Madison ran for president, defeating Federalist Charles Pinckney of South Carolina 122 to 47 in the Electoral College, with 64.7 percent of the popular vote. Four years later, with the Federalists in decline, Madison found himself running against a fellow Democratic-Republican. The son of Madison's recently deceased vice president, DeWitt Clinton was a former US senator from New York and was now in the third of three non-consecutive terms as mayor of New York City. In the election of 1812, Madison took 128 electoral votes to Clinton's 89, as well as 50.4 percent of the popular vote.

opposite: The Bureau of Engraving and Printing's engraved portrait of James Madison as president, and that image in use on a series of 1934 $5,000 Federal Reserve notes. *Bureau of Engraving and Printing*

Montpelier, the Madison family estate, is located in Orange County, Virginia. The original core of the two-story, hipped-roof main house was built by the president's father, James Madison Sr. in the early 1760s. It was one of the largest brick dwellings in Orange County. James and Dolley Madison moved to the house in 1797 and later added the Tuscan portico to the facade. After his presidency, Madison added wings to the main house. He and Dolley lived at Montpelier until his death in 1836. *Bill Yenne*

DOLLEY PAYNE MADISON

Recalled as a popular Washington hostess, she was born Dollie Payne on May 20, 1768, in New Garden, a Society of Friends (Quaker) community in North Carolina, the eldest daughter of the eight children of Mary Coles Payne and John Payne. During her lifetime, her name was often written as "Dolly," though historians have agreed to spell it "Dolley." While she was growing up, the family moved, first to Virginia and then to Philadelphia. Dolley was twenty-four when her father died and her mother returned to Virginia and remarried.

In 1790, Dolley Payne married Quaker attorney John Todd in Philadelphia and they had two sons, John and William. In October 1793, when William was two months old, both he and his father died of yellow fever. She soon met James Madison through a mutual friend from Madison's college days and married him on September 15, 1794. By marrying a non-Quaker, she was expelled from the Society of Friends. They had no children, but Madison adopted John Payne Todd.

Though the term was not coined until 1860, Dolley Madison proved to be the archetypal "first lady," even serving as hostess while widower Thomas Jefferson was in the White House. When the British burned Washington in 1814, she ordered that the famous Gilbert Stuart painting of George Washington be saved, though she did not personally take it down.

She retired to Montpelier with her husband, but after his death, she returned to Washington to live with her sister Anna. She spent her final years selling off her husband's property and papers to pay off the debts incurred by her shiftless, alcoholic son. She died on July 12, 1849, and was buried in Washington, though her remains were later moved to Montpelier.

above: A portrait of James Madison by Gilbert Stuart. *National Gallery of Art*

The biggest event of the Madison years was the War of 1812, which has been seen by some historians as a theater of the Napoleonic Wars still ongoing in Europe, though at the time, it was viewed domestically as a "Second War of Independence" against Britain. The British used their Royal Navy to harass and seize American merchant ships on the high seas, to prevent the United States from trading with France, and to blockade the Eastern Seaboard of the United States. The Royal Navy was also kidnapping American seamen to crew British ships. There were rumors of the British inciting Indian tribes to attack American settlements south of the Great Lakes, although the decisive victory over the Shawnee at Tippecanoe in Indiana Territory by the US Army, under Gen. William Henry Harrison, a future president, had largely eliminated this threat.

Madison asked for a declaration of war, which Congress passed in June 1812, though the downsizing of the United States armed forces that had been ongoing under Jefferson left the country ill equipped. Nevertheless, 1813 proved a good year for the United States in the war. The US Navy defeated the British in the Battle of Lake Erie, and the US Army under William Henry Harrison defeated a British and Indian force in the Battle of the Thames near Chatham, Ontario, effectively eliminating the threat of a British incursion south of the Great Lakes.

In 1814, however, the British launched an offensive against Washington, DC, itself in response to the damage done by American forces to York (now Toronto), Ontario. They captured and briefly held the nation's capital, burning out the White House and the partially completed Capitol building, leaving just the stone shells. The British next attempted to capture Baltimore but were unable to capture Fort McHenry, the bombardment of which was memorialized by Francis Scott Key, who described the attack in "The Star Spangled Banner."

In January 1815, US Army troops under Gen. Andrew Jackson, another future president, achieved a memorable victory in the Battle of New Orleans. Celebration of this event was not overshadowed by the fact that, unbeknownst to the participants, the war was already over. The Treaty of Ghent, ending the war, was signed in December 1814. Neither side gained territory, and the maritime issues were made moot by the final defeat of the Napoleonic armies a few months later.

During Madison's presidency, two states were admitted to the Union. The former Territory of Orleans at the southern tip of Louisiana Territory was admitted as the State of Louisiana in 1812, and Indiana Territory became the state of the same name in 1816. The former Louisiana Territory became Missouri Territory.

After his time in office, Madison retired to Montpelier, where he spent his final years worrying about his finances and sorting—and in many cases, doctoring—his presidential papers. When Jefferson died in 1826, Madison was named as rector of the University of Virginia, and he acted as an advisor to the revision of the Virginia constitution.

Madison died at Montpelier on June 28, 1836, and is interred on its grounds. Dolley Madison sold the property a few years later, but it was acquired by the National Trust for Historic Preservation in 1984 and has undergone restoration.

GEORGE CLINTON

George Clinton was one of only two men to serve as vice president under two presidents, the other being John C. Calhoun. He served from 1801 to 1805 under Thomas Jefferson and from 1805 through his death in 1812 under James Madison. He is profiled in the previous chapter.

ELBRIDGE GERRY

James Madison's second-term vice president was born July 17, 1744, in Marblehead, Massachusetts, a member of a wealthy merchant family, and received his master's degree from Harvard in 1765. A colleague of Samuel Adams, he was active in politics, favored the revolutionary cause, signed the Declaration of Independence, and served in the Second Continental Congress from 1776 to 1780. He participated in the Constitutional Convention of 1787 and was a strong proponent of the Bill of Rights both at the convention and after being elected to the US Congress from Massachusetts as a Democratic-Republican in 1789. After several tries, he was elected governor of Massachusetts in 1810.

A portrait of Elbridge Gerry. *James Bogle*

The practice of creating oddly shaped legislative districts for political purposes was named gerrymandering after Elbridge Gerry when his party created one that looked like a salamander and he approved it as governor. This cost him reelection in 1812.

He was chosen as James Madison's running mate in order to secure northern votes. He fell ill and died on November 23, 1814, leaving Madison without a vice president for most of his second term.

5

James Monroe

DEMOCRATIC-REPUBLICAN PARTY

The fourth Virginian among the first five United States presidents, James Monroe was the last president to have been a member of the Confederation Congress. In 1820, he was the only presidential candidate in history other than George Washington to run unopposed, receiving all but one electoral vote. He was the first president to have served in the US Senate, and the first to ride in a steamboat. He was also the only president since Washington to be the namesake of a national capital—Monrovia, Liberia.

James Monroe was born in Westmoreland County, Virginia, on April 28, 1758, the son of planter Spence Monroe and Elizabeth Jones Monroe. He enrolled at the College of William and Mary in 1774 but dropped out in 1775 to join the Continental Army. He was with George Washington in the famous crossing of the Delaware on Christmas Day 1776 and was wounded in action in the subsequent Battle of Trenton. He served in the Virginia militia while Thomas Jefferson was governor and later studied law under Jefferson. While serving in the Confederation Congress in New York, he met Elizabeth Kortright, whom he married in 1786.

Monroe was elected to the US Senate from Virginia in 1790 but resigned in 1794 to accept an appointment by George Washington as minister to France, where he spoke in support of the revolutionaries against the president's wishes. Running as a Democratic-Republican, he became governor of Virginia in 1799 and was reelected four times. Until 1830, the term was for only one year.

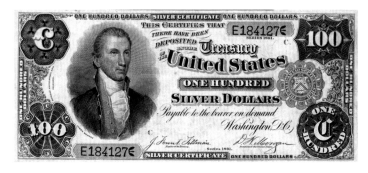

The Bureau of Engraving and Printing's engraved portrait of James Monroe as president and that image in use on a Series of 1891 $100 Silver Certificate. *Bureau of Engraving and Printing*

In 1803, Thomas Jefferson sent Monroe to France to help negotiate the details of the Louisiana Purchase, and later in the year, he was sent to London, where he served as minister to Great Britain until 1807. Monroe then returned to Virginia, where he was elected governor once again in 1811. He served briefly before being tapped by President James Madison to serve as secretary of state, a post that he held until 1817. In the early years of the War of 1812, with things going badly for the United States, Madison fired Secretary of War John Armstrong and asked Monroe to fill in, so that he effectively held two cabinet posts for five months in the winter of 1814 to 1815.

In 1816, Monroe became the Democratic-Republican presidential candidate with the support of both Thomas Jefferson and James Madison, and won the general election

above: The grave of President James Monroe (inside the black cage) at Hollywood Cemetery in Richmond, Virginia. *Library of Congress*

against Federalist Rufus King of New York by a margin of 183 to 34 in the Electoral College with 68.2 percent of the popular vote. By 1820, when Monroe ran for reelection, the Federalist Party had essentially collapsed, and Monroe ran without opposition, taking 228 electoral votes and 80.6 percent of the popular vote. The one electoral vote cast against him was that of a New Hampshire elector delegate who wanted Washington to remain the only president elected unanimously in the Electoral College.

Domestically, Monroe was a popular president whose term coincided with the so-called "Era of Good Feelings," a time of relative peace and prosperity. Monroe received good press for an extensive Great Goodwill Tour of much of the United States, the first by a president. In 1816, he oversaw the chartering of a new "national bank," to help stabilize fiscal matters in the wake of the War of 1812. The Second Bank of the United States (successor to the First, which closed in 1811), was chartered for twenty years through 1836. The Federal Reserve, which was created in 1913, is not technically a bank.

EXCERPT FROM THE MESSAGE TO CONGRESS ANNOUNCING THE MONROE DOCTRINE
December 2, 1823

The occasion has been judged proper for asserting, as a principle in which the rights and interests of the United States are involved, that the American continents, by the free and independent condition which they have assumed and maintain, are henceforth not to be considered as subjects for future colonization by any European powers.

We owe it, therefore, to candor and to the amicable relations existing between the United States and those powers to declare that we should consider any attempt on their part to extend their system to any portion of this hemisphere as dangerous to our peace and safety. With the existing colonies or dependencies of any European power we have not interfered and shall not interfere. But with the Governments who have declared their independence and maintained it, and whose independence we have, on great consideration and on just principles, acknowledged, we could not view any interposition for the purpose of oppressing them, or controlling in any other manner their destiny, by any European power in any other light than as the manifestation of an unfriendly disposition toward the United States.

ELIZABETH "ELIZA" KORTRIGHT MONROE

Born in New York City on June 30, 1768, Elizabeth was the daughter of Hannah Aspinwall Kortright and Lawrence Kortright, a descendant of early Dutch settlers on New Amsterdam. She married James Monroe in New York on February 16, 1786, and accompanied him on his diplomatic missions overseas to Britain and France. While in Paris, their elder daughter, Eliza, became a friend of Napoleon Bonaparte's

A portrait of Elizabeth Monroe.
After a painting by John Vanderlyn

stepdaughter Hortense, and the two families became friends. They were invited back to France for Napoleon's coronation as emperor in 1804.

As first lady, Elizabeth maintained a measure of the courtly exclusivity that she had learned in France, which made her less popular in Washington circles than her predecessor, Dolley Madison. She was also nagged by recurring illness, during which time, her daughters, especially Eliza, served as White House hostesses. In 1820, the younger Monroe daughter, Maria Hester Monroe, wed her cousin Samuel Gouverneur in the first White House wedding.

As had become the rule for former chief executives, the Monroes spent their retirement years wrestling with debts incurred from official duties and from land holdings. Elizabeth died on September 23, 1830, and was buried at Oak Hill in northern Virginia. Her remains were moved twice, first to New York after her husband died, and next to Richmond, Virginia. The latter move was made in 1903, forty-five years after her husband was moved there.

The Children of James Monroe and Elizabeth Monroe
Eliza Monroe Hay (1786–1835)
James Spence Monroe (1799–1801)
Maria Hester Monroe Gouverneur (1804–1850)

A portrait of James Monroe by Samuel F. B. Morse. *White House*

In 1817–1819, Monroe presided over the admission of the former territories of Mississippi, Illinois, and Alabama as states. In 1820, Maine was ceded by Massachusetts as a non-slave state and in 1821, the state of Missouri was carved out of the lower part of Missouri Territory and admitted as a slave state. This was a result of the Missouri Compromise, designed by Henry Clay as a settlement between pro- and anti-slavery factions in Congress. This was to maintain an equal number of slave and non-slave states in the Union.

In that same year, Florida was ceded to the United States by Spain, though it would not become a state until 1845.

Spain figured prominently in the biggest foreign policy initiative of the Monroe Administration. In the wake of the Napoleonic Wars, long-time Spanish colonies in the Western Hemisphere, from Mexico to Chile, along with Portugal's Brazil, experienced rumblings of revolt and declarations of independence. Monroe and Secretary of State John Quincy Adams actively supported the aspirations of those seeking to establish new republics.

On December 2, 1823, the president formally made the landmark announcement of the Monroe Doctrine, stating that the hemisphere should be free of future European colonization. Canada remained British, but Latin America gradually became independent.

After leaving office, James and Elizabeth Monroe retired to Oak Hill in northern Virginia, but after she died in 1830, he moved to New York City to live with his daughter.

Though a slaveholder himself, Monroe grew to oppose the practice. He became a member of the American Colonization Society, formed in 1816 for the purpose of relocating freed slaves to an area of west Africa that became Liberia in 1847. Under Monroe, federal grant money was made available for this purpose. The principal city in this territory was named Monrovia in 1824.

At the Virginia Constitutional Convention in 1829, Monroe called slavery "evil" and proposed that Virginia free all of its slaves.

James Monroe passed away in New York on July 4, 1831, becoming the third president to die on the anniversary of the approval of the Declaration of Independence.

He was originally buried in New York, but in 1858, his remains were moved to the Hollywood Cemetery in Richmond, Virginia.

VICE PRESIDENT
DANIEL D. TOMPKINS

Daniel D. Tompkins was born on June 21, 1774, in Scarsdale, New York, graduated from Columbia College (now Columbia University) in 1795, and was admitted to the New York Bar a year later and served in the New York Assembly. He had no middle name, but added the initial when he was at Columbia. In 1798, he married Hannah Minthorne, the sixteen-year-old daughter of New York City Alderman Mangle Minthorne. They would have eight children.

Tompkins was elected to the US House of Representatives in 1804, but chose instead to accept an appointment to the New York Supreme Court. In 1807, he was elected as governor, a post to which he was reelected three times. During the War of 1812, he earned praise for his reorganization of the state militia, and for using his own money to help finance it. He later moved to free all the slaves still kept in New York.

Having declined James Madison's invitation to serve as secretary of state, he accepted James Monroe's invitation to run for vice president in 1816. He was the last nineteenth-century vice president to serve two terms under the same president. Beset by a serious drinking problem, Tompkins died on June 11, 1825, not long after he left office.

A portrait of Daniel D. Tompkins as governor of New York. *John Wesley Jarvis*

James Monroe acquired Highland, his plantation near Thomas Jefferson's Monticello property outside Charlottesville, Virginia, in 1793. He and his family moved into this modest house in 1799 and lived there for twenty-four years. He sold it in 1825 to pay off debts. After his death it became known as Ash Lawn–Highland. *Bill Yenne*

When Monroe became president, there were nineteen states. During his presidency, the US flag went through a series of variations, first to twenty stars and eventually to twenty-four as Mississippi, Illinois, Alabama, Maine, and Missouri became states. *Author's collection*

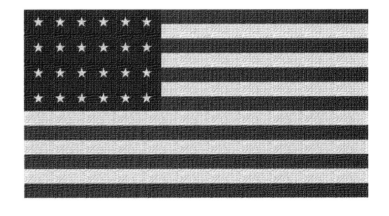

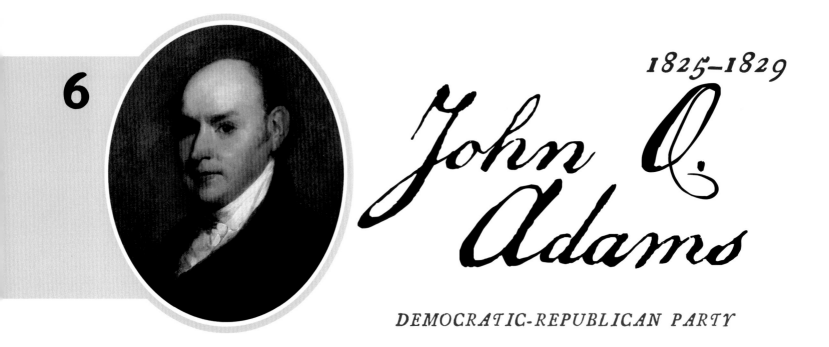

6

John Q. Adams

DEMOCRATIC-REPUBLICAN PARTY

The first son of a president to be elected president, John Quincy Adams was at various times a member of at least five different political parties. He is the subject of the earliest known photograph of an American president, though it was taken after he left office. He is also famous for his nude swims in the Potomac River, though no photographs of this activity exist.

John Quincy Adams was born in Braintree, Massachusetts, on July 11, 1767, the eldest son of future president John Adams and Abigail Adams. His middle name was that of his mother's maternal grandfather. At the time, John Adams was working as an attorney and just beginning to become interested in the cause of independence from Britain. As a young boy, John Quincy learned about the activities of the Continental Congress in the letters that his father wrote from Philadelphia.

Between 1778 and 1782, John Quincy Adams accompanied his father on his overseas missions to France and the Netherlands and attended Leiden University. He then spent three years as secretary to Francis Dana on his diplomatic mission to Russia and eastern Europe. Still a teenager, he had received a practical and diplomatic education unmatched by nearly anyone twice his age, and he had become conversant in French and Dutch. Returning to Massachusetts, he graduated from Harvard in 1787 and was admitted to the Massachusetts Bar in 1791.

Though he would rather have settled down, his father urged him to accept a career as a diplomat. In 1794, the younger Adams was named by President George Washington to serve as minister to the Netherlands, and two years later to the post in Portugal. When John Adams became president in 1797, he sent his son to serve as minister to Prussia, where he remained until 1801. On one of his Atlantic crossings, John Quincy Adams met Louisa Catherine Johnson, the British-born daughter of an American merchant, whom he married in London in 1797.

John Quincy Adams returned to America and was elected to the Massachusetts legislature in 1802, though he was soon elected to the US Senate as Federalist. He served in this office from 1803 to 1808. His support for Thomas Jefferson and the Louisiana Purchase made him unpopular with the Federalists in Massachusetts, which led him to resign his Senate seat and become a Democratic-Republican.

In 1809, after a brief tenure as a Harvard professor, Adams was picked by President James Madison to serve as the first minister to Russia. It was a place with which few America diplomats were familiar, but Adams had worked there twenty years earlier and knew his way around. He was able to convince Tsar Alexander I to aid in securing the release of American ships and sailors that had been seized by Denmark. Adams and his wife fit in well in the diplomatic life and remained until 1814, experiencing Napoleon's capture of Moscow and his ill-starred retreat.

In 1815, after serving as a negotiator on the Treaty of Ghent that ended the War of 1812, Adams moved on to

above: A portrait of John Quincy Adams created in 1858 by George Peter Alexander Healy. *White House.*

opposite: John Quincy Adams in 1818, by Gilbert Stuart. *White House*

London, where he assumed his father's old post as United States minister to Great Britain.

In 1817, when John Quincy Adams returned to the United States to take up the post of James Madison's secretary of state, he was the most qualified man yet—and for many years thereafter—to hold that job. Over the next several years, he negotiated the acquisition of Florida from Spain in 1821, as well as an agreement to set the boundary between the United States and British North America (later Canada) between the Great Lakes and the Rocky Mountains along the 49th Parallel, where it still remains. Secretary of State Adams was also the architect of the Monroe Doctrine.

LOUISA CATHERINE ADAMS

The only first lady not born in the United States, Louisa Catherine Johnson was one of eight children of American merchant Joshua Johnson and his English wife Catherine Nuth Johnson. She was born in England on February 12, 1775, and she married John Quincy Adams in London on July 26, 1797. Her parents relocated to the United States where her father-in-law, President John Adams, aided her now-bankrupt father by giving him a government job.

Louisa accompanied her husband on his many diplomatic missions. In 1809 in St. Petersburg, the attractive and charismatic Louisa charmed Tsar Alexander I and his court, and she and her husband became fixtures on the diplomatic social scene. Their only daughter, named Louisa Catherine after her mother, was born in Russia in 1811. Things soon turned dark, however, as the little girl died shortly after her first birthday. Her mother then had to endure the heartbreak of two sons who died before their parents. Louisa herself died in Washington on May 15, 1852, and was buried next to her husband.

The Children of John Quincy Adams and Louisa Catherine Johnson

George Washington Adams (1801–1829)
John Adams (1803–1834)
Charles Francis Adams (1807–1886)
Louisa Catherine Adams (1811–1812)

above: Louisa Catherine Johnson Adams as a younger woman, by Edward Savage *National Park Service*; and, at top right, as an older woman, by Gilbert Stuart. *White House*

opposite: Taken in 1843, this image of John Quincy Adams is believed to be the oldest photo of a US president. *Philip Haas*

It was natural that Adams should run for president of the United States in 1824, but he faced a stiff challenge from House Speaker Henry Clay of Kentucky and Senator Andrew Jackson of Tennessee, the hero of the 1815 Battle of New Orleans, both of them fellow Democratic-Republicans. When the election was held, Jackson came in first with ninety-nine electoral votes to eighty-four for Adams, but he received only 41.4 percent of the popular vote. Under the Twelfth Amendment, this threw the election into the House of Representatives, where Adams prevailed with Clay's support.

As president, John Quincy Adams emphasized domestic infrastructure projects, such as roads and canals, over foreign policy initiatives. His greatest triumphs in foreign affairs had come when he was secretary of state.

The election of 1828 was a rematch of 1824, but this time, Andrew Jackson soundly defeated his rival.

A US passport issued in 1815 by Adams while he was the US minister to the United Kingdom.

A 2007 John Quincy Adams dollar from the Presidential Coin Program.
US Mint Pressroom Image Library

Adams, unwilling to retire from public life, ran for the US House of Representatives from Massachusetts in 1830, won, and returned to Washington, where he remained until his death in 1848. He was the only ex-president to date to have served in the House. In 1833, while still in Congress, he ran for governor of Massachusetts as a member of the Anti-Masonic Party, but was not elected.

As a congressman, the former president was an outspoken advocate of the abolition of slavery and a critic of the 1846 to 1848 war with Mexico. He was also champion of the creation of a national institution of science and learning, which was realized as the Smithsonian Institution, founded in 1836.

In his personal life, he endured many heartaches, including the deaths of three of his children, including his only daughter, who died in infancy, and suicide of eldest son George Washington Adams, who committed suicide the year his father left the presidency. In 1870, surviving son Charles Francis Adams would establish the first memorial Presidential Library in the United States.

In 1848, two years after having suffered a debilitating stroke from which he never really recovered, John Quincy Adams collapsed on the House floor with a massive cerebral hemorrhage. He died two days later, on February 23, 1848, in the Speaker's Room at the US Capitol. Initially interred in Washington, DC, he was moved to the United First Parish Church in Quincy, Massachusetts, and buried next to his father.

VICE PRESIDENT

JOHN C. CALHOUN

One of the towering figures of American political life in the early nineteenth century, John Caldwell Calhoun served in the US House of Representatives, in the US Senate, in the cabinets of two presidents, and as vice president of the United States under two presidents. During the 1830s and 1840s, he was part of the Congressional Great Triumvirate of statesmen that also included Henry Clay and Daniel Webster. He began his career favoring a strong central government but evolved into a leading proponent of sectionalism and states' rights. Though he is remembered as a leading sectionalist, he was a later convert to that position than Clay or Webster.

Born on March 18, 1782, in Abbeville, South Carolina, Calhoun graduated from Yale College (now Yale University) in 1804 and represented his home state in the House from 1811 to 1817. In 1817, James Monroe selected him as secretary of war, and he served as a Democratic-Republican until 1825. In the election of 1824, when the presidential vote was split between Andrew Jackson and John Quincy Adams, Calhoun won the vice presidency by a landslide. After serving in the Adams administration, he ran again for vice president in 1828, and was again elected. Our sketch of Calhoun continues in the following chapter as we find him as Andrew Jackson's vice president.

A photograph of John C. Calhoun by Mathew Brady, circa 1849.
Library of Congress

7

1829–1837

Andrew Jackson

DEMOCRATIC PARTY

The first president of the United States from west of the Appalachians, Andrew Jackson helped found Tennessee and went on to both command its militia and represent it in Congress. He was the first president to experience an assassination attempt. While the two pistols wielded by the would-be assassin misfired and Jackson was not hit, he carried two bullets within his body from previous incidents, one in his chest from a duel in 1806, and a second in his arm from an 1813 barroom brawl with Senator Thomas Hart Benton.

Jackson was born on March 15, 1767, somewhere in the unsurveyed mountains between the Carolinas at a location that has never been determined. At the time, his mother was en route from burying her recently deceased husband. His

parents, Andrew Jackson and Elizabeth Hutchinson Jackson, had immigrated from Ireland two years earlier with two older sons, Hugh and Robert. Both Hugh and Robert died during the War of Independence, while young Andrew served informally as a militia courier.

Though Jackson was the first president since George Washington not to attend college, he was admitted to the North Carolina Bar in 1787 and he did practice law in that part of North Carolina that later became Tennessee. He served on the Tennessee Constitutional Convention and in 1796, after statehood, he was elected to represent the new state in Congress. After serving briefly in the House of Representatives, he was elected to the US Senate. However, he resigned in 1798 to take a post on the Tennessee Supreme Court. He did return to the US Senate, a few days short of twenty-five years later.

On the personal side, Jackson married Rachel Donelson Robards in 1791 and again in 1794. The reason for the second marriage was that she was still married to Lewis Robards in 1790. The confused legal status of the situation led to impertinent gossip about Rachel to which Jackson took exception. He is reported to have fought around a hundred duels to defend her honor. In 1803, they moved to the Hermitage, a

above: The official White House portrait of Andrew Jackson by Ralph E. W. Earl. *White House*

left: The crowd in front of the White House during President Jackson's first inaugural reception in 1829 as depicted in a work entitled *President's Levee, or all Creation going to the White House.* The Library of Congress notes that "the furnishings of the White House were destroyed by the rowdy crowd during the inaugural festivities." *Library of Congress*

Andrew Jackson's signature military victory as a general came in the Battle of New Orleans, a series of engagements fought in December 1814 and January 1815, marking the final major engagement of the War of 1812. In this Edward Percy Moran painting, Jackson stands on the parapet of his defenses as his troops repulse the attacking Highlanders. *Library of Congress*

plantation that Jackson had purchased near Nashville. She died on the eve of Jackson's inauguration as president and he never remarried. They had no children, though Jackson adopted the son of Rachel's brother Severn Donelson and named him Andrew Jackson Jr.

In 1801, while still on the Tennessee Supreme Court, Jackson was named to command the Tennessee Militia with the rank of colonel, and a year later, he was promoted to major general. Andrew Jackson's stellar military career began in 1813 with the Creek War, during which he commanded Tennessee and Georgia militia troops as well as US Army regulars. The war began between factions of the confederation of Creek (Muscogee) people, in which one faction, the Red Sticks, was actively supported with supplies and arms from the British, who were then fighting the United States in the War of 1812. In turn, the Americans backed the other Creeks militarily in a war that culminated in Jackson's victory in the Battle of Horseshoe Bend in March 1814.

In December 1814, when the British landed troops in preparation for a campaign to capture New Orleans, Jackson intervened with his 4,700-man force. Jackson's significant victory in the Battle of New Orleans, the last major battle of the War of 1812, made him a national hero, while his stubborn demeanor in the face of adversity earned him the nickname "Old Hickory." Overlooked in the victory was that—unbeknownst to those on the battlefield—the Treaty of Ghent ending the war had already been signed.

In 1817, President James Monroe called upon Jackson and his Tennessee volunteers to spearhead a military campaign against the Seminole people of Spanish Florida who were staging cross-border raids into Georgia. Jackson's strategy was to invade Florida to deny the Seminole a base of operations. Spain demanded that Jackson be disciplined, but ultimately the matter merely hastened Spain's cession of Florida to the United States. When this happened in 1821, Jackson served as military governor of Florida.

RACHEL JACKSON

The wife of Andrew Jackson, Rachel Donelson was born on June 15, 1767, and died on December 22, 1828, shortly before he was inaugurated as president, so she was never the first lady. She was born in Pittsylvania County, Virginia, the youngest of the eight children of Rachel Stockley Donelson and Col. John Donelson, one of the founders of Nashville. She endured a bad early marriage to Lewis Robards of Kentucky, but separated from him in 1790.

She met Jackson when he was boarding with Rachel's mother. She assumed that her divorce was final, so the two wed in Natchez, Mississippi, in 1791. After the divorce was finally granted, they remarried in 1794, but accusations of bigamy continued to be hurled at Rachel by her husband's rivals. He defended her honor at every turn, and remained deeply affected by her death for the rest of his life.

EMILY DONELSON

With the death of Rachel Jackson shortly before she became first lady, the role of ceremonial White House hostess was assumed by her niece, Emily Donelson, who had assisted her at the Hermitage before Jackson became president. Born on June 1, 1807, on her father's farm in Donelson, Tennessee, Emily was the daughter of John Donelson, Rachel's brother. In 1824, she married A. J. Donelson, her first cousin, who served in the White House as President Jackson's private secretary.

Emily and the president had a falling out when Emily was perceived as participating in spreading rumors that Secretary of War John Henry Eaton had a pre-marital affair with his then-wife Peggy. When members of Washington society—including the vice president's wife—snubbed Peggy socially, it reminded Jackson of Rachel's ostracism and he reportedly fired Emily, although she remained at the White House for some time. She died of tuberculosis on December 19, 1836.

FIRST LADY
SARAH YORKE JACKSON

The wife of Andrew Jackson Jr., the adopted son of the president, Sarah Yorke Jackson took over as White House hostess after the dismissal of Emily Donelson. Born on July 16, 1803, in Philadelphia, she was the daughter of wealthy merchant Peter Yorke and Mary Haines Yorke, and orphaned as a teenager. She married the younger Jackson in 1831 and they lived at the Hermitage until it was damaged by a fire in 1834.

Andrew and Sarah then moved into the White House, where she acted as a co-hostess or second first lady until Emily Donelson departed. Sarah remained at the White House through Jackson's final term, when she and her husband returned to the Hermitage with the former president. She lived at the estate off and on until her death on August 23, 1887.

A portrait of Rachel Donelson Jackson (left). *Ralph Eleaser Whiteside Earl*

After Rachel's death, Jackson's niece, Emily Donelson (right), acted as First Lady and hostess of the White House. *National Park Service*

In 1822, Jackson was again elected to the US Senate from Tennessee, where he served for only two years.

Encouraged to run against fellow Democratic-Republican John Quincy Adams for the presidency in 1824, Jackson won ninety-nine electoral votes to his opponent's eighty-four, but only 41.4 percent of the popular vote. This left the choice up to the House of Representatives under provisions of the Twelfth Amendment, and the choice was Adams.

When the two faced one another again in 1828, the Democratic-Republican Party had disintegrated. Adams ran under the banner of the National Republican Party, a coalition of anti-Jackson elements of his former party and former Federalists. Jackson ran with the new Democratic Party, which held to Jeffersonian ideals about a small central government and states' rights. This time, Jackson won 178 to 83 in the Electoral College and took 56 percent of the popular vote. When he ran for reelection in 1832, Jackson was challenged by Senator Henry Clay of Kentucky, previously a supporter of Adams and a long-time opponent of Jackson. This time, the Electoral College totals were 219 to 49, with 54.2 percent of the popular vote going to the still-popular Jackson.

As president of the United States, Andrew Jackson cast himself as a man of the people, encouraging a broader electorate that was not dominated by the establishment elite. He invited the general public to his inaugural party at the White House, drawing a chaotic crowd that did considerable damage. He chose his cabinet from outside the political inner circles, and tried without much success to adhere to a merit system for federal employees.

A daguerreotype of Andrew Jackson taken shortly before his death in 1845.
Edward Anthony

In his belief in states' rights Jackson did not go as far as his vice president. John C. Calhoun came to differ with Jackson over the issue of tariffs that helped mainly industrial interests in the North to the detriment of the agricultural South. Calhoun supported Nullification, an interpretation of the Tenth Amendment to the Constitution that would allow states to nullify federal law they considered unconstitutional. This almost led to South Carolina leaving the Union, and it did lead to Calhoun breaking ranks with Jackson and resigning in 1832. Taking an opposite perspective, Jackson vetoed the rechartering of the Second Bank of the United States, the "national bank" that had been chartered for twenty years in 1816, because he felt that it unduly favored the needs of the elite.

Though he presented himself as an advocate of the common man over the elite, Jackson's advocacy stopped at the color barrier. Known as an uncompromising slaveholder in his personal life, he opposed the abolitionist movement in his public life. Nevertheless, he withheld his recognition of the pro-slavery Republic of Texas until after the 1836 election. As president, Jackson oversaw the admission of Arkansas as a slave state in 1836 and Michigan as a non-slave state in 1837.

Jackson's most controversial action as president was his support of the Indian Removal Act of 1830 and his expelling the entire population of Cherokee, Chickasaw, Choctaw, Creek (Muscogee), and Seminole people from the southeastern United States to a tract of land west of the Mississippi that is now eastern Oklahoma. Ironically, these groups were known as the "Five Civilized Tribes" because they had adopted Anglo-American customs, language, farming practices, housing styles, and religion. The removal, ongoing throughout the Jackson administration, was described by one Choctaw commentator as the "Trail of Tears."

After leaving office, Jackson returned to the Hermitage, where he died of a variety of natural causes, including probable heart failure, on June 8, 1845. He was buried beside Rachel at the Hermitage.

VICE PRESIDENTS

JOHN C. CALHOUN

Along with George Clinton, John Caldwell Calhoun was one of only two men to serve as vice president of the United States under two presidents. In 1824, he was elected to serve under John Quincy Adams (see Calhoun sidebar in the previous chapter), and in 1828, he ran with Andrew Jackson, but they came into conflict over Calhoun's more strict interpretation of states' rights, which led to Calhoun's resigning the vice presidency.

Calhoun then ran for the US Senate in 1832 as a member of the Nullifier Party, was elected, and served until 1843, though he joined the new Democratic Party in 1839. He left the Senate in 1844 to serve for one year as President John Tyler's secretary of state, but returned to the Senate in 1845, where he remained until his death in 1850. It was during these years in the Senate that the Great Triumvirate of Calhoun, Henry Clay, and Daniel Webster dominated American legislative and political life. Though they did not always agree on many issues, including slavery, they often compromised in the interest of preserving the Union.

Gradually deteriorating from the effects of tuberculosis, Calhoun died on March 31, 1850, in Washington, DC, even as he was leading the opposition to the Compromise of 1850. He was buried in Charleston, South Carolina, in a grave that remained unmarked until 1871.

MARTIN VAN BUREN

In the face of the friction between Andrew Jackson and John C. Calhoun, the president gravitated toward fellow Democrat and Calhoun rival Martin Van Buren of New York as his running mate in 1832. He had previously named the New York governor as his secretary of state, and in 1831, Jackson appointed Van Buren as minister to Great Britain. In the 1832 election, as Jackson rode a landslide to victory over Henry Clay, Van Buren won 189 electoral votes, more than five times the total of any other challenger. This put him in a good position to be elected as president of the United States in 1836, which he was. He and his presidency are described in detail in the following chapter.

Martin Van Buren

8

DEMOCRATIC PARTY

The first president of the United States who was not born a British subject prior to the Declaration of Independence, Martin Van Buren was also the only president whose first language was not English, but Dutch. He was born Maarten van Buren, the descendant of Dutch settlers, in Kinderhook, New York, on December 5, 1782. His parents were Abraham van Buren and Maria Hoes van Alen van Buren. Maria had previously been married to the late Johannes van Alen, with whom she had two sons and a daughter. Martin—to use his anglicized name—was the middle of Abraham and Maria's five children. In 1807, he married Hannah Hoes, a first cousin, who passed away in 1819 before the high points of his political career. He never remarried.

Like Andrew Jackson, Van Buren never attended college, but he studied law. He apprenticed in New York City with a colleague of Aaron Burr and was admitted to the New York Bar in 1803. He was also active in New York Democratic-Republican politics as a young man, and worked on the state campaigns of Burr, George Clinton, and Daniel Tompkins. He served in the New York Senate from 1812 to 1820, first opposing, then supporting the Erie Canal project. Van Buren was New York's attorney general from 1815 to 1819 and was elected to the US Senate in 1821, where he served through 1829, and where he opposed the infrastructure initiatives of Henry Clay and John Quincy Adams.

In 1828, though recently elected to the Senate with a large majority, Van Buren ran for governor of New York, won, and resigned his Senate seat. He resigned as governor after only ten weeks to accept an appointment as Andrew Jackson's secretary of state. In this role, Van Buren negotiated the return of property in Europe seized during the aftermath of the French Revolution, cut a deal with Turkey for trading

above: The official engraved portrait of Martin Van Buren as president. *Bureau of Engraving and Printing*

left: Lindenwald, the home of Martin Van Buren, is located near Kinderhook, New York. He acquired the thirty-six room mansion in 1839 but did not move in until 1841, after he was defeated for a second term. *Library of Congress*

access to the Black Sea, and opened trade with British colonies in the Caribbean.

In 1831, Washington, DC, was abuzz with the scandal involving the wife of Secretary of War John Henry Eaton. Jackson, who felt that the snubbing of Peggy Eaton was like the early treatment of his own wife, made a show of force by firing cabinet members involved in this.

Van Buren, who had supported Peggy Eaton, resigned in order that Jackson could make a clean sweep. Jackson rewarded Van Buren with the post of minister to Great Britain. When a vengeful John C. Calhoun, now back in the Senate, led the move to overturn this recess appointment, he hoped it to be the nail in Van Buren's political coffin, but instead, it only made him seem that much more appealing as a Calhoun opponent and the Democrats nominated him to run for vice president in 1832. Jackson and Van Buren were elected easily.

In 1836, with Andrew Jackson stepping down, Martin Van Buren was the heir apparent for the Democratic nomination, which he secured by assuring southern delegates that he was no abolitionist. The Democrats, meanwhile, were now opposed by the Whig Party, recently formed by Henry Clay and Daniel Webster to oppose Jackson, and now Van Buren. Fortunately, the Whigs were split with several running for president.

In the general election, Van Buren's biggest competitor was William Henry Harrison, the popular ex-general and Ohio Whig, who earned 73 electoral votes to Van Buren's 170. Webster polled only fourteen. Van Buren captured 50.8 percent of the popular vote.

As president of the United States, Martin Van Buren walked a tightrope between slave-state representatives and abolitionists, rejecting the request of Texas to join the United States because it would upset the balance, and because he did not wish to anger Mexico. Indeed, no states were admitted during his tenure. He took the position of morally opposing slavery, while recognizing its statutory legality.

The Van Buren presidency was cursed by the Panic of 1837 and the subsequent economic downturn. The president was incapable of responding to the emergency and his popularity faded. Thus, when there was a rematch of the previous election in 1840, William Henry Harrison won handily.

Van Buren retired to Lindenwald, his estate at Kinderhook, but made plans for the 1844 election. At the Democratic Convention that year, he was on the ballot but faced the opposition of the pro-slavery faction over his opposition to admitting Texas, and he withdrew. In 1848, he received the

right: A portrait by Henry Inman of First Lady Angelica Singleton Van Buren, the wife of Martin Van Buren's son Abrahm. As Van Buren's wife had died prior to his being elected president, Angelica acted as first lady during her father-in-law's presidency. *White House*

HANNAH HOES VAN BUREN

The wife of Martin Van Buren, whom he affectionately knew as "Jannetje" (Johanna), was born in Kinderhook, New York, on March 8, 1783, the daughter of Johannes Dircksen Hoes and Maria Quakenbush. Martin and Maria, who had known one another as children, were first cousins once removed. They were married on February 21, 1807, at the Catskill, New York, home of Hannah's sister. They had five sons, one of whom died as an infant, and a stillborn daughter. Hannah died of tuberculosis on February 5, 1819, at the age of thirty-five. Nowhere in her husband's 1,247-page autobiographical manuscript is she mentioned.

A miniature of Hannah Hoes Van Buren. *Unknown artist*

The Children of Martin Van Buren and Hannah Van Buren

Abraham Van Buren (1807–1873)
John Van Buren (1810–1866)
Martin "Matt" Van Buren Jr. (1812–1855)
Winfield Scott Van Buren (1814–1814)
Smith Thompson Van Buren (1817–1876)

FIRST LADY
SARAH VAN BUREN

As Hannah Hoes Van Buren died eighteen years before her husband became president, the role of first lady as White House hostess was filled by daughter-in-law, Sarah Van Buren, who had married their son, Abraham Van Buren, on November 27, 1838. She was born on February 13, 1818, in Wedgefield, South Carolina. The daughter of Richard Singleton and Rebecca Travis Coles, she was also a cousin of previous first lady Dolley Madison. At age nineteen, Sarah was the youngest first lady ever to take on this job. After Martin Van Buren left office, Abraham and Sarah joined him in Kinderhook and divided their time between here and her family home in South Carolina. She died in New York City on December 29, 1877.

presidential nomination of the Free Soil Party but received no electoral votes. He remained more active in party politics than previous former presidents, but he was never again considered seriously as a presidential candidate.

Two of his sons, Martin Van Buren Jr. and Smith Thompson Van Buren, who had served him as aides during his time in public life, aided him in compiling his autobiography, which he wrote in part at Villa Falagola in Sorrento, Italy, in 1854. The manuscript was presented to the Library of Congress by Mrs. Smith Thompson Van Buren in 1909. Martin Van Buren died on July 24, 1862, and is buried in the cemetery at the Kinderhook Reformed Dutch Church along with his parents, his wife, and his son Martin.

VICE PRESIDENT

RICHARD M. JOHNSON

Born on October 17, 1780, near Louisville, Kentucky, Richard Mentor "Dick" Johnson was the son of Robert and Jemima Suggett Johnson. His mother became famous for defying threats made by Indians who had surrounded the community Bryan's Station. Refusing to be intimidated, she led other women to make their usual trip to the spring to get water. The Indians waited to attack until they were back in the village, but when they did, an arrow missed two-year-old Richard by inches.

A portrait of Richard Mentor Johnson. *Attributed to Matthew Harris Jouett*

He was admitted to the Kentucky Bar in 1802 and was elected to the state legislature in 1804. Two years later, running as a Democratic-Republican, he was elected to the US House of Representatives, where he served until 1819. During this time, he represented two separate districts and served a term in an at-large seat. He was a great proponent of the War of 1812, and in the war's first two years, he recruited and led his own regiment while Congress was in adjournment. During this time, he distinguished himself heroically in the Battle of the Thames.

After serving again briefly in the Kentucky legislature, he was appointed to fill a vacant US Senate seat in 1819, and won a full term in 1822. In 1828, though, he failed in his reelection bid, reportedly because his common-law wife, Julia Chinn, was one-eighth black. Undaunted, he ran successfully for the House of Representatives and served four terms. In 1836, though he was not Van Buren's first choice, he was picked by the Democratic Party to run for vice president and was elected with almost twice the electoral votes of his nearest Whig competitor.

As vice president, he did not have the confidence of the president, and wielded little power. In 1840, he was dropped by the party and replaced by James Knox Polk as Van Buren's running mate, but the Van Buren–Polk ticket lost. Johnson tried for the nomination for president in 1844 but lost to Polk. Dick Johnson returned to Kentucky, served in the legislature from 1841 to 1843, lost an 1848 bid for governor, and had just been elected again to the legislature when he died on November 19, 1850.

9

1841

William H. Harrison

WHIG PARTY

As president of the United States, William Henry Harrison is remembered for having given the longest inauguration address and serving the shortest term in office. His speech contained more than eight thousand words and lasted more than one hundred minutes. He delivered it in driving sleet without a hat or coat, fell ill with pneumonia—presumably because of this—and died just a month into his first and only term as president. He was also the only president whose grandson became president. Benjamin Harrison was elected in 1888.

William Henry Harrison was born on February 9, 1773, in Charles City County, Virginia, the son of Elizabeth Bassett and Benjamin Harrison, a former Virginia governor, a member of the Continental Congress, and a signatory of the Declaration of Independence. When his father died in 1791, William joined the US Army at the age of eighteen and—thanks to his father's connections—was commissioned as an officer. In this, his first career in the military, he served for seven years, mainly under Gen. "Mad Anthony" Wayne in the Northwest Territory. This entity comprised portions of six present states from Minnesota to Ohio, but Harrison served mainly in Indiana and Ohio, as well as in Kentucky. It was here that he met and married Anna Tuthill Symmes in 1795.

In 1798, Harrison was named as territorial secretary, but often filled in as governor of Northwest Territory while Governor Arthur St. Clair was away. In turn, he was elected to the US House of Representatives as a non-voting territorial delegate. When the Northwest Territory was broken up in

1800, President John Adams named Harrison to serve as the governor of the new Territory of Indiana. As governor, he negotiated a series of treaties under which Indian tribes ceded land to the territory.

Shawnee dissatisfaction over the Treaty of Fort Wayne led to a political standoff between Harrison and two influential Shawnee leaders, the brothers Tecumseh and Tenskwatawa. When the disagreement boiled over into open warfare, Harrison personally led the Indiana Militia to a major victory over the Shawnee in the Battle of Tippecanoe in November 1811, in which Tecumseh was killed, and Harrison became a popular military hero.

Within a few months, the conflict with the Indians in the Northwest became a theater of the War of 1812, and President James Madison named Harrison to command all the militia and US Army units in the region with the rank of major general. He achieved a series of victories across Indiana and Ohio, recaptured Detroit, and chased the British into Canada. Here, he scored a pivotal victory of the British in the Battle of the Thames in 1813, cementing his stellar reputation. Despite this, Secretary of War John Armstrong reassigned Harrison to a minor command, precipitating Harrison's resignation in 1814.

Harrison was elected to the US House of Representatives from Ohio in 1816, and served in the Ohio state legislature from 1819 to 1821, having lost the election for Ohio governor in 1820. In 1824, he was elected to the US Senate and served until 1828, when President James Monroe

opposite top: An engraved portrait of William Henry Harrison. *Bureau of Engraving and Printing*. above: This portrait by Rembrandt Peale originally depicted Harrison in civilian clothes as a congressional delegate in 1800. The uniform was added after he achieved fame in the War of 1812. *National Portrait Gallery*

ANNA SYMMES HARRISON

The only first lady not to set foot in the White House, Anna Harrison was ill and unable to leave Ohio to come to Washington for her husband's inauguration, but planned to travel east in May 1841. By then, she was a widow.

She was born on July 25, 1775, near Morristown, New Jersey, though she was raised on Long Island, where her mother's family lived. She was the daughter of New Yorker Anna Tuthill Symmes and John Cleves Symmes, the chief justice of the New Jersey Supreme Court and a New Jersey delegate to the Continental Congress. In 1788, the family relocated to the newly formed Northwest Territory, settling near what is now North Bend, Ohio. She met William Henry Harrison in 1795 while on a visit to Lexington, Kentucky. When Harrison asked the disapproving Judge Symmes for her hand in marriage, he refused.

Anna Tuthill Symmes Harrison.
Library of Congress

Undaunted, the couple eloped and were married in North Bend on November 22, 1795. When asked by the judge how he planned to support Anna, Harrison famously replied "by my sword, and my own right arm, sir."

After forty-two years of being married to a politician and general, and watching the deaths of six of her ten children, Anna never experienced life as first lady. Ironically, their daughter-in-law, Jane Irwin Harrison, who had been asked to act as White House hostess until Anna arrived, was already a widow.

Anna lived out her years in North Bend, living with son John Scott Harrison, and helped raise his son, Benjamin Harrison. Anna died on February 25, 1864, twenty-four years before Benjamin Harrison was elected as president.

The Children of William Henry Harrison and Anna Harrison
Elizabeth Bassett Harrison (1796–1846)
John Cleves Symmes Harrison (1798–1830)
Lucy Singleton Harrison (1800–1826)
William Henry Harrison Jr. (1802–1838)
John Scott Harrison (1804–1878)
Benjamin Harrison (1806–1840)
Mary Symmes Harrison (1809–1842)
Carter Bassett Harrison (1811–1839)
Anna Tuthill Harrison (1813–1845)
James Findlay Harrison (1814–1817)

appointed him as minister to newly independent Colombia. While in Bogotá, he met Simón Bolívar, whom he perceived as a would-be dictator, and whom he advised to adopt democracy as a form of government. When Andrew Jackson was elected, Harrison returned to Ohio and settled down to life as a gentleman farmer.

Coaxed out of retirement in 1836 by the Whig Party, who saw the national hero as presidential material, Harrison ran for president for the first time. Having four Whigs in the field practically guaranteed failure, and Democrat Martin Van Buren defeated Harrison 170 to 73 in the Electoral College.

Four years later, the economic downturn made Van Buren deeply unpopular, while Harrison was still a war hero, and he chose the popular John Tyler as a running mate. The winning campaign slogan in 1840 was "Tippecanoe and Tyler too."

Harrison won with 234 electoral votes to 60 for Van Buren, and 52.9 percent of the popular vote. There then followed the shortest presidency ever, in which Harrison did little but to call Congress into a special session to consider fiscal matters, a session that he would never see.

Inaugurated on March 4, 1841, William Henry Harrison passed away on April 4, the first American president to die in office.

JOHN TYLER

Senator John Tyler of Virginia had first run for vice president as a Whig Party candidate in the 1836 election, but had come in second among the Whigs and a distant third behind Democrat Richard Mentor Johnson, who was elected as vice president when Martin Van Buren defeated William Henry Harrison for president.

In 1840, when Harrison faced Van Buren a second time, Tyler was again on the Whig ticket in a rematch with incumbent Democrat Johnson. This time, Tyler won 234 electoral votes to Johnson's 48. In March 1841, Tyler took office, little knowing that his would be the shortest vice presidency ever. A month later, he found himself president of the United States. John Tyler and his presidency are described in detail in the following chapter.

This lithograph, published by Endicot in New York around the time of the 1840 election, graphically depicts events from the life and military career of William H. Harrison, from his log cabin origins to the Battle of Tippecanoe. *Library of Congress*

10

John Tyler

WHIG PARTY

T he first president to assume the presidency after having been elected as vice president, Tyler is also the only one to have served in the legislatures of two countries, the United States of America and the Confederate States of America. However, he is perhaps best remembered for his family life rather than for his accomplishments in office. When his first wife died in the White House, he remarried twenty-one months later, becoming the first president to be wed in the White House.

Tyler had more children than any other president, eight with his first wife and seven with his second. There was a forty-five-year span between the birth of his first child and the birth of his youngest. Indeed, Mary Tyler, his oldest, died at the age of thirty-three, a dozen years before his youngest, Pearl Tyler, was born. He had two grandsons still living in the twenty-first century.

John Tyler was born on March 29, 1790, in Charles City County, Virginia, the son of Mary Marot Armisted and John Tyler Sr., a college roommate of Thomas Jefferson. Tyler was admitted to the Virginia Bar in 1809 and practiced in Richmond. He was elected to the Virginia House of Delegates in 1811, and in 1816, he was picked to fill a vacant seat in the US House of Representatives. He returned to his law practice in 1821, but ran again for the House of Delegates in 1823.

In 1825, he was elected to his first of two one-year terms as governor of Virginia, a post in which his father had served from 1808 to 1811. In 1827, Tyler resigned the governorship to serve in the US Senate. As a Democrat, he supported Andrew Jackson—at least in most of his policy initiatives. In 1832, Tyler allied himself with John C. Calhoun and broke ranks with Jackson over the president's opposition to Nullification, the interpretation of the Tenth Amendment to the Constitution

top: John Tyler as president of the United States. *Library of Congress*

left: John Tyler receiving the news of President William Henry Harrison's death from Chief Clerk of the State Department Fletcher Webster. *Library of Congress*

opposite page: The official presidential portrait of John Tyler by George Peter Alexander Healy. *White House*

The official presidential portrait of John Tyler by George Peter Alexander Healy. *White House*

FIRST LADY
LETITIA CHRISTIAN TYLER

Born on November 12, 1790, in New Kent County, Virginia, Letitia Christian was the daughter of Col. Robert Christian and Mary Brown Christian. She met John Tyler in 1808 when he was studying law, though they were not married until March 29, 1813. By the time that Tyler became president, they had seven children and had lost another as an infant.

In the White House, Letitia was one of the most reclusive of first ladies, remaining in the residential quarters and not participating in social activities. She did, however, venture downstairs to attend the White House wedding of her daughter, Elizabeth, in January 1842. Only eight months later, on September 10, she became the first of three first ladies, along with Caroline Harrison and Ellen Wilson, to die in the White House.

The Children of John Tyler and Letitia Christian Tyler

Mary Tyler (1815–1848)
Robert Tyler (1816–1877)
John Tyler (1819–1896)
Letitia Tyler (1821–1907)
Elizabeth Tyler (1823–1850)
Anne Contesse Tyler (1825)
Alice Tyler (1827–1854)
Tazewell Tyler (1830–1874)

An oil portrait of Letitia Tyler. *Unknown artist*

that would allow states to nullify federal law they considered unconstitutional. Tyler joined the Whig Party and resigned from the Senate in 1836. Later that year, he was one of the Whigs who ran for vice president, but the party lost to the Democrats on the general election.

In the 1840 election, Tyler again ran for vice president as William Henry Harrison headed the Whig Party in a rematch of his unsuccessful bid for the presidency against Martin Van Buren. This time, Harrison won, and so did John Tyler.

A month after being sworn in as vice president, Tyler found himself serving out Harrison's term—though there were many, from Henry Clay to John Quincy Adams, who thought of him as a mere "acting president" and addressed him as such. Clay engineered the resignation of the cabinet—previously picked by Harrison—in an effort to force Tyler out, but he stood fast and Secretary of State Daniel Webster stayed on for two years. Nevertheless, the Tyler administration was nagged by problems with Congress, including fellow Whigs as well as Democrats.

As there was no constitutional provision for a replacement vice president, Tyler had none, and this office remained vacant throughout his presidency.

In the last days of his presidency, Florida achieved statehood and Tyler signed legislation annexing the Republic of Texas, an action that had long been discussed and debated. The majority in Texas, which had been independent of Mexico since 1836, favored such a move, but there was still much opposition in the United States to the admission of another slave state, and threats of war from Mexico. Because of the ongoing disagreement, Tyler chose not to run for reelection in 1844. Early in 1845, the annexation bill was approved by the US Congress and signed by Tyler, though statehood did not occur until December, after Tyler had left office—and this resulted in the Mexican War, a major event in the presidency of James K. Polk.

Tyler retired to his plantation in Virginia, and remained out of public life until 1861, when he became active in efforts to prevent the Civil War. Later in the year, after Virginia had seceded from the Union, John Tyler, former president of the United States, was elected to represent Virginia in the Confederate House of Representatives. However, his health had been deteriorating for some time, and he died of a stroke on January 12, 1862, before he took office. A Confederate state funeral was held, and he was interred at Hollywood Cemetery in Richmond.

FIRST LADY
JULIA GARDINER TYLER

She was born on May 4, 1820, on Gardiner's Island off New York's Long Island, the daughter of New York State Senator David Gardiner and Juliana McLachlan Gardiner. As a teenager, she was more outgoing than usual by contemporary standards and was sent aboard to learn the social norms of a proper young lady in upper crust society. The family began living in Washington, DC, after David Gardiner was elected to the US House of Representatives, and it was here that Julia met John Tyler in 1842.

In February 1844, Julia and her father were among a group who joined President Tyler and his entourage for a cruise on the Potomac River aboard the USS *Princeton*. During a gunnery demonstration, one of the guns exploded, and several people, including Gardiner, were killed. Julia fainted and was carried to safety by Tyler himself. A romance ensued.

Julia refused Tyler's first marriage proposal—he was fifty-four and she was just short of twenty-four—but she later reconsidered, and they were married in an understated ceremony in New York City on June 26, 1844. His children, three of whom were older than Julia, disapproved and did not attend.

Unlike Letitia Tyler, who rarely appeared in public, Julia Tyler took to the role of first lady with boundless energy and enthusiasm, hosting events with guest lists in the thousands.

After leaving the White House, the Tylers retired to his estate in Virginia, where Julia, a daughter of New York, thoroughly embraced her new life as a southerner, both socially and politically. After her husband died in 1862, she spent the duration of the Civil War in New York, but was observed flying a Confederate flag. In the 1870s, she converted to Roman Catholicism and returned to Virginia, where she died on July 10, 1889.

The Children of John Tyler and Julia Gardiner Tyler
David Gardiner Tyler (1846–1927)
John Alexander "Alex" Tyler (1848–1883)
Julia Gardiner Tyler (1849–1871)
Lachlan Tyler (1851–1902)
Lyon Gardiner Tyler (1853–1935)
Robert Fitzwalter Tyler (1856–1927)
Pearl Tyler (1860–1947)

Julia Gardiner Tyler. *Francesco Anell*

John and Julia Tyler's home at Sherwood Forest, near Charles City, Virginia, is the only private residence to have been owned by two unrelated presidents. William Henry Harrison owned the plantation, then named Walnut Grove, in 1790–1793, but never lived in the house. Harrison's successor, Tyler purchased the plantation in 1842 and lived there after leaving the White House. *National Park Service*

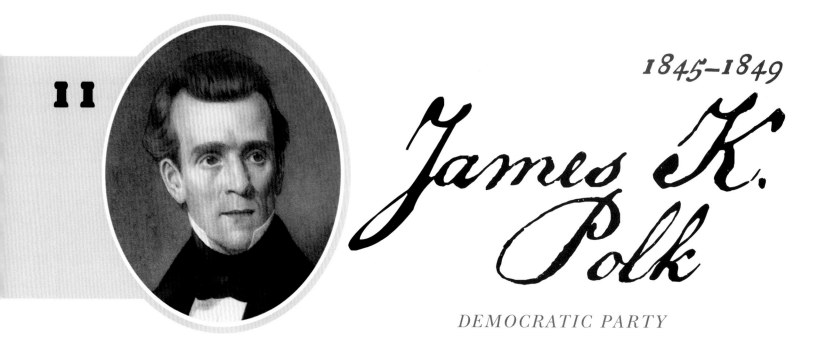

1845–1849

James K. Polk

DEMOCRATIC PARTY

A number of important technological changes coincided with the presidency of James Knox Polk. He was the first president whose nomination and election were widely reported via telegraph, he was the first president to install gas lighting inside the White House, and he was the first president to be photographed while in office. The United States issued its first postage stamps on his watch. Many important entities, including the Smithsonian Institution and the US Naval Academy, got their start during his presidency, as did the Department of the Interior, the first new cabinet department in nearly half a century.

He is perhaps best remembered for adding more territory to the contiguous United States than any president since Thomas Jefferson had made the Louisiana Purchase. He was a believer in the idea of "Manifest Destiny," a term coined in 1845 by columnist John Louis O'Sullivan to describe the widely held notion that it was the destiny of the United States to comprise all of the territory between the Atlantic and Pacific that it now occupies.

James Knox Polk was born on November 5, 1795, in a farmhouse in Mecklenburg County, North Carolina, the eldest of the ten children of Jane Knox Polk and Samuel Polk, who eventually became a prosperous farmer. An incident often related in describing Polk's early life came when he had bladder stones removed from his body without the benefit of anesthetic.

Polk graduated from the University of North Carolina in 1818 and moved to Nashville to study law, being admitted to the Tennessee Bar in 1820. In 1822, he joined the Tennessee Militia and was appointed to the governor's staff with the rank of colonel, a title he used for the rest of his life. In 1823, he was elected to the state legislature, and in 1825, he was elected to the US House of Representatives.

In the meantime, he met Sarah Childress, whom he married in 1824 but whom he did not take with him to Washington, DC, until 1826. In the House, Polk worked diligently for the policies of Democratic presidents Andrew Jackson and Martin Van Buren. In 1833, in his fifth term, Polk became chairman of the House Ways and Means Committee, and in 1835, he became Speaker of the House. In 1839, he left Congress to run for governor of Tennessee, where he won, but faced difficulties with an uncooperative legislature.

Polk had long entertained dreams of making a serious presidential bid, and he got his chance in 1844. The major issue was the admission of Texas to the Union as a slave state. President John Tyler and the Democrats promoted it, while Henry Clay and the Whigs opposed it. Clay was nominated to carry the party's banner as its presidential candidate. Van Buren was the presumptive Democratic nominee, but when his candidacy failed to win broad support, Polk emerged as a dark-horse candidate and captured the nomination. In a close general election, Polk defeated Clay 170 to 105 in the Electoral College, earning 49.5 percent of the popular vote.

Immediately upon being inaugurated, Polk stepped into crisis. After he was elected, Congress and President John Tyler, now a lame duck, authorized the annexation of the Republic of Texas, though the move was opposed by abolitionists, and Mexico had threatened war. Polk attempted to negotiate with Mexico and also offered to buy land in the West that Mexico had inherited when it achieved its independence from Spain but in which most of the non-indigenous population was American.

In early 1846, when Mexican troops killed US Army troops in a disputed area north of the Rio Grande, Polk asked Congress for a declaration of war, which came on May 13. United States forces under Gen. Zachary Taylor invaded Mexico in 1847, capturing Mexico City and other major population centers.

A month later, California, where the majority population consisted of Americans, Europeans, and Californios (descendants of Spanish settlers), declared its independence. The Mexican War concluded in February 1848 with the Treaty of Guadalupe Hidalgo, which called for Mexican recognition of Texas annexation, a withdrawal of American troops from Mexico south of Texas, and a substantial cash payment to Mexico for California and the land between there and the Mississippi River.

In December 1846, one year after the admission of Texas as a slave state, Iowa was admitted as a non-slave state, and Wisconsin was admitted as

left: An official oil portrait of James Knox Polk by George Peter Alexander Healy. *White House*

opposite top: James Knox Polk in a lithograph published by C. S. Williams in 1846. *Library of Congress*

FIRST LADY
SARAH CHILDRESS POLK

Born in Murfreesboro, Tennessee, on September 4, 1803, Sarah Childress was one of the six children of Elizabeth Whitsitt Childress and businessman and planter Joel Childress. She was educated in North Carolina and first met James K. Polk in 1815. They were married on January 1, 1824, in Murfreesboro. They had no children but raised a nephew, Marshall Tate Polk, in their household.

Sarah was interested in politics and active in her husband's political campaigns, and she advised him on policy matters. She reportedly held a narrow view of societal norms, not permitting hard liquor or dancing at the White House. Nevertheless, she did permit wine and champagne and hosted the first Thanksgiving dinner at the White House.

After their time in Washington, she and her husband retired to Polk Place in Nashville, where the former president died three months later, and where she lived for forty-two years, mourning his passing by always dressing in black. She died on August 14, 1891, and was buried next to her husband. Two years later, they were reinterred together on the Tennessee State Capitol grounds.

A portrait of Sarah Childress Polk.
White House

the same in May 1848. The question of California statehood would be resolved on the watch of Polk's successor.

In the meantime, Polk negotiated a deal with Britain over the disputed area between the Rocky Mountains and the Pacific Ocean that lay north of California and south of the 54th Parallel. The British wanted everything north of the Columbia River, and many Americans wanted it all, but the agreement was made to extend the boundary at the 49th Parallel, negotiated in 1818 for land east of the Rocky Mountains, all the way to the Pacific.

James K. Polk left office having significantly changed the shape and breadth of the United States, but the strain took its toll. He died at Polk Place, his home in Nashville, Tennessee, on June 15, 1849, only three months after leaving office. He and his wife were interred on the grounds of their home, but the remains were moved to the Tennessee State Capitol complex in 1893.

VICE PRESIDENT
GEORGE M. DALLAS

A former US senator from Pennsylvania, George Mifflin Dallas was chosen by the Democratic Party to run for vice president in the election of 1844. During his career, he had a long-running political rivalry with fellow Pennsylvania Democrat and future president of the United States James Buchanan.

Born on July 10, 1792, in Philadelphia, Dallas graduated from the College of New Jersey (now Princeton University) in 1810 and was admitted to the Pennsylvania Bar in 1813. During the War of 1812, he traveled to Europe as part of a team led by Secretary of the Treasury Albert Gallatin to negotiate and end to the war.

Elected as mayor of Philadelphia, he resigned in 1829 to accept a post as a US attorney for Pennsylvania. Two years later, he was picked to fill a vacant US Senate seat and served for two years before declining to run for reelection and returning to his law practice. He remained in private practice until 1844, except for a stint as Martin Van Buren's minister to Russia between 1835 and 1837. In the 1844 election, Dallas defeated Whig candidate Theodore Frelinghuysen of New York 170 to 105 in the Electoral College.

In 1856, Dallas was called out of private practice by President Franklin Pierce to succeed his old rival James Buchanan as the United States minister to Great Britain, where he remained until 1861. Dallas passed away in Philadelphia on December 31, 1864.

POLK. THE YOUNG HICKORY.   DALLAS AND VICTORY.

JAMES K. POLK.   GEO: M. DALLAS.

PRESIDENT
AND

VICE-PRESIDENT

GRAND, NATIONAL, DEMOCRATIC BANNER.

PRESS ONWARD.

12

1849–1850

Zachary Taylor

WHIG PARTY

Standing for election at the end of a three-decade military career, Zachary Taylor was elected as the first president of the United States not to have had previous civilian experience in government. A military hero in campaigns from the War of 1812 through the Mexican War, he earned the nickname "Old Rough and Ready" for his tough disposition.

Born on November 24, 1784, in Orange County, Virginia, Zachary Taylor was the third son of Sarah Dabney Strother Taylor and Lt. Col. Richard Taylor, a veteran of the Continental Army in the War of Independence. He was also a second cousin of President James Madison. The family moved west to what is now Louisville, Kentucky, when Zachary was a boy, so he grew up on the frontier. He married Margaret Mackall Smith in 1810 and bought a plantation near Louisville.

Zachary Taylor joined the US Army in 1808 and was commissioned as a first lieutenant with the 7th Infantry Regiment. He served initially in Louisiana, and later in Indiana Territory, where he assumed command of Fort Knox at Vincennes. During the War of 1812, he saw action against the Shawnee in Indiana Territory. He mustered out of the service after the war, but rejoined in 1816 with the rank of major. After commanding Fort Howard, near Green Bay, Wisconsin, Taylor was promoted to lieutenant colonel in 1819 and given command of the 7th Infantry on the Red River in Louisiana. While here, he acquired a plantation and moved his family to Jefferson County, Mississippi. When he eventually ran for president, he chose Louisiana as his "home" state.

top: An official portrait of Gen. Zachary Taylor. *Bureau of Engraving and Printing*

above: An 1848 campaign poster engraved by Thomas Strong. *Library of Congress*

opposite: For the official presidential portrait of President Zachary Taylor, Joseph Henry Bush depicted him as a general. *White House*

FIRST LADY
MARGARET SMITH TAYLOR

Recalled today as one of the most obscure first ladies, of whom little is known and no portraits exist, Margaret Mackall Smith was born in Calvert County, Maryland, on September 21, 1788. Known to the family as "Peggy," she was the daughter of Ann Mackall Smith and Walter Smith, a successful planter and former Continental Army officer. She married Zachary Taylor on June 21, 1810, at her sister's home near Louisville, Kentucky. While he was serving in combat during a string of wars, she lived much of the time at the family plantation in Jefferson County, Mississippi. In 1820, the Taylors lost two young daughters to "bilious fever," a term widely used in the early nineteenth century for gastrointestinal maladies. Another daughter, Sarah, died shortly after her 1835 marriage to Jefferson Davis.

Peggy is recalled as having lived in fear for Zachary's life, not only while he was campaigning with the US Army, but while he was president. Like Letitia Christian Tyler, she was a reclusive first lady, rarely venturing outside the family quarters of the White House and letting her daughter, Betty Taylor, act as official hostess.

After her husband's death, she returned to Mississippi, where she died two years later, on August 14, 1852. She was interred next to her husband near Louisville.

The Children of Zachary Taylor and Margaret Mackall Taylor
Ann Margaret Mackall Taylor Wood (1811–1875)
Sarah Knox "Knoxie" Taylor Davis (1814–1835)
Octavia Pannill Taylor (1816–1820)
Margaret Smith Taylor (1819–1820)
Mary Elizabeth "Betty" Taylor Bliss (1824–1909)
Richard "Dick" Taylor (1826–1879)

Margaret "Peggy" Taylor. *White House*

In 1826, Taylor was called to US Army headquarters in Washington, DC, for two years before being given command of Fort Snelling, Minnesota, and later Fort Crawford, Wisconsin, both on the Mississippi River. Promoted to colonel, Taylor also saw action in the 1832 Black Hawk War.

Around this time, the colonel's daughter, Sarah Knox Taylor, age twenty-one, met a young lieutenant named Jefferson Davis. They married in 1835, but she died of malaria three months later, well before Davis became the president of the Confederate States of America.

In 1837, having been sent to Florida during the Second Seminole War, Taylor achieved a decisive victory in the Battle of Lake Okeechobee, one of the largest Indian Wars battles to date. He remained to command all US Army forces, and in 1841, now a brigadier general, he took command US Army's entire Western Division.

In 1844, in anticipation of a Mexican invasion in response to the impending annexation of Texas, Maj. Gen. Zachary Taylor deployed with a force to Louisiana, and later into Texas. In March 1846, he advanced south from the now state of Texas to the disputed territory along the Rio Grande, where some of his troops were killed by Mexican troops. When war was declared in May, he led his troops into Mexico, where he defeated the Mexican Army in the Battle of Monterrey in September. Having contributed part of his command to Gen. Winfield Scott's action at Veracruz, Taylor was attacked by the Mexican Gen. Antonio López de Santa Anna. Taylor's defeat of Santa Anna and a force nearly four times as large as his own in the Battle of Buena Vista was his greatest victory, and one that propelled him toward consideration for the presidency.

Though he had not previously announced a political preference, Taylor chose the Whigs, and was chosen by them over veteran Senator Henry Clay as their nominee. In the 1848 general election, Taylor defeated Lewis Cass of Michigan, the Democratic Party nominee, 163 to 127 in the Electoral College and won 47.3 percent of the popular vote.

As president of the United States, Taylor appointed a geographically diverse group of Whigs to his cabinet and made a point of touring the Northeast, a region of the country with which he was unfamiliar. As Texas statehood had been a major issue for his predecessor, admission of California loomed large for Taylor. The California Gold Rush of 1849 and a massive surge of Americans toward the West was underway even as Taylor took the oath of office. With a growing population and the source of immense quantities of mankind's favorite yellow metal, California was ripe for

Nathaniel Currier entitled this lithograph *Give Them a Little More Grape, Captain Bragg*, a phrase attributed to Zachary Taylor at the Battle of Buena Vista in 1847. In fact, Taylor ordered artillery battalion commander (and future Confederate general) Braxton Bragg to "double-shot your guns and give 'em hell," *not* to use grapeshot. The phrase was nevertheless popular as a slogan in the campaign of 1848. *Library of Congress*

statehood. There were also the other recently acquired regions to contend with.

Zachary Taylor never lived to see the resolution of the issue. Having come down with food poisoning at a Fourth of July celebration, he died in Washington on July 9, 1850, after just sixteen months in office. Vice President Millard Fillmore became the second holder of that office to assume the presidency.

Initially, Taylor was interred at the Congressional Cemetery in Washington, but his remains were later moved to the original Taylor homestead near Louisville. His only son, Richard "Dick" Taylor, was active in Louisiana politics and served as a general with the Confederate Army during the Civil War.

VICE PRESIDENT

MILLARD FILLMORE

An upstate New York lawyer, Millard Fillmore was chosen by the Whigs in 1848 to balance the ticket headed by Zachary Taylor of Louisiana. When Taylor died on July 9, 1850, Fillmore was sworn in as the second vice president to unexpectedly assume the presidency. He and his own presidency are described in detail in the following chapter.

13

Millard Fillmore

WHIG PARTY

Born on January 7, 1800, in Moravia in New York's Cayuga County, Millard Fillmore was the eldest son and second child of Nathaniel Fillmore and Phoebe Millard. He did not graduate from college but apprenticed to an attorney and was admitted to the New York Bar in 1823. He started a law practice in East Aurora, New York, and later joined with Nathan Hall in a law partnership. The only president to have married a teacher who had taught him in high school, he wed Abigail Powers in 1826 and they had two children. In 1846, he was one of the founders of the University of Buffalo.

Fillmore served three years in the New York legislature before being elected to the US House of Representatives in 1832. Here, he was an opponent to the admission of Texas as a slave state. In 1844, he failed in a New York gubernatorial bid, but served as the state's comptroller from 1848 to 1849. While in this office, he was picked as a vice presidential candidate to balance the Whig slate in the 1848, and was swept into office on the tide of Zachary Taylor's popularity as a war hero.

On July 9, 1850, he was sworn in as president on the same day that Taylor died. The first significant items to reach his desk from Congress were the bills that constituted the Compromise of 1850, which Taylor was thought to have opposed. Signed into law by Fillmore, the Compromise included statehood for California as a non-slave state, a ban on the slave trade in the District of Columbia, and an agreement whereby land claimed by Texas was incorporated into New Mexico Territory. Also included was the Wilmot

above: The official portrait of Millard Fillmore by George Peter Alexander Healy. *White House*

top: An engraving of Millard Fillmore as a presidential candidate.

Proviso, which called for the formation of Utah and New Mexico as territories that would make their own choice with regard to the slave issue. Most controversial was the Fugitive Slave Act that called for fugitive slaves to be returned to their owners even if found in non-slave states.

Internationally, Fillmore is remembered for sending Commodore Matthew Perry and the US Navy to open trade with insular Japan.

A photograph by Mathew Brady of Fillmore as a former president. *Library of Congress*

Like John Tyler, Fillmore served out most of the term of his predecessor and did so with no vice president.

In 1852, Fillmore decided to run for a full term as his own, but his having signed the Fugitive Slave Act made him unpopular at the Whig Convention, where he was opposed by Gen. Winfield Scott. The Whigs went through fifty-three ballots before achieving a majority. Fillmore gradually lost ground, and eventually, he lost the nomination. In the general election, Scott lost to Democrat Franklin Pierce.

Fillmore retired to New York, where he served as chancellor of the University of Buffalo. After the deaths of his wife in 1853 and his daughter in 1854, Fillmore spent time in Europe. He returned to the United States in 1856 to accept the presidential nomination of the anti-Catholic American Party, better known by its later nickname, the "Know-Nothing" Party, because of the secrecy that surrounded its internal workings. In his second bid for the White House, Fillmore earned only eight electoral votes.

During the Civil War, Fillmore was a constant critic of Abraham Lincoln and his war policy, and a supporter of George McClellan, who ran against him in 1864.

Fillmore died of a stroke on March 8, 1874, and was survived by his second wife, Catherine McIntosh, whom he had married in 1858. He was interred at Forest Lawn Cemetery in Buffalo.

FIRST LADY
ABIGAIL POWERS FILLMORE

Born on March 13, 1798, in Stillwater, New York, Abigail Powers was the daughter of a Baptist minister, Reverend Lemuel Powers, and Abigail Newland Powers. As a young woman of twenty-one, she got a job as a teacher in New Hope, where one of her students was the nineteen-year-old Millard Fillmore. After a long romance, they were married on February 5, 1826, in Moravia, New York, and settled down in East Aurora. They had a mutual interest in things literary and built a sizable library to which their two children were exposed.

A portrait of Abigail Fillmore.
Library of Congress

Abigail traveled to Washington, DC, accompanying her husband as a congressman and as vice president. When she joined him in the White House as the unexpected president of the United States, her health was deteriorating, so she depended upon her daughter to shoulder the challenges of first lady. At age eighteen, Mary Abigail "Abby" Fillmore had the stamina that her mother did not.

Abigail came down with pneumonia at the inauguration of her husband's successor and died less than a month later on March 30, 1853. She was buried at Forest Lawn Cemetery in Buffalo, where her husband would be interred eleven years later. Young Abigail died the following year of cholera at the age of twenty-two.

The Children of Millard Fillmore and Abigail Powers Fillmore
Millard Powers Fillmore (1828–1889)
Mary Abigail "Abby" Fillmore (1832–1854)

CAROLINE CARMICHAEL FILLMORE

The second wife of Millard Fillmore, Caroline Carmichael was born on October 21, 1813, in Morristown, New Jersey, the daughter of Charles Carmichael and Temperance Blachley Carmichael. In 1832, she married Ezekiel McIntosh, the wealthy and influential president of the Schenectady & Troy Railroad. When he died in 1855, she inherited a fortune so immense that when she married Millard Fillmore on February 10, 1858, her attorneys required him to sign a then-rare prenuptial agreement.

The social status of being married to a former president of the United States greatly appealed to her, just as the freedom from financial worry that came from being married to a wealthy heiress appealed to him. After his death in 1874, she remained in their mansion in Buffalo until her death on August 11, 1881. She was interred at Forest Lawn Cemetery in Buffalo near her husband and his first wife.

Franklin Pierce

DEMOCRATIC PARTY

Born on November 23, 1804, in a log cabin on his father's homestead near Hillsborough, New Hampshire, Franklin Pierce was the son of a former officer in the Continental Army, Benjamin Pierce, and Anna Kendrik Pierce, Benjamin's second wife. He did poorly in primary school, which he disliked, but attended the Philips Exeter Academy prep school and graduated from Bowdoin College in 1834. He worked for a while as a teacher in Hebron, New Hampshire, and became politically active as a Democrat in support of Andrew Jackson—as well as his father, Benjamin Pierce, who was elected as New Hampshire governor in 1827. Franklin was elected to the state legislature the following year. In 1832, as Jackson was elected to a second term as president of the United States, Franklin Pierce was elected to the US House of Representatives.

In 1834, he married Jane Means Appleton, with whom it seems he had nothing in common. She was from a pro-temperance Whig family, while he was a hard-drinking Democrat. He had developed a keen interest in pursuing his considerable political ambitions, while Jane detested both politics and Washington, DC.

In 1836, Pierce was elected to a seat in the US Senate, where he voted the Democratic Party line. The primary issue was the divide between the abolitionists and the pro-slavery Democrats. Though a northerner, Pierce opposed abolition. In 1842, Pierce resigned from the Senate and settled down in Concord, New Hampshire, to pursue a law career and to ponder his political future. An officer in the state militia, he

had always wanted to serve in combat, and in 1846, during the Mexican War, he got his chance. Promoted from colonel to brigadier general, and from regimental to brigade command, Pierce served under Gen. Winfield Scott in a series of battles culminating in the capture of Mexico City in 1847. He returned to New Hampshire, where he used his status as a perceived war hero to his political advantage.

At the 1852 Democratic Convention, the front-runners were Lewis Cass of Michigan and James Buchanan of Pennsylvania, neither of whom could get a majority. Pierce, a dark horse, received no votes until the still-deadlocked convention cast the thirty-fifth ballot. Thereafter, dispirited delegates migrated away from the front-runners and Pierce won on the forty-ninth ballot. In the general election, Pierce found himself running against his wartime commander, Gen. Winfield Scott, the Whig nominee, whom he defeated 254 to 42 in the Electoral College, with 50.8 percent of the popular vote. The victory was, however, clouded by tragedy. On their way to the inauguration, the rail car carrying the president-elect, his wife, and their only surviving son derailed and eleven-year-old Benjamin Pierce was killed.

Pierce was president when the Gadsden Purchase added a final slice of territory to the southern border to define the present shape of the contiguous United States, but the deal was done not by a member of Pierce's Administration, but by railroad executive James Gadsden.

The pivotal event of the Pierce years came with the passage in 1854 of the Kansas-Nebraska Act, which he supported. It was intended to open new territory for westward expansion

top left: An engraved portrait of Franklin Pierce. *Bureau of Engraving and Printing* above: Franklin Pierce, painted in 1853, by George Peter Alexander Healy. *National Portrait Gallery*

FIRST LADY
JANE APPLETON PIERCE

The wife of Franklin Pierce was born on March 12, 1806, in Hampton, New Hampshire, the daughter of Elizabeth Means Appleton and Congregationalist minister Reverend Jesse Appleton, who served as president of Bowdoin College. How she met Pierce is uncertain, but they were wed on November 19, 1834, in Amherst, New Hampshire. She is recalled as having been shy and sickly, even melancholy. Given the deaths of two of their three children before the age of five and that she disliked her husband's career and his drinking habits, there is probably an easy explanation. When her son Benny died, Jane considered it divine punishment for her husband's ambitions. She became withdrawn and did not appear in public in the White House until 1855. Jane suffered from tuberculosis in her later years and died in Andover, Massachusetts, on December 2, 1863. She was interred at Old North Cemetery in Concord, New Hampshire, where Franklin Pierce would be buried six years later.

The Children of Franklin Pierce and Jane Appleton Pierce
Franklin Pierce Jr. (1836–1836)
Franklin "Frank" Robert Pierce (1839–1843)
Benjamin "Benny" Pierce (1841–1853)

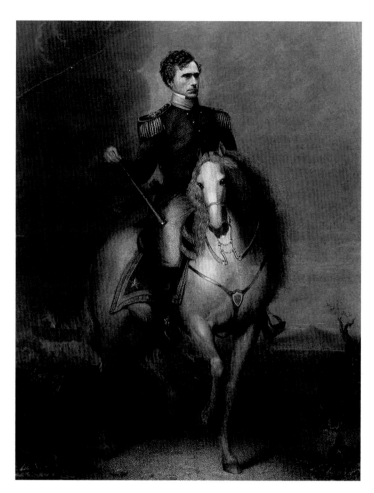

above: A heroic equestrian lithograph of Franklin Pierce. *Library of Congress*

Jane Appleton Pierce, circa 1886. *Library of Congress*

by creating the two territories of Kansas and Nebraska, but it essentially nullified the Missouri Compromise of 1820 by allowing the citizens of these territories to chose to be pro-slave or not. Open warfare ensued in "Bleeding Kansas" as settlers from opposing sides swarmed into the new territory. With this, Pierce's popularity fell, and so too his support within his own party. In 1856, he became the only incumbent president of the United States to have his bid for renomination rejected by his own party. Instead, they nominated James Buchanan, who won the election.

After leaving the White House, Pierce and his wife traveled in Europe for several years before returning to New Hampshire. Pierce would continue to be outspoken in his opposition to abolitionism, and during the Civil War, he was a blunt and acerbic critic of Abraham Lincoln.

The death of his wife in 1863, combined with ill health and an uncontrolled drinking problem, made Pierce's final years a misery. He died on October 8, 1869, in Concord.

A pro-Whig cartoon showing rival candidates Winfield Scott and Franklin Pierce in a game of "Cock and Goose" during their race for the presidency in 1852. Scott, in uniform and looking uncharacteristically trim, rides a giant gamecock. He is clearly in the lead here and tips his hat to Pierce, also in uniform but riding a large goose, an unflattering symbol also associated with Pierce's Democratic predecessor, James Knox Polk. *Library of Congress*

VICE PRESIDENT

WILLIAM R. KING

The only vice president to be sworn into office in a foreign country, William Rufus DeVane King also served the shortest term—just three weeks. Born on April 7, 1786, in Sampson County, North Carolina, King graduated from the University of North Carolina in 1803, and was admitted to the bar in 1806. He was elected to the US House of Representatives in 1811, serving until 1816, when he was appointed as minister to Russia. In 1818, he returned to the United States, taking up residence in Alabama, where he served in the state legislature from 1819 to 1844, when he resigned to take the post of minister to France. In 1846, he was elected to a vacant US Senate seat.

At the 1852 Democratic Convention, where it took forty-nine ballots to nominate Franklin Pierce, King received the vice presidential nomination on the second ballot, thanks to the support of his friend James Buchanan. Ill with tuberculosis, King traveled to the warmer climate of Cuba after being elected, and took the oath of office in the American consul's office in Havana, nearly three weeks later than Pierce. King hurried back to the United States, but to Alabama, where he died on April 18, 1853, and was buried at Live Oak Cemetery in Selma. He never spoke with Pierce as vice president. The office remained vacant for the remainder of Pierce's term as president.

right: A portrait of William Rufus King, painted by George Cooke in 1839. *Library of Congress*

James Buchanan

1857–1861

DEMOCRATIC PARTY

The only bachelor president of the United States, James Buchanan was the last president born in the eighteenth century. He was born on April 23, 1791, in Franklin County, Pennsylvania, the son of businessman James Buchanan Sr. and Elizabeth Speer Buchanan, and grew up in nearby Mercersburg. He graduated from Dickinson College in Carlisle, Pennsylvania, in 1809 and was admitted to the Pennsylvania Bar in 1812. He opposed the War of 1812, but volunteered for the US Army when the British invaded neighboring Maryland. He served in the Pennsylvania state legislature from 1814 to 1816, and in 1820, he was elected to the US House of Representatives, where he served five terms as a Federalist.

Buchanan went abroad in 1832 as Andrew Jackson's minister to Russia, and in 1834, he was elected as a Democrat to fill a vacant US Senate seat. Reelected twice, he headed the Committee on Foreign Relations for five years, but resigned from the senate in 1845 to take over as James K. Polk's secretary of state. In this post until 1849, he helped negotiate the treaty with Britain that created the Oregon Territory. Buchanan intended to use the job as a springboard to the presidency.

Buchanan and Lewis Cass of Michigan were the front-runners at the 1852 Democratic Convention and dueled with one another for forty-eight ballots until dark horse Franklin Pierce emerged from behind to clinch the nomination. In 1853, as a consolation, Pierce named Buchanan as minister to Great Britain, where he remained until 1856. At the Democratic Convention that year, Buchanan beat Pierce for the nomination and went on to win the general election. He defeated John Charles Frémont of California, the first presidential candidate of the new Republican Party, 174 to 114 in the Electoral College, with 45.3 percent of the popular vote.

When Buchanan took office, the nation was careening toward disaster over the slavery issue on myriad tracks, all of which were headed toward the collision that tipped the nation into the Civil War. In this environment, his indecisive management style served himself and the nation poorly.

The Bleeding Kansas crisis continued, and when Buchanan supported its admission to the Union as a slave state, he lost support within his own party. When Kansas was finally admitted, in 1861 in the final weeks of the Buchanan presidency, it was as a non-slave state. In the meantime, in 1858 and 1859, respectively, Minnesota and Oregon were admitted, both as non-slave states.

Buchanan hoped that the Dred Scott case, then before the US Supreme Court, would resolve the slavery question without his intervention. Dred Scott, a former slave living in a non-slave state but claimed by former owners, had sued for his freedom. The court ruled against Scott in 1857, citing the property rights of the owners, a ruling that only inflamed the passions of the abolitionists. Meanwhile, Buchanan's restrained reaction to the Panic of 1857 did little to alleviate the effects of the economic downturn. This, along with the Kansas problem, cost the Democrats control of the House of Representatives in 1858, and threw the government into stalemate.

opposite top: Buchanan in his later years. *Library of Congress* above: An official portrait of James Buchanan by George Peter Alexander Healy. *National Portrait Gallery*

James Buchanan **71**

James Buchanan's presidential inauguration at the US Capitol in Washington in 1857 was the first inauguration to have been photographed. *Library of Congress*

HARRIET REBECCA LANE JOHNSTON

Being unmarried, James Buchanan invited his niece, the daughter of his sister, Jane Ann Buchanan Lane, to serve as his first lady in the role of White House hostess. As Harriet Rebecca "Hal" Lane had lost both her parents by age eleven, her uncle had become her legal guardian. She was born on May 9, 1830, in Franklin County, Pennsylvania, and was educated, along with her sister, in boarding schools in the Washington, DC, area, near where Buchanan was serving in Congress and as secretary of state. Harriet also joined him in London in 1854, while he was minister to Great Britain, and was well liked by Queen Victoria.

Popular on the Washington society scene as first lady, Harriet was referred to as the "Democratic Queen." She was active both socially and philanthropically, more in the style of a late twentieth-century first lady than of her predecessors. It was after the Civil War when she finally married, to Baltimore banker Henry Elliott Johnston, but lost both him and their two sons by 1884. She lived much of her later life in Washington, but died in Narragansett, Rhode Island, on July 3, 1903.

Harriet Lane, the niece of James Buchanan and his acting first lady, circa 1860. *Library of Congress*

JOHN C. BRECKINRIDGE

A future Confederate general and James Buchanan's vice president, John Cabell Breckinridge was born near Lexington, Kentucky, on January 16, 1821, the only son and one of six children of Joseph "Cabell" Breckinridge and Mary Clay Smith Breckinridge. He graduated from Centre College in Danville, Kentucky, in 1838, briefly attended the College of New Jersey (now Princeton University), and was admitted to the Kentucky Bar in 1841. He practiced law in Iowa briefly before settling back in Kentucky in 1843. He led the 3rd Kentucky Infantry in the final days of the Mexican War but saw little action.

Breckinridge became active in the Democratic Party and was in the Kentucky legislature before serving in the US House of Representatives between 1851 and 1855. In 1856, he was a delegate at the Democratic Convention when his name was one of those put forward for the party's vice presidential nomination. Easily nominated, Breckinridge campaigned hard for himself and Buchanan, and they won. In office, however, the two remained distant, met infrequently, and disagreed on most issues.

In 1860, John Breckinridge sought the Democratic nomination for president, but lost to an old friend recently turned rival, Senator Stephen Douglas of Illinois. However, the southern wing of the party split off to form the Constitutional Democratic Party, and they nominated Breckinridge as their candidate. In the general election, Breckinridge came in second to Abraham Lincoln, the Republican candidate. Named to fill a vacant US Senate seat, Breckinridge remained in Washington until October 1861. At that time, he resigned from the Senate, joined the Confederate Army as a general, and was indicted as a traitor to the United States. He saw action in numerous battles, mainly in the Mississippi Valley through 1862 and in Virginia thereafter. In January 1865, he was named as Confederate secretary of war .

With the end of the Civil War, Breckinridge escaped to Britain via Cuba, and later lived off and on in Canada and traveled extensively in Europe. Back in the United States in 1869, he went into the railroad business, avoiding calls for him to reenter politics. He died in Lexington, Kentucky, on May 17, 1875.

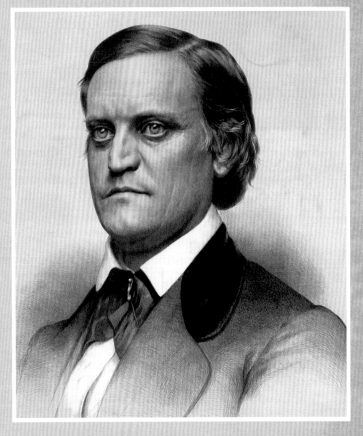

above: John Cabell Breckinridge, painted by Jules Émile Saintin, circa 1860, after a photograph by Mathew Brady. *Library of Congress*

By 1860, the crisis had mushroomed out of control, with the southern states on the verge of secession. In the face of this, Buchanan insisted they had no right to secede, but that the federal government had no power to stop them. James Buchanan's presidency was a disaster for himself, his party, and the country. He did make good on one promise that he made at his inauguration—that he would not run for a second term. Abraham Lincoln had been elected, but not yet inaugurated, when the southern states began to leave the Union in December 1860.

Blamed for having caused the Civil War by his inaction, Buchanan spent his final years defending himself in the court of public opinion. Depressed and in ill health, he withered and died on June 1, 1868, and is buried at Woodward Hill Cemetery in Lancaster, Pennsylvania. On his deathbed, Buchanan famously remarked that "history will vindicate my memory." So far, this prediction has not yet come true.

Abraham Lincoln

REPUBLICAN/NATIONAL UNION PARTIES

Regarded as one of America's three greatest presidents in most scholarly and popular polls, Abraham Lincoln is best remembered for winning the Civil War—which consumed his entire presidency—and for preserving the Union. He is also highly regarded for his Emancipation Proclamation, which was a step toward ending slavery, and for the Pacific Railway Acts, which paved the way for the Transcontinental Railroad. His 1863 Gettysburg Address is the best-known and most highly regarded speech in American history.

Abraham Lincoln was born on February 12, 1809, in Hardin (now LaRue) County, Kentucky, the son of farmer Thomas Lincoln and Nancy Hanks Lincoln. They had two other children, Sarah, born in 1807, and another son, who died as an infant. Much has been made of Lincoln's having been born in a log cabin, but this was also the case for several earlier presidents. Another often-told story about him was his reading by the light of an open fire, which is true. He was an avid reader, though he had no formal education. He was a self-taught lawyer who built a successful practice and a successful career in public service.

The image of "Lincoln the rail-splitter" is another story often ascribed to the Lincoln legend, and he was good with an axe. However, he reportedly disliked physical labor, despite his imposing presence. At just under six feet four inches, Lincoln was the tallest United States president, a foot taller than James Madison, the shortest.

The Lincoln family moved across the Ohio River to Indiana in 1816, where Nancy and Sarah died in 1818 and 1828 respectively. Thomas Lincoln remarried in 1819, and when he moved west to Illinois in 1830, Abraham went as well. Here, Abraham found work crewing aboard a flatboat carrying goods down the Mississippi to New Orleans, which is where the future "emancipator" first witnessed slavery. In 1832, he served briefly as a captain in the state militia during the Black Hawk War and became a partner in a general store in New Salem, Illinois. In 1834, while studying to be a lawyer, he was elected to the state legislature as a Whig. Having passed the bar in 1836, he set up his practice in Springfield, the state capital.

On the personal side, he had courting relationships with several women before marrying Mary Todd on November 4, 1842, nearly two years after they had cancelled earlier wedding plans. They had four sons, one of whom died before Lincoln became president of the United States, and one who died while Lincoln was in the White House.

A four-term Illinois legislator, Lincoln was elected to the US House of Representatives as a Whig in 1846, where—as he had promised—he remained for one term before going back to his lucrative legal practice. He earned fame for winning *Hurd v. Rock Island Bridge Company*, a case involving a steamboat that hit the first bridge across the Mississippi. As a result of the case, Lincoln invented a flotation device, which would make him the only president of the United States to hold a patent.

Meanwhile, Lincoln had become outspoken in his moral opposition to slavery and to laws such as the Kansas-Nebraska Act of 1854, which allowed popular sovereignty, the right of

opposite top: An official engraving of Abraham Lincoln. *Bureau of Engraving and Printing*

above: A contemplative Abraham Lincoln, painted by George Peter Alexander Healy in 1869. *White House*

An 1860 lithograph by Leopold Grozelier of Abraham Lincoln, without a beard, as the Republican candidate for the presidency. *Library of Congress*

FROM ABRAHAM LINCOLN'S HOUSE DIVIDED SPEECH
June 16, 1858

A house divided against itself cannot stand. I believe this government cannot endure, permanently, half slave and half free. I do not expect the Union to be dissolved—I do not expect the house to fall—but I do expect it will cease to be divided. It will become all one thing or all the other. Either the opponents of slavery will arrest the further spread of it, and place it where the public mind shall rest in the belief that it is in the course of ultimate extinction; or its advocates will push it forward, till it shall become lawful in all the States, old as well as new—North as well as South.

local jurisdictions to permit slavery. In 1854, he ran unsuccessfully for the US Senate as a Whig against Democrat Lyman Trumbull. Four years later, having joined the new Republican Party, he ran for the other Illinois Senate seat. This pitted him against the powerful Senator Stephen Douglas, a strong proponent of popular sovereignty and the architect of the Kansas-Nebraska Act. The Lincoln-Douglas Debates are easily the most famous American political debates of the nineteenth century. Lincoln spoke eloquently and passionately, predicting that slavery would be the force that would tear the Union apart. He established himself as a political power to be reckoned with, especially within his party, but he lost the election. It should be noted that until the Seventeenth Amendment of 1913, federal senatorial balloting took place in state legislatures.

In 1860, the Republican Convention nominated Lincoln as its presidential candidate on the third ballot. In the general election, he faced a split Democratic Party and the three challengers, including his nemesis Stephen Douglas. Lincoln won with 180 electoral votes and 39.8 percent of the popular vote. Former vice president John Breckinridge of the Southern Democrats came in second with seventy-two, trailed by Whig John Bell with thirty-nine and Douglas, running as a Northern Democrat, with just twelve—though Douglas was second in the popular vote.

Lincoln famously formed his cabinet from the most prominent men of the Republican Party, including those who had opposed him for the nomination. William Seward became his secretary of state, while Salmon Chase, later the originator of the national banking system and of United States paper currency, became secretary of the treasury.

The issues that had long plagued American politics—from slavery to popular sovereignty, to the rights of states versus the federal government—came to a head in 1860. Southern states, which were firmly on the opposite side of all these issues from the president-elect, had threatened to secede from the Union if he was elected. By the time he was inaugurated on March 4, 1861, seven states (South Carolina, Mississippi, Florida, Alabama, Georgia, Louisiana, and Texas) had done so and four more (Virginia, Arkansas, Tennessee, and North Carolina) followed by June. In February, they had come together to form a new country, the Confederate States of America (CSA). Jefferson Davis, the one-time son-in-law of President Zachary Taylor, was elected as president of the CSA.

In addition to the eleven southern states forming the CSA, rebel factions in the "border states" of Missouri and Kentucky established pro-CSA provisional governments that paralleled the "legitimate" pro-Union governments. Maryland, also a border state, stayed in the Union under martial law.

The CSA took military action to capture US Army facilities in their territory. The siege and capture of Fort Sumter in Charleston harbor in South Carolina in April was the first major battle of the Civil War.

As Lincoln mobilized the US Army to protect Washington, DC, it was widely assumed that the Civil War would be short and that the Union would prevail. However, in July, when the Confederate Army defeated the US Army at Manassas, Virginia—less than thirty miles from Washington—in the first large field battle between the opposing armies, it became apparent that the Civil War would be long and difficult.

Lincoln's biggest challenge in prosecuting the war was the selection of the right general to lead the Union Army. When the war began, the general in chief of the US Army was seventy-five-year-old Gen. Winfield Scott, the Mexican War hero and 1852 presidential candidate, who was past his prime. In late 1861, Lincoln turned to Gen. George Brinton McClellan, a bright young West Point graduate from Pennsylvania who had served under Scott in Mexico. McClellan formed the US Army's Army of the Potomac to lead offensive actions against the Confederate Army's Army of Northern Virginia, commanded by Robert E. Lee. McClellan's ensuing Peninsula Campaign was a disaster. Moving sluggishly, he was consistently and repeatedly outmaneuvered by Lee both tactically and strategically.

In July 1862, Lincoln replaced McClellan as general in chief with Gen. Henry Halleck, whose armies in the West had secured Missouri for the Union and had occupied much of Tennessee. However, McClellan remained in command of the Army of the Potomac, the largest component of the US Army.

In September 1862, having defeated the US Army at Manassas a second time, Lee took the war onto Union ground by invading Maryland. It was assumed that a major Confederate victory in the North would result in international recognition of the CSA as a country. The two armies, comprising more than one hundred thousand troops, met in the Battle of Antietam, near Sharpsburg, Maryland. This was the bloodiest single day in American military history, with a total of nearly twenty-three thousand casualties. Neither side won the battle tactically, but Lee was compelled to withdraw south of the Potomac, making it a strategic victory for the Union. However, McClellan refused Lincoln's orders to pursue Lee, thereby losing the opportunity for a decisive end to the Civil War.

An 1864 Republican presidential campaign poster showing incumbent candidate Abraham Lincoln with his running mate, Andrew Johnson. Above the portraits is a "Temple of Liberty," within which stands a female figure holding a staff and liberty cap. Perched on the temple's dome is an eagle with spread wings holding a banderole in his mouth and arrows in his talons. A vignette below the portraits shows a man plowing with a team of horses in front of farm buildings. The peace and prosperity promised by the candidates is indicated by cornucopias on either side spilling over with fruit.
Library of Congress

Lincoln replaced McClellan with Gen. Ambrose Burnside, who lost to Lee in the Battle of Fredericksburg in December 1862, precipitating a drop in Union morale. Lincoln then replaced Burnside with Gen. Joseph "Fighting Joe" Hooker, who lost to Lee in the Battle of Chancellorsville in May 1863, precipitating a steeper drop in Union morale and Lincoln's replacing Hooker with Gen. George Meade.

In June and July 1862, with Congress now devoid of the delegations from the southern states who had blocked such

MARY ANN TODD LINCOLN

The daughter of banker Robert Smith Todd and Elizabeth Parker Todd, Mary was born into a comfortably affluent life in Lexington, Kentucky, on December 13, 1818. After having dated his future archrival, Stephen Douglas, she married Abraham Lincoln in Springfield, Illinois, on November 4, 1842. Being a fellow Whig, she supported her husband both politically and socially throughout his career. During the Civil War, she was active in visiting wounded veterans and accompanying her husband on his visits to the troops in the field.

She suffered from ill health, both physically and mentally, which got worse in later life. Her migraines increased after a head injury during her White House years. She exhibited a violent temper and unpredictable behavior, which future psychologists have attributed to bipolar disorder. Other personal hardships included the loss of three children, the second of whom died of typhoid fever at age twelve while she was first lady, and the anguish of having several half-brothers fighting and dying with the Confederate Army. She was also seated next to her husband when he was shot and fatally wounded.

After his death, she retired to Chicago to be near her son, Robert, where she began receiving a federal pension in 1870. As she became more and more erratic and paranoid, she was committed to an asylum, from which she briefly escaped. She later attempted suicide. Eventually confined to the home of her sister in Springfield, she died on July 16, 1882. She is buried next to her husband.

above: Mary Todd Lincoln, as photographed in 1861 by Mathew Brady
Library of Congress

inset: A photograph of Mary Todd Lincoln taken in 1846 or 1847.
Nicolas H. Shepherd

The Children of Abraham Lincoln and Mary Todd Lincoln

Robert Todd Lincoln, (1843–1926)
Edward Baker "Eddie" Lincoln (1846–1850)
William Wallace "Willie" Lincoln (1850–1862)
Thomas "Tad" Lincoln (1853–1871)

measures in the past, the two Confiscation Acts were passed, calling for the freeing of slaves owned by anyone supporting the "rebellion," meaning those who supported and fought for the CSA and with its army. Lincoln signed the laws hesitantly, fearing that they might tip the border states, which he considered not yet "in rebellion," into joining the CSA.

In September 1862, Lincoln went a step further with the Emancipation Proclamation. Under his powers as commander in chief of US armed forces, he declared that slaves in the states "in rebellion" would be freed effective January 1, 1863, as that territory was occupied by the US Army.

The border states as well as Tennessee, which was then mostly under US Army control, were exempted from the Emancipation Proclamation. To ban slavery outright and in all states and territories, Lincoln would spend the next two years pressing Congress for a constitutional amendment.

In the meantime, given the unfavorable progress of the war for the Union Army, occupation of CSA territory seemed more wishful thinking than probability. Buoyed by his successes in Maryland, Robert E. Lee prepared for a decisive battle on Union soil, and led his Army of Northern Virginia north into Pennsylvania. His objective was to destroy the Army of the Potomac and to march deep into Pennsylvania, capturing Harrisburg and penetrating as far as Philadelphia. With Washington, DC, surrounded, Confederate leaders hoped to negotiate an armistice and recognition of the independence of the CSA.

The turning point in the Civil War came during the first three days of July 1863 in the Battle of Gettysburg, one hundred miles west of Philadelphia. Lee's seventy-two thousand troops were met by ninety-four thousand Union troops, now commanded by Meade, who had replaced Hooker only a few days earlier. The three days at Gettysburg cost around fifty thousand total casualties, but when it was over, Lee had been defeated on his deepest penetration into the Union and he was withdrawing toward Virginia.

The dead were buried in a huge cemetery at the battle site. The dedication of this cemetery on November 19, 1863, gave Lincoln the opportunity to deliver his Gettysburg Address, which has been called the greatest, and certainly the most famous, speech in American history.

It is also worth noting that, thanks to an October 1863 proclamation by Abraham Lincoln, Thanksgiving was first celebrated as a national holiday exactly one week after Gettysburg.

After the disasters of 1861 and 1862, 1863 had been a good year for the Union Army. In addition to Gettysburg, the Union Army had achieved important victories in the Battle of Shiloh in Tennessee in April 1863, and in the end of the Vicksburg campaign in Mississippi, which concluded successfully during the same week as Gettysburg. What Shiloh and Vicksburg had in common was the leadership of Gen. Ulysses S. Grant. Grant's subsequent success in the Chattanooga Campaign, which secured Tennessee and opened the Deep South to invasion, convinced Lincoln that he had found his long-sought general. In March 1864, Grant replaced Halleck as general in chief of the US Army and took direct command of the campaign against Lee in Virginia, the war's most contested theater.

In 1864, Abraham Lincoln ran for reelection as president of the United States, a nation at war and a nation torn apart. While eleven seceded states would not cast ballots, three other states voted in a presidential election for the first time. These included Kansas, admitted at the end of the Buchanan presidency, and Nevada, admitted in October 1864, just before the election. Also voting was West Virginia, consisting of fifty northwestern counties of Virginia, which seceded from Virginia and were admitted back into the Union as a permanent separate state in June 1863.

A photographic portrait of Abraham Lincoln taken by Mathew Brady on February 27, 1860. *Library of Congress*

Lincoln easily won the renomination of the Republican Party, which used the name National Union Party for the 1864 presidential election to convey a message of national unity. The Democrats, meanwhile, nominated George McClellan in an effort to unify a party that was divided over the issue of supporting the war or negotiating an armistice with the CSA. Lincoln won with 212 electoral votes to only 21 for McClellan, and with 55 percent of the popular vote.

A major issue in the campaign was the effort to outlaw slavery. Lincoln had succeeded in getting Congress to consider his proposal of a constitutional amendment, though the idea

ABRAHAM LINCOLN'S GETTYSBURG ADDRESS
November 19, 1863

Four score and seven years ago our fathers brought forth on this continent a new nation, conceived in liberty, and dedicated to the proposition that all men are created equal.

Now we are engaged in a great civil war, testing whether that nation, or any nation so conceived and so dedicated, can long endure. We are met on a great battlefield of that war. We have come to dedicate a portion of that field, as a final resting place for those who here gave their lives that that nation might live. It is altogether fitting and proper that we should do this.

But, in a larger sense, we cannot dedicate, we cannot consecrate, we cannot hallow this ground. The brave men, living and dead, who struggled here, have consecrated it, far above our poor power to add or detract. The world will little note, nor long remember what we say here, but it can never forget what they did here. It is for us the living, rather, to be dedicated here to the unfinished work which they who fought here have thus far so nobly advanced. It is rather for us to be here dedicated to the great task remaining before us—that from these honored dead we take increased devotion to that cause for which they gave the last full measure of devotion—that we here highly resolve that these dead shall not have died in vain—that this nation, under God, shall have a new birth of freedom—and that government of the people, by the people, for the people, shall not perish from the earth.

David Bachrach took the only known and confirmed photograph of Abraham Lincoln at the dedication of the Soldiers' National Cemetery in Gettysburg, Pennsylvania. It was taken about three hours before Lincoln delivered the Gettysburg Address and then lost for nearly a century. It was identified in the Mathew Brady collection of photographic plates in the National Archives and Records Administration in 1952. To locate Lincoln, look for the man in the top hat to the right of the flag at the top of the picture. Lincoln is the second man directly beneath this man. He is hatless and looking slightly down and to his right. *National Archives*

fell short of a two-thirds majority in June 1864 before finally passing in January 1865.

By the time that Lincoln began his second term, the critical mass of momentum in the Civil War was with the Union Army. Grant's relentless campaign against Lee gave the Confederates little room to maneuver, while Gen. William Tecumseh Sherman had literally cut the Confederacy in half at the end of 1864 with his "March to the Sea" from Chattanooga to Savannah by way of Atlanta.

Even as the war was still raging, Lincoln had turned his attention to the postwar Reconstruction of the South and the readmission of the eleven rebel states back into the United States. He now saw the country defined as a single, albeit federal, nation, not a grouping of states with a weak central government. Indeed, it was around this time that the name

Lincoln appeared on this ten-dollar Demand Note issued in 1861 while he was still alive. He is one of five people to be depicted on federally issued United States paper currency during their lifetimes. The others were Salmon P. Chase, Francis E. Spinner, Spencer M. Clark, and Winfield Scott. He is currently on the United States five-dollar bill. *Bureau of Engraving and Printing*

VICE PRESIDENTS

HANNIBAL HAMLIN

A staunch Republican, Hamlin supported Abraham Lincoln and the positions for which he stood. He was born in Paris, Maine, on August 27, 1809, the son of farmer Cyrus Hamlin and Anna Livermore Hamlin. Having been admitted to the Maine Bar in 1833, he maintained a practice in Hampden, Maine, near Bangor until 1848. Also in 1833, he married Sarah Jane Emery, and when she died in 1855, he married Ellen Vesta Emery, her half sister.

Hamlin served in the state legislature from 1836 to 1841, and was elected to the US House of Representatives in 1842. He was elected to fill a vacant US Senate seat in 1848, and was reelected to a full term in 1850. Originally a Democrat, he opposed slavery, the Compromise of 1850, and the Kansas Nebraska Act. In 1856, he left the Democratic Party to join the Republican Party, which nominated him as their candidate for governor of Maine, to which he was elected. He served only briefly before returning to the US Senate.

At the Republican Convention in 1860, he was nominated on the second ballot as Lincoln's vice presidential running mate, though the two did not meet until after their election. As vice president he had little impact aside from advocating for Lincoln's initiatives, such as the Emancipation Proclamation, in Congress. In 1864, the party rejected Hamlin and nominated Andrew Johnson.

Hamlin was reelected to the US Senate in 1868, where he served until 1881, when President James Garfield named him as the United States minister to Spain. On July 4, 1891, he collapsed while playing cards at his club in Bangor, Maine, and died shortly thereafter.

ANDREW JOHNSON

In 1864, the Republican Party renamed itself the National Union Party in order to attract "War Democrats," who supported the defeat of the Confederacy, rather than a negotiated acceptance of the CSA. With this in mind, they dumped Hannibal Hamlin in favor of Andrew Johnson, a War Democrat who had distinguished himself as military governor of Tennessee. He did not distinguish himself at the inauguration, arriving drunk and incoherent. Embarrassed, he made himself scarce and was rarely seen. The next time he saw Lincoln was on April 14. That night, Lincoln was shot, and the next day, Andrew Johnson was the president of the United States. He and his own presidency are described in detail in the following chapter.

left: A photograph of Hannibal Hamlin as vice president. *Library of Congress*

Painted by Francis Bicknell Carpenter in 1864, this image depicts Lincoln presenting the first draft of the Emancipation Proclamation to his cabinet in July 1862. The scene is Lincoln's office, which also served as the Cabinet Room, and which is now known as the Lincoln Bedroom. From left to right, those pictured are Secretary of War Edwin M. Stanton (seated), Secretary of the Treasury Salmon P. Chase, the president, Secretary of the Navy Gideon Welles, Secretary of the Interior Caleb Blood Smith (standing), Secretary of State William H. Seward, Postmaster General Montgomery Blair, and Attorney General Edward Bates. Paintings of former secretary of war Simon Cameron and former president Andrew Jackson are on the wall behind. Carpenter reported that he avoided "imaginary curtain or column, gorgeous furniture or allegorical statue." Carpenter spent six months in the White House as he painted the picture. It is now displayed at the United States Capitol. *Architect of the Capitol*

of the country subtly changed from plural "the United States are" to singular "the United States is."

Other elements of his presidency, overshadowed by emancipation and the Civil War, included his support for land grant colleges, creation of the Department of Agriculture, a strong national banking system, and a national currency, including Salmon Chase's idea for paper money. The Pacific Railway Acts of 1862 and 1864 supported the building of the transcontinental railway. Lincoln saw railroads as a vital tool to bind the nation east to west as he hoped to bind the nation north to south by successfully waging the Civil War.

On April 2, 1865, Grant captured Richmond, Virginia, and began his final pursuit of Lee's army to the west. A few days later, Lincoln came to Richmond and toured the city, walking through the home of President Jefferson Davis, who had fled. On April 9, at Appomattox Court House, ninety miles west of Richmond, Lee formally surrendered to Grant, effectively ending the Civil War.

above: Abraham Lincoln delivering his second inaugural address at the US Capitol in 1865 in a photograph by Alexander Gardner. *Library of Congress*

From Abraham Lincoln's Second Inaugural Address
March 4, 1865

Fondly do we hope—fervently do we pray—that this mighty scourge of war may speedily pass away. Yet, if God wills that it continue, until all the wealth piled by the bond man's 250 years of unrequited toil shall be sunk, and until every drop of blood drawn with the lash, shall be paid by another drawn with the sword, as was said three thousand years ago, so still it must be said, "the judgments of the Lord, are true and righteous altogether." With malice toward none; with charity for all; with firmness in the right, as God gives us to see the right, let us strive on to finish the work we are in; to bind up the nation's wounds; to care for him who shall have borne the battle, and for his widow, and his orphan—to do all which may achieve and cherish a just and lasting peace, among ourselves, and with all nations.

above: A depiction of John Wilkes Booth leaning forward to shoot President Abraham Lincoln as he watches *Our American Cousin* at Ford's Theater in Washington on April 15, 1865. To the right of Booth and Lincoln are Mary Todd Lincoln, Clara Harris, and Henry Rathbone. *Library of Congress*

opposite: Abraham Lincoln, his war weariness clearly in evidence, as photographed by Alexander Gardner in February 1865, about two months before he was assassinated. *Library of Congress*

On April 14, Lincoln and his wife, along with Maj. Henry Rathbone and his wife, went to Ford's Theater in Washington, DC, to attend the play *Our American Cousin*. At 10:13 p.m., John Wilkes Booth surreptitiously stepped into the presidential box. A member of a family of famous actors, he was a Confederate sympathizer who passionately disliked Lincoln. Booth fired a bullet into the back of Lincoln's head, knifed Rathbone, and escaped by awkwardly jumping onto the stage. He was tracked down by Union troops and killed twelve days later.

Lincoln, who was not dead, was taken to a house across the street. He received medical attention, but died at dawn the following day. His son, Robert Todd Lincoln, who was present when his father passed away, would be present or nearby at the assassinations of two other American presidents, James Garfield and William McKinley. He served as Garfield's secretary of war.

When Lincoln's body was taken by train to Springfield for burial, the route was lined with tens of thousands of mourners. Though controversial in life, especially during the acrimony of the Civil War, Lincoln was celebrated for preserving the Union, and soon enshrined along with George Washington as one of the most beloved presidents. Tributes were many. There are cities or towns named "Lincoln" in more than two dozen states, not including a dozen in Wisconsin alone. The Lincoln Memorial on the Capitol Mall in Washington, dedicated in 1922, is among the most impressive of the monuments that were constructed.

above: The Lincoln Memorial at sunset, illuminated from within. *Erich Robert Joli Weber, licensed under Creative Commons*

below: Lincoln has appeared on US postage stamps more often than anyone but George Washington, and more times than all the other presidents combined. From left are the ninety-cent issue of 1869, the four-cent 1890 issue, the 1903 five-cent stamp designed by R. Ostrander Smith, the two-cent 1909 centennial issue, the sixteen-cent stamp from the 1938 Presidential Series, and the 1954 four-cent stamp that was used on most first class letters until 1963. *US Postal Service*

above: The statue of Abraham Lincoln sitting in contemplation inside the Lincoln Memorial was designed by Daniel Chester French and carved by the Piccirilli Brothers under his supervision over four years. It was assembled in the memorial on the National Mall in 1920, and unveiled at the memorial's formal dedication on May 30, 1922. *Jeff Kubina, licensed under the Creative Commons*

below: The 1948 three-cent commemorative of the Gettysburg Address, the 1958 four-cent commemorative of the Lincoln-Douglas Debate, and a four-cent Lincoln Sesquicentennial commemorative depicting the Daniel Chester French statue in the Lincoln Memorial. Finally, there is the 1960 twenty-five-cent airmail stamp. Lincoln was the only American president to appear on a US airmail stamp. *US Postal Service*

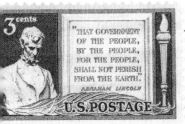   

17

1865–1869

Andrew Johnson

REPUBLICAN/NATIONAL UNION PARTIES

Perhaps best known for succeeding Abraham Lincoln and for being the first president of the United States to be impeached, Andrew Johnson was born on December 29, 1808, in Raleigh, North Carolina, the son of Jacob Johnson and Mary McDonough Johnson, who was better known as "Polly." Andrew and his brother William were apprenticed as tailors as boys, but broke their apprenticeship bond to their master and ran away. By his late teens Andrew landed in Greenville, Tennessee, where he put down roots and became a successful tailor. He married Eliza McCardle in 1827, and they had five children.

Johnson's political career began in 1827 with local office in Greenville, of which he was elected mayor in 1834. He served several terms in the state legislature until being elected to the US House of Representatives as an anti-abolitionist Democrat in 1842 and served five terms. He then served as governor of Tennessee from 1853 to 1857, when he was elected to the US Senate. He was a proponent of westward expansion and the homestead concept, and he introduced the legislation that became the Homestead Act of 1862.

In 1861, Johnson opposed Tennessee's secession from the Union and aligned himself with the War Democrats who wished to preserve the Union though war with the Confederacy. In 1862, as the Union Army occupied large parts of Tennessee, Johnson was appointed as military governor. This put him in a good position to be selected as Abraham Lincoln's running mate on the National Union ticket in 1864, though once in office, they did not meet until

the day Lincoln was killed. On April 15, 1865, Johnson was sworn in as president of the United States within hours of Lincoln's death.

Reconstruction dominated Johnson's presidency. In favoring an expeditious readmission of seceded states, he faced a Republican Congress more bent on retribution and excluding southern Democrats from holding Congressional office.

In December 1865, the Thirteenth Amendment finally freed the slaves, and the Civil Rights Act of 1866 was passed over Johnson's veto, granting citizenship to former slaves. Johnson opposed it because the states of the former Confederacy were not yet represented in Congress.

Congress went a step further by passing the Fourteenth Amendment, which precluded states from denying equal protection to all citizens. Congress further stipulated that states could be readmitted to the Union only after ratifying the amendment. Having been ratified, it became part of the Constitution in 1868. In turn, Johnson pardoned most Confederates except the top leadership and those who were former United States officials who had sworn allegiance to the Confederacy.

As Congress clashed with Johnson over Reconstruction, there was a groundswell of support for impeachment. The catalyst came on a technicality in the Tenure of Office Act when Johnson dismissed Secretary of War Edwin Stanton. Johnson was impeached, but not convicted when tried in the US Senate. Stanton resigned and Johnson served out the term he inherited from Lincoln. In 1868, Johnson sought to run for reelection in his own right, but was denied the nomination of the Democratic Party, who nominated Horatio Seymour of New York.

Overshadowed by the ongoing Reconstruction debate was the fact that on Johnson's watch, Secretary of State William Seward acquired Alaska from the Russians at a bargain price. Those who called the purchase "Seward's Folly" would be proven wrong.

During the years following his presidency, Johnson lost a Congressional bid and one for the US Senate. In 1875, he tried again for the Senate, winning narrowly. He died of a stroke on July 31, 1875, four months after taking office, and was interred in Greenville, Tennessee. Having steered an unpopular middle ground in polarized times, he died with few political friends and little to show for his troubled presidency.

opposite: An official engraved portrait of Andrew Johnson. *Bureau of Engraving and Printing*

right: A portrait photograph of Andrew Johnson, circa 1870. *Library of Congress*

FIRST LADY
ELIZA MCCARDLE JOHNSON

Born on October 4, 1810, in Telford, Tennessee, Eliza McCardle married Andrew Johnson on May 17, 1827, in her mother's home, while they were both still in their teens.

She was the only child of Sarah Phillips McCardle and shoemaker John McCardle, who died when Eliza was young. Because Johnson had not attended school and was barely literate, his new wife became his tutor. Though she supported her husband politically, she did not come to Washington until after he became president. As with several of her predecessors, she did not take to the role of White House hostess, leaving that chore almost exclusively to her daughter, Martha, who was married to David Trotter Patterson, who was elected to the US Senate in 1866 after Tennessee was readmitted to the Union. Eliza died of tuberculosis on January 15, 1876, and was buried next to her husband, who had died six months earlier.

left: Eliza McCardle Johnson, circa 1883. *Library of Congress*

The Children of Andrew Johnson and Eliza Johnson

Martha Johnson Patterson (1828–1901)

Charles Johnson (1830–1863)

Mary Johnson Stover Brown (1832–1883)

Robert Johnson (1834–1869)

Andrew Johnson Jr. (1852–1879)

18

Ulysses S. Grant

1869–1877

REPUBLICAN PARTY

The general who led the Union Army in its crushing defeat of the Confederacy was the president who finally reincorporated the Confederate states back into the Union. The military man who began his career as an Indian fighter was the president who named Ely Parker of the Seneca as Commissioner of Indian Affairs. It was also on his watch that Yellowstone became America's first national park.

He was born Hiram Ulysses Grant on April 27, 1822, in Point Pleasant, Ohio, the eldest of the five children of Hannah Simpson Grant and Jesse Root Grant. When he appointed the younger Grant to the US Military Academy at West Point in 1839, Congressman Thomas Hamer used the name "Ulysses S. Grant," intending the "S" to stand for "Simpson." Grant let it stand, favoring the initials "US." At West Point and through his career, his nickname was "Sam."

Young Lieutenant Grant graduated in 1843 and was posted to Missouri, where he met and married Julia Dent, the sister of a classmate. During the Mexican War, he served heroically, leading a charge in the Battle of Resaca de la Palma in 1846. During the march on Mexico City, he dragged a cannon up a tall building in Chapultepec. After the war, he reenlisted and served in the Indian Wars in the Pacific Northwest.

Grant resigned from the US Army in 1854, allegedly because of a drinking problem, but civilian life did not agree with him. He was unsuccessful in business and farming, and wound up working for his father in a tannery in Galena, Illinois. In 1861, when Abraham Lincoln visited Galena and personally asked for volunteers to fight the Confederacy, Grant organized a militia regiment. Once he rejoined the US Army, he rose quickly, being promoted to colonel in July 1861 before receiving a promotion—back-dated to May—as brigadier general.

During the Civil War, Grant won a series of battles, beginning with the capture of Fort Henry, Tennessee, in February 1862 and the Battle of Shiloh two months later, that established a prominent reputation. Promoted to major general, he now commanded the Army of the Tennessee. Grant led US Army forces in the lengthy Vicksburg Campaign, which lasted from December 1862 through July 1863 and gave the Union control of the Mississippi River. In a series of battles in the fall of 1863, Grant led three field armies to take control of Tennessee and lay Georgia bare to an invasion.

In March 1864, Grant's successes led Lincoln to promote him to lieutenant general and to make him general in chief of the entire US Army. Leaving Gen. William Tecumseh Sherman in command in the West, Grant came to Virginia to face Confederate Gen. Robert E. Lee head on. Grant's yearlong campaign was relentless and determined, slowed by the skill and determination of Lee and the Army of Northern Virginia, the largest Confederate field army. It was ultimately successful, though at great cost. Grant captured Richmond, the Confederate capital, on April 2, and pursued Lee's army westward for ninety miles. Lee finally sent word that he was ready to surrender,

and on April 9, they met in Appomattox Court House, and signed the paperwork.

Immensely popular as a war hero, Grant remained in command of the US Army as it transitioned to its postwar mission of military occupation of the South, while dealing with increasing tensions between settlers and Indian tribes on the Plains and in the Southwest.

Though he opposed slavery and obviously supported the Union, Grant remained politically inactive until after the war—but both the Democrats and Republicans courted him because of his popularity. In 1867, when President Andrew Johnson fired Secretary of War Edwin Stanton, Grant reluctantly accepted the job. When the Senate reinstated Stanton, Grant ignored Johnson's demands that he refuse to step aside, telling the president that to remain in the post would be illegal. This only served to increase Grant's popularity as Johnson's plummeted.

In 1868, after the Republican Party nominated Grant unanimously for president, he went on to defeat Democrat Horatio Seymour 214 to 80 in the Electoral College while taking 52.7 percent of the popular vote.

As president, Grant promoted passage of the Fifteenth Amendment, which prohibited the use by the states of "race, color or previous condition of servitude" to prohibit the right to vote. By March 1870, when the amendment was certified as part of the Constitution, it had been ratified by all of the states that had seceded, and they had all been readmitted to the Union.

In 1872, Grant signed the Amnesty Act, restoring citizenship and voting rights to all but around five hundred high-ranking Confederate leaders.

Fiscally, Grant took steps to phase out "greenbacks," legal tender notes not backed by gold, which had been issued during the Civil War. By selling off gold, he was able to stabilize the dollar and curb inflation, but it led to charges that he was enriching his cronies. Internationally, Grant settled a series of disputes with Britain, including damage claims for the harm to American maritime interests done by Confederate warships built in Britain.

In 1872, despite scandals over political cronyism that tarnished his reputation, the Republican Party renominated Grant unanimously. In the general election, he did better than he had in 1868, garnering 286 electoral votes, while taking 52.7 percent of the popular vote. Nominated by the Democrats and Liberal Republicans, newspaperman Horace Greeley took 43.8 percent of the vote, but died before the Electoral College met.

Grant's second term began against the backdrop of the Panic of 1873, and the beginning of a five-year "Long Depression," the worst economic downturn since before the Civil War. It was also a period of bribery scandals and rampant corruption within the Grant administration that

right: Ulysses S. Grant as president, circa 1870s. *Library of Congress*

below: An 1888 lithograph of Grant leading Union Army troops to victory at the Battle of Shiloh in April 1862. Illustrated by Thure de Thulstrup, with restoration by Adam Cuerden. *Library of Congress*

opposite page: An 1885 engraving by Thure de Thulstrup depicting Grant's achievements through the Civil War. Clockwise from lower left, they show his graduation from West Point (1843), Grant in the tower at Chapultepec (1847), drilling his Volunteers (1861), Fort Donelson (1862), the Battle of Shiloh (1862), the Siege of Vicksburg (1863), the Battle of Chattanooga (1863), Grant as general in chief (1864), and the surrender of Lee at Appomattox (1865). *Library of Congress*

Ulysses S. Grant **93**

FIRST LADY
JULIA DENT GRANT

Julia Boggs Dent married Ulysses S. Grant, after multiple proposals and a four-year engagement. She was introduced to her future husband by Frederick Dent, her brother, who was a West Point classmate of Grant's. She was born on January 26, 1826, near St. Louis, Missouri, the daughter of Ellen Wrenshall Dent and Col. Frederick Dent, a planter and merchant. The fact that the Dents were slaveholders and the Grants were abolitionists created a great deal of strain between the two sides of the family while they were courting. She finally accepted his proposal in 1844, but the Mexican War intervened and they were not married until August 22, 1848.

Julia Dent Grant. *Library of Congress*

Unlike many of her predecessors, Julia greatly enjoyed being first lady and readily embraced her role as White House hostess, and she became a popular Washington socialite. One of the society high points of the Grant years was the lavish White House wedding of Nellie, the Grant's only daughter, to British entertainer Algernon Charles Frederick Sartoris May 21, 1874. The president didn't approve, and the couple eventually separated after having four children.

Thanks to proceeds from her husband's autobiography, Julia's final years were comfortable. She wrote her own memoirs, but they remained unpublished until long after her death on December 14, 1902. She was laid to rest next to her husband.

The Children of Ulysses S. Grant and Julia Dent Grant
Frederick Dent Grant (1850–1912)
Ulysses Simpson "Buck" Grant Jr. (1852–1929)
Ellen Wrenshall "Nellie" Grant Sartoris (1855–1922)
Jesse Root Grant (1858–1934)

above right: The General Grant National Memorial, better known as "Grant's Tomb," on Riverside Drive in New York City. Dedicated on April 27, 1897, it was designed by John H. Duncan. It is the final resting place of Ulysses S. Grant and his wife, Julia Dent Grant. Library of Congress

the former general seemed powerless to control. When the Democrats took control of the US House of Representatives in the 1874 midterm election, Grant's hands were further tied. Nevertheless, there were rumors that the president would run for a third term. He had the distinction of being in office during the celebrations of the Centennial of the Declaration of Independence, and had his popularity been what it had been, he might have run again, but he did not.

In retirement, Grant and his wife embarked on a round-the-world tour that lasted two years. They dined with Queen Victoria and German Chancellor Otto von Bismarck, had an audience with Pope Leo XIII, sailed through the Suez Canal, and toured India and Siam. Grant even paused to mediate a dispute between China and Japan. In 1880, back in the United States with his image enhanced by his international statesmanship, Grant was again a candidate for the Republican nomination. He led James G. Blaine for thirty-five ballots, but never had quite enough to win. Ultimately, the convention turned to James A, Garfield as a compromise candidate.

Leaving politics, Grant settled in New York City and gambled on various railroad schemes, but these ventures left him bankrupt. Meanwhile, his lifelong fondness for cigars had left him with throat cancer.

He had written several well-received magazine articles, and it was suggested that he write his memoirs. Working long hours and encouraged by a number of friends and literary figures, including Mark Twain, he completed the work shortly before his death on July 23, 1885. The two-volume work was a critical success and is still highly regarded by historians. Meanwhile, it earned his widow around $10 million in current dollars.

He is interred in the General Grant National Memorial, better known as "Grant's Tomb," a massive mausoleum in New York City.

VICE PRESIDENTS

SCHUYLER COLFAX

Ulysses Grant's first-term vice president was born in New York City on March 23, 1823, the son of Schuyler Colfax Sr. and Hannah Delameter Stryker Colfax. The elder Colfax died before his son was born, Hannah remarried, and the family moved west to Indiana in 1836. Colfax found his career as a newspaperman at a young age and bought his first paper at age twenty-two. He dabbled in politics as a Whig and was elected to the US House of Representatives on his second try in 1854. As with most Whigs, Colfax migrated to the new Republican Party, and by 1862, he had become Speaker of the House. In 1865, Colfax and two companions made an extensive trip across the West to the Pacific Coast.

At the Republican Convention in 1868, he was nominated as Grant's running mate. Having been involved in a financing scandal involving the Union Pacific Railroad, Colfax was not renominated as a vice presidential candidate in 1872. In his later years, he achieved some success on the public speaking circuit. Colfax died of a heart attack on January 13, 1885, in the railroad station at Mankato, Minnesota, while waiting for a train.

right: Schuyler Colfax. *Library of Congress*

HENRY WILSON

Grant's second-term vice president was born in Farmington, New Hampshire, on February 16, 1812, the son of Winthrop Colbath (also spelled Colbreath) and Hannah Rollins Colbath. The boy was named Jeremiah Jones Colbath after a wealthy man in the community as part of a scheme hatched by Winthrop to get money from Jones. As soon as he could, Jeremiah changed his name to Henry Wilson, a name that he found in a book.

Wilson worked as a shoemaker before serving in the Massachusetts state legislature. Opposed to slavery, he was affiliated with the short-lived Free Soil Party and the "Know Nothings" before becoming a member of the young Republican Party. In 1855, he was elected to the US Senate, where he served until 1873. In the meantime, in 1861, when the Civil War began, Wilson organized the 22nd Massachusetts Volunteer Infantry Regiment.

An intriguing part of his story is his extramarital affair with Washington socialite and notorious Confederate spy Rose O'Neil Greenhow, to whom he was long rumored to have betrayed secrets of US Army tactical deployments.

At the 1872 Republican Convention, he ran as an alternative against scandal-plagued incumbent Schuyler Colfax for the vice presidential nomination and won. Elected along with Grant, he was paralyzed by a debilitating stroke in 1873, not long after taking office. Though in diminished capacity, he continued to act in the vice presidential role of president of the Senate until suffering a fatal stroke on November 22, 1875.

Left: Henry Wilson. *Library of Congress*

19

1877–1881

Rutherford B. Hayes

REPUBLICAN PARTY

Having received a minority of both popular vote and uncontested electoral votes, Rutherford Birchard Hayes ultimately won the closest presidential election in American history by a single vote in the Electoral College.

Hayes was born on October 4, 1822, in Delaware, Ohio, the son of Rutherford Hayes Jr. and Sophia Birchard Hayes. Sophia raised the boy alone when she was widowed shortly before his birth. He graduated from Kenyon College in Gambier, Ohio, as the valedictorian of the Class of 1842. He went on to graduate from Harvard Law School in 1845 and was admitted to the Ohio Bar the same year. He practiced law initially in Lower Sandusky (now Fremont) but moved to Cincinnati in 1850. It was here that he met Lucy Webb, whom he married in 1852.

Having tried a number of runaway slave cases, Hayes became a staunch abolitionist and joined the Republican Party. He also served for a time as city solicitor in Cincinnati. When the Civil War began in 1861, Hayes was appointed to lead the 23rd Ohio Volunteer Infantry, which first saw combat in September. Having been wounded, Hayes saw little action until the Shenandoah Campaign of 1864, by which time he had been promoted to brevet brigadier general. Here he

top: An official engraving of Hayes. *Bureau of Engraving and Printing*

above: New York Governor Samuel Tilden opposed Hayes in the 1876 election, winning both the popular and electoral votes. However, the House of Representatives awarded disputed electoral votes to Hayes. *Frank Fowler*

saw considerable action, and was cited by Gen. Ulysses S. Grant for "conspicuous gallantry."

In 1864, Hayes was nominated to run for the US House of Representatives, but refused to leave the battlefront to campaign. Elected nevertheless, he left the field to take office, where he was a backer of the Fourteenth Amendment. In 1867, he resigned from Congress for a successful run for the Ohio governorship, where he helped engineer ratification of the Fifteenth Amendment. He returned to private life in 1872, but was nominated to run again for governor in 1875. His successful election and his popularity in Republican circles made him a potential presidential candidate in 1876 when Grant chose not to run for a third term.

At the Republican Convention, Hayes narrowly defeated front-runner James G. Blaine of Maine on the seventh ballot. In the general election, Democrat Samuel J. Tilden captured 50.92 percent of the popular vote, and 184 electoral votes to 165 for Hayes. There were, however, twenty contested votes in four states. Under the Constitution, the matter went to the US House of Representatives for resolution. The House came up with the Compromise of 1877, in which the Republicans agreed to a removal of federal occupation forces from the southern states, and the Democrats agreed that Hayes could have all twenty contested votes.

The Compromise of 1877 committed Hayes to end Reconstruction and restore the autonomy of southern states, which he did while making efforts to protect the voting rights of former slaves. Another initiative of the Hayes administration was a reform of the Civil Service system in order to reverse the tide of corruption which had blighted the Grant administration. Internationally, Hayes is remembered for signing the Chinese Exclusion Act of 1879, which was passed in response to the economic

An official oil portrait of Rutherford Birchard Hayes as president by Daniel Huntington. *White House*

LUCY WARE WEBB HAYES

Known as "Lemonade Lucy" (though not during her tenure in the White House) for her support of the Women's Christian Temperance Union, Lucy Ware Webb was born in Chillicothe, Ohio, on August 28, 1831. She was the daughter of Dr. James Webb and Maria Cook Webb, and like her future husband, she was raised by a widowed mother. The first first lady to graduate from college, she was a member of the class of 1850 at Wesleyan Women's College, now part of Ohio Wesleyan University. She married Rutherford B. Hayes at her mother's home in Cincinnati, Ohio, on December 30, 1852.

Five of their eight children grew to adulthood. The most famous was James Webb Cook Hayes, who served as his father's presidential secretary and received the Medal of Honor in the Philippines during the Spanish-American War. In 1886, he was a co-founder of the National Carbon Company, which later became a component of Union Carbide.

Though she was a temperance advocate and a devout Methodist, it was her husband, not "Lemonade Lucy," who banned alcohol from the White House. The ban was famously not enforced when Grand Duke Alexei Alexandrovich of Russia came to visit. She is credited with originating the tradition of the annual White House lawn Easter egg roll. She and her husband retired to Fremont, Ohio, where she died of a stroke on June 25, 1889.

The Children of Rutherford B. Hayes and Lucy Ware Webb Hayes

Sardis "Birchard Austin" Birchard Hayes (1853–1926)
James Webb Cook Hayes (1856–1934)
Rutherford Platt Hayes (1858–1931)
Joseph Thompson Hayes (1861–1863)
George Crook Hayes (1864–1866)
Frances "Fanny" Hayes Smith (1867–1950)
Scott Russell Hayes (1871–1923)
Manning Force Hayes (1873–1874)

The official portrait of First Lady Lucy Webb Hayes, painted in 1881 by Daniel Huntington. *White House*

---

downturn following the Panic of 1873 and the perception that Chinese immigrants to the West Coast were adversely impacting the labor market.

Having promised early in his presidency that he would not run for reelection, Hayes left office at the end of his term and returned home to serve on the Board of Trustees of Ohio State University, of which he had been a founder. In 1878, he was called upon to arbitrate a territorial dispute between Argentina and Paraguay, which led to a Paraguayan province being named for him.

He died of a heart attack on January 17, 1893. His funeral at Oakwood Cemetery in Fremont, Ohio, was attended by president-elect Grover Cleveland and future president William McKinley.

VICE PRESIDENT

WILLIAM A. WHEELER

Born in Malone, New York, on June 30, 1819, William Almon Wheeler was admitted to the New York Bar in 1845. He served as Franklin County district attorney from 1846 to 1849, and as state legislator from 1850 to 1859. A Republican, he was elected to the US House of Representatives in 1860, where he served until 1877. At the 1876 Republican Convention, where Hayes was not nominated for president until the seventh ballot, Wheeler was the overwhelming choice for vice president on the first. As vice president, Wheeler was one of the first to be on cordial terms with the president with whom he served. After his term, Wheeler retired and did not promote himself as an 1880 presidential candidate. He died in Malone on June 4, 1887, and is interred there.

A campaign poster for the 1876 Republican presidential ticket that was produced by Currier & Ives. Library of Congress

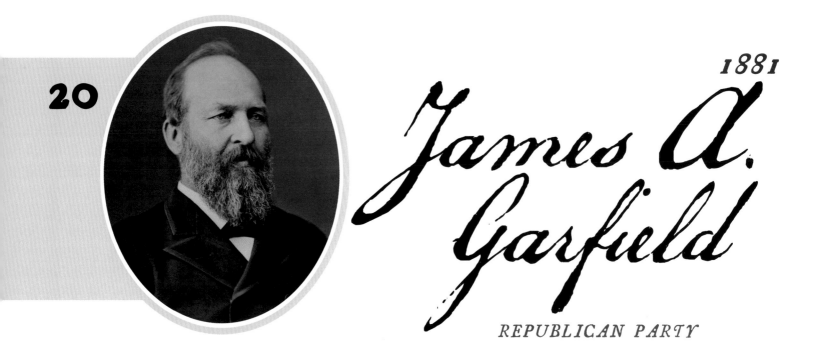

20

1881

James A. Garfield

REPUBLICAN PARTY

The second president of the United States to be assassinated, James A. Garfield also had the second shortest presidency to date. He spent eighty of his two hundred days in office not actually *in* his office, but writhing in pain with a bullet lodged in his body. During his brief tenure, he was also the first president to talk on a telephone, conversing with the inventor, Alexander Graham Bell.

Garfield was born on a farm in Cuyahoga County, Ohio, on November 19, 1831, the son of Eliza Ballou Garfield and Abram Garfield, who died when James was an infant. He grew up poor and worked for a canal boat company while in his teens. Between 1848 and 1850, he attended at the Geauga Seminary, a Free Will Baptist school in Chester, Ohio, which is where he met his future wife, Lucretia Rudolph, whom

he married in 1858. Through 1854, he attended Western Reserve Eclectic Institute (now Hiram College), becoming fluent in classical Greek and Latin. While pursuing a career as a traveling preacher, he attended Williams College in Massachusetts, from which he graduated in 1856. He then returned to a faculty post at Western Reserve. He studied law, was admitted to the Ohio Bar in 1861, and served briefly in the state legislature.

In 1861, as the Civil War began, Garfield was commissioned as a colonel in the 48th Ohio Infantry, which was dispatched to fight in Kentucky. In January 1862, under his command, the 48th defeated the Confederates in the Battle of Middle Creek, and Garfield was promoted to brigadier general. Placed in command of the 20th Brigade of the Army of

top: James Abram Garfield as president. *Library of Congress*

left: On July 2, 1881, four months into his presidency, James A. Garfield was shot by Charles Guiteau at the Baltimore & Potomac Railroad Station in Washington, but he survived the injury. This illustration was published on July 16, 1881, in *Frank Leslie's Illustrated Newspaper*. The caption read, "The attack on the President's life—Scene in the ladies' room of the Baltimore and Ohio Railroad depot—The arrest of the assassin from sketches by our special artist's [sic] A. Berghaus and C. Upham." Garfield is at center right, leaning after being shot. He is supported by Secretary of State James G. Blaine, who is wearing a light-colored top hat. At left, assassin Charles Guiteau is restrained by members of the crowd. Garfield died eleven weeks later on September 19. *Library of Congress*

The official presidential portrait of James Abram Garfield painted in 1881 by Calvin Curtis. *White House*

FIRST LADY
LUCRETIA RUDOLPH GARFIELD

Born on April 19, 1832, in Hiram, Ohio, Lucretia "Crete" Rudolph was the daughter of Arabella Green Mason Rudolph and Zebulon Rudolph, who was a founder of the Western Reserve Eclectic Institute (now Hiram College), where both Lucretia and her future husband were educated. The two actually met at the Geauga Seminary in Chester, Ohio, and both later moved to the Eclectic Institute. They were married on November 11, 1858, at the home of her parents in Hiram.

When he was elected to Congress, they divided their time between Washington and Mentor, Ohio. By all accounts, their marriage was close and they provided one another with intellectual stimulation. During her brief time as first lady, she was a cordial, though not ostentatious, hostess and dabbled in researching White House history. Unfortunately, she contracted malaria shortly after moving into the executive mansion. She was recuperating at Elberon on the New Jersey shore when her husband was shot, and she returned to Washington immediately. They both traveled two months later to Elberon, where he died.

She survived for nearly four decades, living out of the public eye while conserving the records of Garfield's years in public life. She moved to South Pasadena, California, where she passed away on March 14, 1918. She was interred along with her husband at Lake View Cemetery in Cleveland, Ohio.

The Children of James A. Garfield and Lucretia Garfield
Harry Augustus Garfield (1863-1942)
James Rudolph Garfield (1865-1950)
Mary "Mollie" Garfield Stanley Brown (1867-1947)
Irvin McDowell Garfield (1870-1951)
Abram Garfield (1872-1958)

A portrait of Lucretia Garfield taken at the Washington studio of Mathew Brady and his nephew Levin Corbin Handy. *Library of Congress*

---

the Ohio, Garfield participated in the Battle of Shiloh. He later served as chief of the staff of Gen. William Rosecrans, commander of the Army of the Cumberland, whose own career collapsed after he retreated during the Battle of Chickamauga.

In 1862, while serving in the US Army, Garfield allowed himself to be nominated by the Republicans for an Ohio seat in the US House of Representatives. He was elected, though because of his war service, he did not take his seat until late in 1863. In Congress, he supported the Emancipation Proclamation, though he considered Lincoln a "second-rate Illinois lawyer." After the war, he supported Andrew Johnson's initiatives to restore the southern states to the Union, passage of the Fifteenth Amendment, and the gold standard as the underpinning of United States currency.

He was, like many, tainted by scandal during the Grant years, but he landed on his feet. Indeed, after the Republicans lost control of the House of Representatives in 1874, Garfield became Minority Leader. When the inconclusive

1876 presidential election was referred to the House for resolution, Garfield was among those who successfully pressed for the certification of Rutherford B. Hayes. Like Hayes, Garfield was a proponent of Civil Service reform to curb patronage appointments.

In January 1880, the Ohio legislature elected Garfield to a term in the US Senate that was to begin in 1881, but he did not serve. Instead, he became a dark-horse candidate for the 1880 Republican presidential nomination, which he won on the thirty-sixth ballot. It was a contest between Ulysses S. Grant, going for a third term, and James G. Blaine of Maine. The two dueled through the earlier balloting without achieving a majority until the anti-Grant elements coalesced around Garfield.

In the 1880 election, James A. Garfield won the presidency with 48.31 percent of the popular vote, edging out Democratic Winfield Scott Hancock, who took a 48.22 percent share. In the Electoral College, Garfield took 214 electoral votes to Hancock's 155.

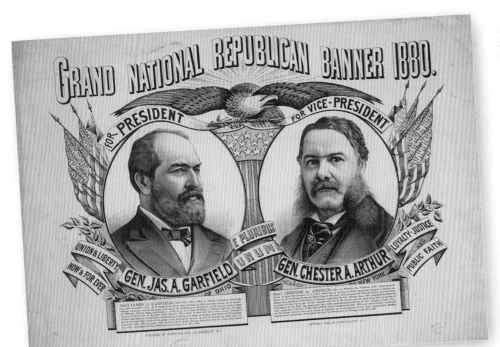

A poster for the 1880 Grand National Republican ticket of James A. Garfield and Chester A. Arthur that was published by Currier & Ives. *Library of Congress*

Garfield's brief presidency was devoted to a less than successful effort toward building a cabinet to achieve Republican Party unity. This included naming Blaine, his rival, as secretary of state. He intended to continue efforts begun under Hayes to reform Civil Service and appointed African Americans to important federal posts. Frederick Douglass was named as Recorder of Deeds in Washington. Many of his initiatives were stymied by a House of Representatives that was evenly divided between Democrats and Republicans.

On July 2, 1881, as Garfield entered the Baltimore & Potomac Railroad station in Washington to prepare to board a train to the New Jersey shore to escape the summer heat in the capital, Charles Guiteau shot him twice with a .44-caliber British Bulldog revolver. Guiteau had contacted the president several times, unsuccessfully seeking a government job as reward for having actively supported Garfield during the election.

One bullet grazed Garfield's arm, but the other lodged near his pancreas. It was a wound easily survivable today, but the president's trauma team did everything wrong, including probing the wound with unwashed hands and instruments. Indeed, Garfield survived, and even improved slightly over the coming days, but the infection, which would have been a non-issue if he had received the correct treatment, became rampant. Meanwhile, he had difficulty eating and developed pneumonia. In early September, a special train took him to Elberon, New Jersey, where his wife was convalescing from malaria. It was here that he died on September 19, 1881, within earshot of the Atlantic.

Apprehended at the scene, Guiteau was tried, convicted, and finally executed in June 1882.

Garfield is interred along with his wife in Lake View Cemetery in Cleveland, Ohio, where a massive memorial mausoleum was completed in 1890.

VICE PRESIDENT

CHESTER A. ARTHUR

The man who would serve out the majority of James A. Garfield's presidential term came to be nominated as his running mate not because of long legislative experience, which he did not have, but because of his being part of the New York Republican political machine, which was considered essential to winning the election for the Republicans.

At the 1880 Republican Convention, Garfield was not nominated until the thirty-sixth ballot. On the first ballot for the vice presidential nominee, Chester Alan Arthur—presented as a party unity candidate—polled nearly twice as many votes as all of his challengers combined. The two men were elected and inaugurated, and six months later, Chester A. Arthur was president of the United States. He and his own presidency are described in detail in the following chapter.

Chester A. Arthur

REPUBLICAN PARTY

The fourth vice president to ascend to the presidency upon the death of his predecessor, Chester Alan Arthur was born in Fairfield, Vermont on October 5, 1829, the son of Malvina Stone Arthur and William Arthur, a Free Will Baptist preacher who had immigrated from Ireland by way of Canada. The family relocated to upstate New York when Chester was a young boy, and lived in a number of cities there. He graduated from Union College in Schenectady in 1848, and worked as a schoolteacher for several years while studying law.

He moved to New York City, and was admitted to the bar in 1854. As a partner in the firm that became Culver, Parker, and Arthur, one of his often-cited cases was a case against a slaveholder passing through New York with his slaves. The firm successfully argued that because slavery was illegal in New York, the slaves should be freed. On the personal side, Arthur married Ellen Herndon in 1859.

In 1860, Arthur earned a patronage appointment to the military engineering staff of Republican Governor Edwin Morgan. In 1861, as the Civil War began, Arthur served in a recruitment role, at which he was a success. Returning to his law practice in 1863, Arthur found that the contacts he had made in state and federal government were good for business, and he found a place in the New York Republican machine—which was a rival to the Democrat-controlled Tammany Hall. In 1871, Ulysses S. Grant named Arthur to the powerful position of Collector of the Port of New York, to which numerous patronage appointments would

be made. In 1878, Arthur was among those who lost his job when President Rutherford B. Hayes made it a priority to clean up the patronage system in the federal government.

In 1880, the Republican Party was deeply divided between reformers and the "Stalwart" faction, those who relied on the patronage system. Arthur was among the latter, and among the Stalwarts backing the return of Ulysses S. Grant. When Garfield was nominated, the convention chose Chester Arthur as his running mate to balance the ticket and unify the party. When Garfield died, Arthur became president.

As president, Arthur found himself surrounded by Garfield's reform-minded cabinet—notably James G. Blaine—and a tide of public opinion favoring the Civil Service reform begun under Hayes. Unexpectedly, Arthur allowed his own actions to be swept along with that tide and soon, even jobs at the New York Customs House were being assigned on merit, not patronage.

On Arthur's watch, with Blaine as secretary of state, the United States intervened to mediate the end of the War of the Pacific between Bolivia, Peru, and Chile in an effort to checkmate British intervention in South America.

In 1884, despite failing health, Arthur made plans to run for a full term as president. However, his standing among the Stalwarts within the Republican Party had declined, dividing that faction and increasing the prospects of James G. Blaine, who had been seeking the nomination since 1876. At the convention, Blaine led from the start and gained the necessary

ELLEN HERNDON ARTHUR

The wife of Chester A. Arthur, Ellen Lewis "Nell" Herndon was born on August 30, 1837, in Culpeper Court House, Virginia, the daughter of naval officer William Lewis Herndon and Frances Elizabeth Hansbrough. In 1857, her father died saving the passengers of a ship of which he was captain in the worst commercial maritime disaster to date. Nell met her future husband in 1856, and they were married in New York City on October 25, 1859. Though they were personally close, their marriage was strained by his continuous absences

Ellen Arthur. *Library of Congress*

related to his political activities. During the Civil War, the relationship was complicated because Nell had numerous Virginia relatives fighting for the Confederacy. They had three children, the oldest of whom died in 1863 at the age of three before his siblings were born. The second-born, Chester A. Arthur II, largely ignored by his father, lived abroad for extended periods and became a notorious playboy.

Nell Arthur did not live to see her husband become president, nor to live in the White House as first lady. She died on January 12, 1880, shortly after contracting pneumonia and was buried at Albany Rural Cemetery in New York. Her husband kept a portrait of her in the White House, before which fresh cut flowers were placed every day.

The Children of Chester A. Arthur and Ellen Herndon Arthur
William Lewis Herndon Arthur (1860–1863)
Chester Alan Arthur II (1864–1937)
Ellen Hansbrough Herndon Arthur Pinkerton (1871–1915)

FIRST LADY
MARY ARTHUR McELROY

After the death of his wife, Chester A. Arthur never remarried. When he became president, he invited his youngest sister to act as first lady at White House social events. Mary Arthur was born on July 5, 1841, in Greenwich, New York, the youngest of the president's eight siblings. She attended the Emma Willard School Seminary, and married salesman John McElroy. Not terribly forward thinking, she was a member of the Albany Association Opposed to Women's Suffrage.

Mary continued to live with her husband and family in Albany, spending only a month or so each year in Washington as first lady. She shared her duties with former First Ladies Julia Tyler and Harriet Lane, who were both still living in Washington, DC. She died on January 8, 1917, and is interred at Albany Rural Cemetery.

opposite: An engraving of Chester Alan Arthur. *Bureau of Engraving and Printing*

above: The official portrait of Chester Arthur by Daniel Huntington. *White House*

majority. Chester Arthur became the fifth sitting president to be denied the renomination of his own party.

Arthur refused to campaign for Blaine, declined a suggestion that he run for the US Senate, and returned to his law practice in New York City. In late 1886, with his health failing, he and his son destroyed most of his personal and official papers, and on November 16, he died. He was interred at Albany Rural Cemetery in New York.

Grover Cleveland

DEMOCRATIC PARTY

Perhaps best known as the only president of the United States to serve two non-consecutive terms, Stephen Grover Cleveland was also the only president who was older than his father-in-law, albeit by only eight months. Cleveland was born in Caldwell, New Jersey, on March 18, 1837, the son of Reverend Richard Falley Cleveland and Ann Neal Cleveland, and a distant relative of Gen. Moses Cleveland, the namesake of Cleveland, Ohio. Grover grew up in upstate New York, where he graduated from the Clinton Liberal Academy. He later settled in Buffalo, where he studied law. Admitted to the bar in 1859, he was named Erie County district attorney in 1863. Rather than serving in the US Army during the Civil War, he paid another man to serve in his place, which was considered acceptable at the time. After a term as county sheriff—during which he personally hanged two murderers—he returned to his private law practice in 1873.

Having become active on Democratic Party politics, Cleveland was elected as mayor of Buffalo in 1881, but served only one year before being elected as governor of New York. In both posts, he earned a reputation as an active opponent of corruption and wasteful spending, which brought him public praise, but opposition from the powerful Tammany Hall Democratic machine in New York City.

In 1884, Cleveland's popularity earned him the Democratic presidential nomination. He led by a substantial margin on the first ballot and won on the second. In the general

election, the popular vote was close, with 48.85 percent going to Cleveland and 48.28 percent going to Republican James G. Blaine. In the Electoral College the margin was a more comfortable 219 to 182.

During the campaign, Cleveland was embarrassed when a story emerged that he had an affair with a widow named Maria Crofts Halpin, and that he had fathered her child. The Republicans coined the campaign slogan "Ma, Ma, where's my Pa?" After the election, the Democrats countered with "Gone to the White House, ha, ha, ha." The paternity charge is widely believed, but was never conclusively proven.

Cleveland entered the White House as the first bachelor president since James Buchanan, with his sister, Rose, acting as first lady. Two years into his first term, he married Frances Folsom, the daughter of a deceased friend for whom he had been acting as guardian.

As president, Cleveland was as a reformer, continuing the trend of his two predecessors toward merit appointments. Addressing another divisive issue of the day, he stood firm on the gold standard as a backing for United States currency, despite calls from western, silver-producing states to use both metals. He also created the Interstate Commerce Commission and undertook to revoke land grants given to railroads that had not actually built track on the land as promised. Given that the federal budget was running a surplus, Cleveland advocated reducing tariffs on imported goods which had been raised during the

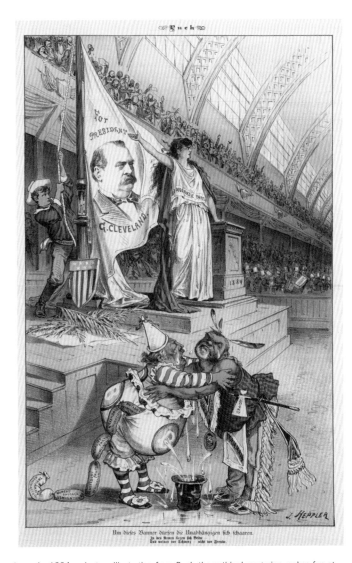

above: An 1884 caricature illustration from *Puck*, the satirical magazine, pokes fun at the Democratic Party machine. At the convention, the woman representing an independent Democratic Party points to Cleveland. In the foreground are former Massachusetts governor and party insider Benjamin F. Butler in dressed as a clown, and Tammany Hall boss John Kelly is dressed as an Indian. The caption reads, "When party lifts a flag like this on high, small wonder clowns and demagogues should cry." *Library of Congress*

opposite: An engraving of Grover Cleveland. *Bureau of Engraving and Printing*

Civil War and remained high, but this idea was opposed by manufacturers and their employees. This and his vetoes of a wave of Civil War pension bills were controversial and hurt his popularity.

In 1888, Cleveland was unanimously renominated at the Democratic Convention, and faced Republican Benjamin Harrison, the grandson of President William Henry Harrison, in the general election. Cleveland won the popular vote, albeit by less than a percentage point, but lost in the Electoral College. There would, however, be a rematch in 1892.

FIRST LADY
ROSE CLEVELAND

The sister of Grover Cleveland, Rose Elizabeth "Libby" Cleveland acted as her brother's first lady for fifteen months until his marriage to Frances Folsom in 1886. Rose Cleveland was born on June 14, 1846, in Fayetteville, New York, the youngest child of Reverend Richard Falley Cleveland and Ann Neal Cleveland. After her father died, when she was seven, she was raised by her widowed mother. She worked as a schoolteacher, including time at the Collegiate Institute in Lafayette, Indiana, but later returned home to care for and support her mother until Ann's death in 1882.

At the White House, she was criticized within the Washington social scene for her reservedly academic inclination. After Cleveland married, and young Frances Folsom became first lady, Rose divided her time between the Collegiate Institute and editing a literary magazine.

Around 1890, she became romantically involved with a wealthy widow named Evangeline Marrs Simpson. Evangeline remarried to Bishop Henry Benjamin Whipple, but after he died in 1901, the two women moved to Tuscany, where they lived together until Rose died on November 22, 1918, during the global influenza pandemic.

VICE PRESIDENT
THOMAS A. HENDRICKS

Born in Muskingum County, Ohio, on September 7, 1819, Thomas Andrew Hendricks was the son of John Hendricks and Jane Thomson Hendricks. He graduated from Hanover College in Indiana in 1841, was admitted to the bar in 1843, and became active in the Democratic Party. After having served in the Indiana state legislature, he was first elected to the US House of Representatives in 1850, where he served until 1855. Defeated in his Congressional bid, Hendricks was appointed as commissioner in the General Land Office in Washington by Franklin Pierce. After an unsuccessful run for governor of Indiana in 1860, Hendricks began a private law practice in Indianapolis. Elected to the US Senate in 1862, he served until 1869. On his third attempt, he was finally elected governor of Indiana in 1872, serving until 1877.

In 1876, Hendricks was nominated as the running mate of Democratic presidential candidate Samuel Tilden. They won the popular vote and a thin margin in the Electoral College, but the House of Representatives awarded twenty contested votes to the Republicans.

Eight years later, Hendricks had his second chance as Grover Cleveland's running mate. This time he was elected, but served only eight months until his death on November 25, 1885. For the majority of Cleveland's first term, as with most of Arthur's term, which preceded it, there was no vice president.

23

Benjamin Harrison

REPUBLICAN PARTY

The grandson of President William Henry Harrison, Benjamin was the son of Ohio Congressman John Scott Harrison and Elizabeth Ramsey Irwin Harrison. He was born in North Bend, Ohio, on August 20, 1833, and grew up on the family farm. He attended Farmers' College near Cincinnati, but transferred to Miami University in Oxford, Ohio, where he graduated in 1852. In 1853, he married Caroline Lavinia Scott, whom he had met at Farmers'. Having been raised as a Whig, Harrison joined and became active in the new Republican Party in 1856.

In 1862, during the Civil War, Harrison was commissioned as a colonel in the 70th Indiana Infantry and dispatched to Kentucky. In 1864, he and his regiment participated in the Georgia Campaign under Gen. William Tecumseh Sherman, and Harrison was later promoted to command a brigade in the action. He mustered out of the service in 1865 as a brevet brigadier general, promoted by Abraham Lincoln himself.

Having been the losing candidate in an 1876 run for governor of Indiana, he also failed in a US Senate bid in 1878. In 1880, though, with Republicans now in control of the state legislature, Harrison finally won a Senate seat, where he served until 1887.

At the 1888 Republican Convention, when perennial candidate James G. Blaine announced that he would not seek the nomination, Harrison was one of several candidates that were considered. He trailed for five ballots, but then emerged as a front-runner and gained the necessary majority on the seventh. In the 1888 general election, Harrison trailed

top: President Benjamin Harrison. *Bureau of Engraving and Printing*

above: Benjamin Harrison as a student, circa 1850. *Unknown photographer*

Democratic incumbent President Grover Cleveland in the popular vote by 47.8 percent to 48.63 percent, but won in the Electoral College 233 to 168.

Once in office, Harrison, like his predecessors of both parties, made a priority of continuing reforms to Civil Service to favor the merit system. Cleveland had been defeated in part because of his advocacy of lowering tariffs, so Harrison maintained them, while advocating reciprocity, or lowering tariffs on goods from countries that reduced tariffs on American exports. Meanwhile, Congressman and future president William McKinley promoted the Tariff Act of 1890, which resulted in the highest tariffs to date.

With a surplus in the Treasury, thanks to the high tariffs, what came to be known to critics as the "Billion-Dollar Congress" embarked on a spending spree that included infrastructure projects and an expanded US Navy. With both houses of Congress and the White House in the hands of the same party for the first time since 1875, a great deal of far-reaching legislation was passed. The Land Revision Act of 1891 created the National Forest System, the Disability and Dependent Pension Act expanded the scope of Civil War pensions, and the Morrill Land Grant Colleges Act paved the way for the creation of what evolved into many major educational institutions. Senator John Sherman of Ohio sponsored the Sherman Antitrust Act, outlawing monopolies that restricted trade, and the Sherman Silver Purchase Act, requiring the federal government to mint silver coinage.

These were expansive, changing times. During one eight-month stretch of Harrison's presidency, more new states were admitted to the Union in a shorter span of time than at any other time since the admission of the first eleven in 1787 to 1788. Between November 1889 and July 1890, North Dakota, South Dakota, Montana, Washington, Idaho, and Wyoming joined as the thirty-ninth through forty-fourth states, and Oklahoma was organized as a territory.

As the 1892 presidential election approached, however, the wind behind the sails of expansion was starting to abate, just as the Treasury surplus dwindled. Harrison easily won Republican renomination, but a fickle electorate was ready to give Grover Cleveland another try and restore him to the presidency. Harrison's electoral defeat in a rematch election, combined with the death of his wife two weeks earlier, was deeply depressing for him.

An 1890 caricature illustration from *Puck*, the satirical magazine. It pokes fun at President Benjamin Harrison, sitting at his White House desk, wearing the large hat of his grandfather, President William Henry Harrison. Referencing "The Raven," the poem by Edgar Allan Poe, Secretary of State James G. Blaine is shown as a raven, sitting atop a bust of Harrison's grandfather, nagging Harrison to urge Congress to add reciprocity provisions to the proposed McKinley Tariff. *Library of Congress*

CAROLINE LAVINIA SCOTT HARRISON

Born on October 1, 1832, in Oxford, Ohio, Caroline Lavinia "Carrie" Scott was the second daughter of Mary Potts Neal and Reverend John Witherspoon Scott, a professor at Miami University. Fired from this job for his abolitionist views, Scott moved on to Farmers' College, near Cincinnati, which is where his daughter met Benjamin Harrison, who was a student, in 1848.

Carrie graduated from the Oxford Female Institute in 1852 with a degree in music and took a teaching job in Kentucky. After a long courtship, she and Harrison wed on October 20, 1853, married by Reverend Scott. They settled initially in Indianapolis, but spent much of their time apart because of the time and energy that he devoted to his law practice, and later his political career.

When he was elected president, she took a great interest in her role as first lady, hosting events, supporting charities, and successfully lobbying Congress for funding to do a major renovation of the White House, including the installation of electrical wiring. She also began the tradition of a White House Christmas tree. She was a founder of the National Society of the Daughters of the American Revolution and its first president general.

In 1891, Caroline Harrison contracted tuberculosis, which resulted in her death on October 25, 1892. When she died, her daughter, Mamie McKee, who had been living in the White House with her husband and their two children, assumed the role of unofficial first lady during the last months of the Harrison presidency. Mamie's husband, J. Robert McKee, was later a founder of General Electric.

The Children of Benjamin Harrison and Caroline Harrison
Russell Benjamin Harrison (1854–1936)
Mary "Mamie" Scott Harrison McKee (1858–1930)

The official portrait of Caroline Scott Harrison by Daniel Huntington, painted in 1894. *White House*

MARY SCOTT LORD DIMMICK HARRISON

The second wife of Benjamin Harrison, Mary Scott Lord was born on April 30, 1858, in Honesdale, Pennsylvania, the daughter of Russell Farnham Lord and Elizabeth Mayhew Scott and the niece of Harrison's first wife, Caroline Scott. In 1881, she wed Walter Erskine Dimmick and was widowed three months later. After Benjamin Harrison was elected, she moved into the White House, where she and her aunt's daughter, Mamie Harrison, assisted the first lady. The two women were almost the same age, with Mamie being only three weeks older than Mary.

On April 6, 1896, Mary Scott Lord Dimmick married Benjamin Harrison, twenty-five years her senior, at St. Thomas Protestant Episcopal Church in New York City. Harrison's children, Russell and Mamie, who were both older than their father's bride, strenuously disapproved and did not attend the wedding. The couple had one daughter, who was born less than a year later.

Mary outlived her husband by forty-seven years but never remarried. She died of asthma in New York City on January 5, 1948, and was buried next to her husband and his first wife.

The Daughter of Benjamin Harrison and Mary Harrison
Elizabeth Harrison Walker (1897–1955)

After leaving the presidency, Harrison returned to Indianapolis, though he traveled a great deal. He lectured at Stanford University in California, and traveled to Europe to attend the International Peace Conference that resulted in the Hague Convention of 1899, which dealt with such issues as rules of war, maritime law, and mechanisms for resolving international disputes without war. Harrison remarried in 1896 to the niece of his deceased wife.

Benjamin Harrison died of influenza or related causes on March 13, 1901, and was buried next to his first wife at Crown Hill Cemetery in Indianapolis. His second wife was interred next to them forty-seven years later.

The official portrait of Benjamin Harrison by Eastman Johnson. *White House*

VICE PRESIDENT

LEVI P. MORTON

Born in Shoreham, Vermont, on May 16, 1824, Levi Parsons Morton began his business career as a clerk in a general store and eventually became a New York banker. A Republican, he ran unsuccessfully for the US House of Representatives from New York in 1876, but was elected two years later. He declined an invitation from James A. Garfield to be his 1880 running mate, but accepted the post as Minister to France. It was here that he drove the first rivet in the Statue of Liberty.

In 1888, Morton was nominated as the Republican vice presidential candidate on the first ballot and was swept into office along with Benjamin Harrison. In office, he frustrated Harrison by his doing little to help move legislation through Congress. In 1892, Morton chose not to run again, and was replaced by fellow New Yorker Whitelaw Reid on the ultimately unsuccessful ticket with Harrison. Morton returned to New York, where he served as governor from 1895 to 1896. He went into the private sector as a real estate investor, and died in Rhinebeck, New York, on May 16, 1920.

Levi P. Morrison *Library of Congress*

24

Grover Cleveland

DEMOCRATIC PARTY

Having been defeated by Republican Benjamin Harrison in the 1888 presidential election, Democrat Grover Cleveland won their rematch four years later with 46 percent of the popular vote to 43 percent for Harrison. In the Electoral College, the margin was 277 to 145. Cleveland had little time to relish the triumph. Even before his inauguration, the cracks in the economy that would become the Panic of 1893 had already appeared. The Philadelphia & Reading Railroad, one of the most powerful in the Northeast, went bankrupt ten days before the inauguration and it was downhill from there. Stock prices collapsed, there was a run on gold, and the United States fell into the worst depression in its history thus far. Cleveland's response was to undo McKinley's 1890 Tariff Act, end silver coinage, and veto disability pensions.

Labor unrest ensued, of which the nationwide 1894 Pullman Strike by railroad workers was emblematic. The Republicans rebounded in the 1894 midterm election, and Cleveland lost support from within the Democratic Party, in whose ranks there was a rising tide of populism.

Whereas Harrison saw six states admitted to the Union on this watch, only Utah was admitted under Cleveland, and this because its people favored the Democrats. There was still a cloud over Utah because of its Mormon majority and the practice of polygamy favored by the Mormons, which met with disapproval elsewhere in the United States. Though the Mormons disavowed polygamy in 1890, there were still suspicions. Meanwhile, Cleveland moved to block annexation of Hawaii, which had been favored by Harrison.

In 1896, Cleveland chose not to run for the nomination, as the center of gravity within the Democratic Party swung toward the populists, personified by the great orator William Jennings Bryan, who was the party's standard-bearer that year.

Cleveland and his wife retired to Princeton, New Jersey, where he served on the board of trustees at Princeton University, and where he often disagreed with Princeton's president and future Democratic president of the United States Woodrow Wilson. Gradually, Cleveland's health began to fail, though it was considered lucky that he had lived so long considering the major surgery he had undergone—kept secret from the public—when he was diagnosed with cancer of the mouth in 1893. Grover Cleveland died of a heart attack on June 24, 1908, and was buried in the cemetery at Nassau Presbyterian Church.

top: A portrait of Grover Cleveland as an older man. *National Archives*

above: A 1934 series $1,000 banknote featuring Cleveland. *Bureau of Engraving and Printing*

The official portrait of Grover Cleveland by Eastman Johnson. *White House*

Grover Cleveland **113**

FIRST LADY
FRANCES FOLSOM CLEVELAND

Grover Cleveland first met his future wife when she was an infant, and he was twenty-seven. Frances Clara Folsom was born in Buffalo, New York, on July 21, 1864, the daughter of Emma Harmon Folsom and Oscar Folsom, an attorney friend of Cleveland. As she was growing up, Cleveland was a constant presence, taking on the role of doting "uncle." After Folsom was killed in an accident in 1875, Cleveland became the court-appointed guardian of the eleven-year-old Frances. In 1885, she was attending Wells College in Aurora, New York, when her guardian proposed marriage in a letter.

Serenaded by John Philip Sousa and the Marine Corps Band, they were married in a White House wedding on June 2, 1886. At age twenty-one, Frances was the youngest wife of a president to become first lady, and he was the first president to get married in the White House. Their twenty-seven-year age difference is surpassed by the thirty years that separated John Tyler and his second wife, Julia Gardiner.

Frances leapt into her role as first lady with boundless energy, planning and hosting social events several times a week. When Cleveland left office in 1889, she told the White House staff that she would be back, and in 1893, she was. One of their five children, Esther Cleveland, was born in the White House. Esther later married British military officer William Bosanquet. Their daughter, Cleveland's granddaughter, was the British philosopher Philippa Ruth Foot.

After leaving office in 1897, Grover and Frances settled in Princeton, New Jersey. After his death in 1908, she remarried in 1913 to Thomas Preston, an archaeology professor at Wells College. Frances died on October 29, 1947, and was buried next to Cleveland.

The Children of Grover Cleveland and Frances Cleveland
Ruth Cleveland (1891–1904)
Esther Cleveland Bosanquet (1893–1980)
Marion Cleveland Dell Amen (1895–1977)
Richard Folsom Cleveland (1897–1974)
Francis Grover Cleveland (1903–1995)

An Alleged Child of Grover Cleveland and Maria Halpin
Dr. James E. King Jr. (born Oscar Folsom Cleveland) (1874[?]–1947
(According to the story, the child was raised by Dr. James E. King Sr., who delivered him, but neither King ever commented on this narrative. An alternate version of the story is that the boy was actually the son of Oscar Folsom, Cleveland's father-in-law.)

above: The White House wedding of Grover Cleveland and Frances Folsom. *Harper's Weekly*

above: A political cartoon lampooning Cleveland for the widely circulated rumor that he had an illegitimate child. He was dogged for years by the taunt, "Ma, Ma, where's my Pa?" *Library of Congress*

A painting of Grover Cleveland relaxing by Anders Leonard Zorn. *National Portrait Gallery*

VICE PRESIDENT

ADLAI E. STEVENSON

Born in Christian County, Kentucky, on October 23, 1835, Adlai Ewing Stevenson was the son of John Turner Stevenson and Eliza Ewing Stevenson. In 1850, when his tobacco crop failed, John Stevenson freed his slaves and moved to Illinois. Adlai Stevenson graduated from Centre College in Danville, Illinois, and was admitted to the bar in 1858. During his practice in Woodford County, Illinois, Stevenson, a Democrat, met Abraham Lincoln, whom he disliked.

Stevenson was elected to the US House of Representatives in 1874, was defeated two years later, but was reelected in 1878. Defeated again in 1880 and 1882, he stopped running. He received a patronage appointment as assistant postmaster general during the first Cleveland administration, but left the post when Benjamin Harrison came in. At the 1892 Democratic Convention, it was decided that Stevenson might be useful in helping Cleveland carry Illinois and he received the nomination. As vice president, he diverged from Cleveland's point of view on the question of silver coinage.

In 1896, Stevenson considered running for the Democratic presidential nomination, but there was little enthusiasm for him compared to that for the rising star, William Jennings Bryan. In 1900, however, the Democrats did pick Stevenson, but as Bryan's running mate. He thus became the first candidate to run for vice president with two different presidential candidates. After his defeat, he went back into private practice, coming out only for an unsuccessful bid for Illinois governor in 1908. Adlai Stevenson died on June 14, 1914. His grandson, also named Adlai Stevenson, was the unsuccessful Democratic Party candidate for president in 1952 and 1956.

Adlai Ewing Stevenson.
Library of Congress

25

1897–1901

William McKinley

REPUBLICAN PARTY

The man who presided over the unanticipated acquisition of nearly two hundred thousand square miles
of overseas territory by the United States, William
McKinley enjoyed the good fortune to have come into office
just as the ill effects of the Panic of 1893 were fading, but
suffered the ill fortune to leave office by assassination.

He was born on January 29, 1843, in Niles, Ohio, the son
of Nancy Allison McKinley and an iron foundry owner also
named William McKinley. He attended Allegheny College
in Pennsylvania and Mount Union College in Ohio, but
graduated from neither. In 1861, when the Civil War began,
McKinley volunteered for service and was assigned to the
23rd Ohio Infantry as a sergeant. He saw action in Virginia
during 1863 and 1864, and was promoted to brevet major
in 1865 shortly before the war ended. While in uniform,
McKinley developed a lasting friendship with Rutherford B.
Hayes.

After the war, McKinley studied law and was admitted to the
Ohio Bar in 1867. He became active in the Republican Party,
and briefly held office as a prosecutor. In 1871, he married
Ida Saxton, who encouraged his political career. They had
two daughters, both of whom died very young, which brought
great sadness to their lives.

In 1876, as his friend Hayes was elected as president,
McKinley was elected to the US House of Representatives,
where he served a half dozen terms, albeit from different
districts as boundaries were being redrawn. In Congress, he
is perhaps best remembered for sponsoring the Tariff Act

above: A tabloid illustration by T. Dart Walker depicting the assassination of President
William McKinley by Leon Czolgosz on September 6, 1901. *Library of Congress*

top: A portrait of William McKinley as president. *Library of Congress*

opposite: An 1896 campaign poster showing William McKinley dramatically standing
on golden "sound money," against a backdrop of ships representing "commerce" and
factories symbolizing "civilization." *Library of Congress*

of 1890. In 1891, he was elected as governor of Ohio, which
had been Hayes's springboard to the presidency. Ohio
was indeed an important state as five of the preceding six
men to serve as president were from the state. And so it
was for McKinley, who would make it six of seven. In 1896,

FIRST LADY
IDA SAXTON MCKINLEY

Born on June 8, 1847, in Canton, Ohio, Ida Saxton was the daughter of banker James Saxton and Katherine DeWalt Saxton, and she was employed at the father's bank, a rare thing for a woman in the mid-nineteenth century. She met William McKinley in 1867, though she went off on an extensive European tour and they did not begin their courtship for several years. They were married on January 25, 1871, and had two daughters, both of whom died young. Ida suffered a nervous breakdown as a result of the loss, developed epilepsy, and became an invalid. Doctors prescribed drugs, including tincture of opium, which kept her sedated for much of her life.

Even as president, McKinley doted on his wife, who accompanied him as he traveled. At the White House, the role of hostess was largely filled by Jennie Tuttle Hobart, wife of Vice President Garret Hobart, with the president's wife as a mere figurehead. She was in Buffalo at the time of the assassination, but was not a witness. Her health declined after his death, and she died on May 26, 1907. She and her daughters are interred with the president at the McKinley Memorial Mausoleum.

The official portrait of First Lady Ida McKinley, painted by Emily Drayton Taylor.
White House

The Children of William McKinley and Ida McKinley
Katherine McKinley (1871–1875)
Ida McKinley (1873–1873)

The recently deceased William McKinley commemorated on a US postage stamp issued in 1904. *US Postal Service*

the Republicans nominated him on the first ballot, while the Democrats nominated Congressman William Jennings Bryan, whose famous "Cross of Gold" speech and advocacy of silver coinage put him in direct conflict with the Republican advocacy of the gold standard. McKinley defeated Bryan 271 to 176 in the Electoral College, while capturing 51 percent of the popular vote.

McKinley had run for president as a booster of high tariffs and the gold standard and these concepts guided his legislative agenda. As prosperity returned, both remained popular.

However, it was the Spanish-American War that overshadowed everything during McKinley's first term. Cuba had been a simmering issue since the beginning of the nineteenth century. There had been calls for the United States to intercede to help Cubans liberate themselves from Spain, and calls for the United States to annex Cuba, but nothing happened until 1898. The Cuban war for independence had heated up and rioting was taking place in Havana, so McKinley sent the battleship USS *Maine* to Havana as a show of force to protect American interests, while attempting the negotiate with Spain for Cuban independence. When the battleship blew up with the loss of most aboard—the exact cause has never been definitively determined—Congress declared war on Spain, though McKinley did not request such a declaration.

Between April and July, the US Army defeated the Spanish in Cuba and occupied Puerto Rico, while the US Navy scored decisive victories against the Spanish off Cuba and in the Battle of Manila Bay in the Philippines. By December, paperwork had been signed by which the Spanish withdrew from Cuba, while agreeing to sell Guam, the Philippines, and Puerto Rico to the United States. In the meantime, McKinley had concluded a deal to annex Hawaii. Practically overnight, the United States had gained an empire spreading for ten thousand miles across the globe.

In 1900, McKinley was renominated unanimously, while the Republican Party chose the popular governor of New York, Theodore Roosevelt, as his running mate. The Democrats nominated William Jennings Bryan again, making 1900 a rematch of 1896 at the head of the tickets. Once again,

GARRET A. HOBART

Vice President Garret Augustus Hobart. *Library of Congress*

Born in Long Branch, New Jersey, on June 3, 1844, Garret Augustus Hobart was the son of Sophia Vanderveer Hobart and elementary school founder Addison Hobart. He graduated from Rutgers College in 1863, studied law, and was admitted to the bar in 1866. An active Republican, he was elected to the first of several terms in the state legislature in 1872, where he served as Speaker of the Assembly and later president of the New Jersey Senate. He had an active career in private legal practice and in business, where he specialized in turning around failing railroads.

In 1896, he was picked as William McKinley's running mate to balance the ticket with a northeasterner. As vice president, Hobart had a good relationship with McKinley and served as a close advisor, a role not often performed by previous vice presidents.

With his previous legislative experience, Hobart was also more active than many of his predecessors when it came to presiding over the US Senate. Though energetic, Hobart had a failing heart, a fact that he hid as long as possible. In late 1899, Hobart's health declined precipitously, and he died on November 21. He was buried at Cedar Law Cemetery in Paterson, New Jersey.

THEODORE ROOSEVELT

The death in office of Garret Hobart left William McKinley without a vice president in the last year of his presidency, and left the Republican Party with an opening as McKinley's running mate for the 1900 election. The popular choice was New York Governor Theodore Roosevelt. At the convention, both McKinley and Roosevelt were nominated on the first ballot without opposition. Roosevelt and his own presidency are described in detail in the following chapter.

The official portrait of William McKinley by Harriet Anderson Stubbs. *White House*

McKinley prevailed and by a slightly greater margin, 291 to 155 in the Electoral College and with 51.64 percent of the popular vote.

On September 6, 1901, six months after his second inauguration, McKinley was visiting the Pan-American Exposition in Buffalo, New York, when anarchist Leon Czolgosz fired two bullets into the president's abdomen. William McKinley died on September 14. As had been the case with the shooting of James Garfield, the gunshots were not immediately fatal, and the ultimate cause of death was infection, which would not have occurred had sanitary conditions prevailed during McKinley's treatment. Czolgosz received a speedy trial and was executed six weeks after McKinley's death.

McKinley was interred at West Lawn Cemetery in Canton, Ohio, where the McKinley Memorial Mausoleum was dedicated in 1907.

26

Theodore Roosevelt

REPUBLICAN PARTY

The youngest man ever to become president of the United States, Theodore Roosevelt was also probably the most widely accomplished president since Thomas Jefferson. He was an author, an explorer, a collegiate boxer, a taxidermist, and a pioneer conservationist. He was a Dakota Territory rancher and New York City's police commissioner. He organized a cavalry detachment to fight in the Spanish-American War and was the first president of the United States to be awarded the Medal of Honor and the Nobel Peace Prize.

Roosevelt, often called simply "TR," was born on October 27, 1858, in New York City. He was the son of Martha Stewart "Mittie" Bulloch and the wealthy philanthropist Theodore Roosevelt Sr. The younger Roosevelt was a sickly boy, whose asthma rendered him a near invalid. At an early age, however, he discovered that physical exercise controlled his symptoms and greatly improved his health. With this, he became a confirmed outdoorsman.

He attended Columbia Law School, but transferred to Harvard, where he boxed, rowed, and graduated Phi Beta Kappa in the top 12 percent of the class of 1880. While at Harvard, he penned a landmark history and analysis of the US Navy in the War of 1812.

Also in 1880, Roosevelt married Alice Hathaway Lee. She died in 1884, two days after the birth of their daughter and eleven hours after the death of Roosevelt's widowed mother.

top: Theodore Roosevelt, circa 1902. *Library of Congress*

above: Roosevelt with the hunting rifle he used as a Dakota rancher, photographed by George Grantham Bain in 1885. *Library of Congress*

The official portrait of Theodore Roosevelt painted by John Singer Sargent in 1903. *White House*

He thereafter plunged himself into his work in state legislature to which he had been elected in 1882 and where his legislative focus was fighting corruption. He became so active that he is credited with having written more legislation than any of his colleagues. He ran for mayor of New York City in 1886, but came in third. In that same year, Roosevelt married his second wife, Edith Kermit Carow, with whom he would have five children. During their honeymoon in Europe, Roosevelt led a climbing expedition to the summit of Mont Blanc, the tallest mountain on the continent.

In the meantime, his interest in the outdoors had taken him to the Badlands of Dakota Territory, specifically into the area that is now western North Dakota. He first came in 1883 on a two-week buffalo-hunting trip, but he wound up acquiring the Chimney Butte Ranch (also known as the Maltese Cross Ranch) and going into the cattle business. After Alice's death, Roosevelt decided to leave the East and live full time in the West. He then bought a second property, the Elkhorn Ranch, where he was joined by two friends from Maine, who had a similar interest in the West, and who relocated to the Elkhorn with their families.

Roosevelt became thoroughly involved in his new life, working as a cowboy on his property. At one point he single-handedly tracked and captured a trio of outlaws. He also authored three books about life on the frontier. The terrible blizzards of the winter of 1886 to 1887, still

above: Theodore Roosevelt's home at Sagamore Hill in Oyster Bay on Long Island is now preserved as the Sagamore Hill National Historic Site. *Library of Congress*

below: William Dinwiddie photographed Roosevelt and his Rough Riders (the 1st Volunteer Cavalry) at the top of Kettle Hill, which they captured on July 3, 1898, during the Spanish-American War. The hill is often misidentified as San Juan Hill. *Library of Congress*

opposite: Theodore Roosevelt, in Rough Rider uniform, as photographed on October 26, 1898, by George Gardner Rockwood. *Library of Congress*

ALICE HATHAWAY LEE ROOSEVELT

The Official portrait of First Lady Edith Roosevelt by Theobald Chartran. *White House*

The first wife of President Theodore Roosevelt was born in Chestnut Hill, Massachusetts, on July 29, 1861, the daughter of banker George Cabot Lee and Caroline Watts Haskell Lee. She met Roosevelt, who fell in love with her on the spot, in 1878, but the feeling was not mutual. She found him bookish and "eccentric," and rejected his initial proposals of marriage. She finally warmed to him and accepted, and they were married on October 27, 1880, in Brookline, Massachusetts, at the home of the Alice's parents. They settled into the sprawling family home at Sagamore Hill in Oyster Bay, New York, that was still home to Roosevelt's widowed mother, Mittie.

He was on the floor at the state assembly in Albany on February 12, 1884, when he learned that their daughter, Alice, had just been born. He arrived home to find his wife lingering near death with typhoid fever and was with her when she died on Valentine's Day, February 14, in the same house, and on the same day as Mittie Roosevelt died. With Alice's death, Theodore confided in his diary that "the light has gone out of my life." Alice and her mother-in-law were interred at Green Wood Cemetery in Brooklyn.

In 1906, the younger Alice, known as "Princess Alice," married Congressman Nicholas Longworth III and remained as one of the most important of Washington, DC, socialites for the rest of her life. Indeed, she was called "the other Washington Monument."

FIRST LADY
EDITH KERMIT CAROW ROOSEVELT

The second wife of Theodore Roosevelt was a childhood friend who had been a guest at his wedding to Alice Hathaway Lee. Born on August 6, 1861, in Norwich, Connecticut, Edith Kermit Carow was the daughter of Charles Carow and Gertrude Elizabeth Tyler Carow. She grew up next door to the Roosevelts, and was a companion of Theodore's until he left for Harvard in 1876. They reconnected after Alice died, and he proposed in late 1885. They were married on December 2, 1886, at St. George's Church in London, England, and took up residence at the Roosevelt family home in Oyster Bay, New York.

When she became first lady in 1901, she found the White House "dark" and "musty," and undertook the first substantial remodel since Carrie Harrison had lived there. Whereas some first ladies had remained aloof from the Washington social scene, Edith made the executive mansion the social center of Washington. One of the biggest events was the White House wedding of Edith's stepdaughter, Alice, to Congressman Nicholas Longworth III. Relations between Edith and Alice were strained, though apparently businesslike, and they thawed over time. Edith had five children of her own, all of whom served in the US Army (Ethel was a nurse during World War I), and three of whom preceded her in death— Quentin was killed in action in World War I, Ted died of a heart attack in Normandy during World War II, and Kermit committed suicide.

After Theodore's death, Edith visited Kermit's grave in France, and traveled elsewhere, but continued to live at the family home in Oyster Bay until her death on September 30, 1948. She is buried with her husband at Youngs Memorial Cemetery in Oyster Bay.

The Daughter of Theodore Roosevelt and Alice Roosevelt
Alice Lee Roosevelt Longworth (1884–1980)

The Children of Theodore Roosevelt and Edith Roosevelt
Theodore "Ted" Roosevelt III (1887–1944)
Kermit Roosevelt (1889–1943)
Ethel Carow Roosevelt Derby (1891–1977)
Archibald Bulloch "Archie" Roosevelt (1894–1979)
Quentin Roosevelt (1897–1918)

Alice Hathaway Lee Roosevelt.
Library of Congress

above: Theodore Roosevelt with naturalist and Sierra Club founder John Muir at Glacier Point in Yosemite National Park in 1906. Upper and lower Yosemite Falls are visible in the left background. *Library of Congress*

right: Perhaps the most significant political cartoon in the history of American popular culture was this one drawn by Clifford Berryman in November 1902. It depicts an incident on a bear hunting trip to Mississippi when Theodore Roosevelt refused to shoot a bear restrained by a rope. From this came the immensely popular plush toys in the form of bears that became known as "Teddy Bears." *Library of Congress*

remembered as a High Plains turning point, wiped out most of Roosevelt's cattle, and he made the decision to return to New York—although he did later make visits to the West.

After the 1888 election, Benjamin Harrison appointed Roosevelt to the Civil Service Commission, on which he pursued corruption with vigor and enthusiasm. His reputation as a reformer led to his being considered as a New York mayoral candidate in 1894 and to his being appointed as a New York City Police Commissioner in 1895. In the latter post, he is credited with cleaning up one of the most corrupt police departments in the United States. He went so far as to walk their beats with police officers to keep his hand on the pulse of things.

In 1897, William McKinley named Roosevelt to the post of assistant secretary of the navy based on his interest in naval matters going back to his years at Harvard. As acting secretary in 1898, he mobilized the US Navy for war after the sinking of the USS *Maine*. He then resigned to organize the 1st US Volunteer Cavalry Regiment, specifically recruiting a core group of cowboys and Western outdoorsmen. Known as the "Rough Riders," they arrived in Cuba in June 1898. Under the direct leadership of Roosevelt, now a colonel, they spearheaded the US Army's successful assault on Kettle Hill on

A 1904 Republican Party campaign poster depicting candidates Theodore Roosevelt and his vice presidential running mate Charles Warren Fairbanks. The slogan reads that "Protection, which guards and develops our industries, is a cardinal policy of the Republican Party." In the party platform, though not in the poster, that thought was followed by the words "The measure of protection should always at least equal the difference in the cost of production at home and abroad. We insist upon the maintenance of the principle of protection, and therefore rates of duty should be readjusted only when conditions have so changed that the public interest demands their alteration, but this work cannot safely be committed to any other hands than those of the Republican party. To intrust it to the Democratic party is to invite disaster." *Library of Congress*

July 1. Roosevelt's role in the battle, for which he was belatedly awarded the Medal of Honor, was a defining moment in his life and career.

After the war, Roosevelt's popularity made him a star figure in the Republican Party, and led to his election as governor of New York in 1898. In office, his energetic war on corruption and advocacy of the merit system angered machine politicians, but revolutionized state government. He also made himself the enemy of monopolistic corporate interests and a champion of the common man.

In 1900, the death of William McKinley's vice president opened a spot on the Republican ticket for which Roosevelt was the favored candidate. His political friends were anxious to see him in national office, while his political foes were happy to see him out of New York government.

It was as vice president that he coined his famous commentary on foreign policy, "speak softly, and carry a big stick," which he defined as "the exercise of intelligent forethought and of decisive action sufficiently far in advance of any likely crisis."

On September 14, 1901, half a year into his vice presidency, Theodore Roosevelt was sworn in as president of the United States upon the death of William McKinley.

In 1904, the Republican Party unanimously renominated Roosevelt, who went on to a landslide victory over fellow New Yorker Alton Parker, the Democratic nominee, in the general election. He won 336 electoral votes to 140 for Parker. His 56.42 percent of the popular vote was the greatest earned by any presidential candidate since James Monroe's uncontested reelection in 1820.

In office, Theodore Roosevelt's leadership style was one of strong executive leadership, using the office of the president as a "bully pulpit" to push to his agenda as hard as possible. Through his two terms, his domestic agenda, which would help to define public policy in the new twentieth century, was called the "Square Deal," implying a philosophy of all-around fairness. It centered on three fundamental concepts, known as the "Three Cs": natural resource conservation, consumer protection, and control of the corporate roguery represented by the so-called "robber barons" of the late nineteenth century.

Under the conservation heading, Roosevelt championed such initiatives as the creation in 1905 of the US Forest Service to manage the National Forests, and the passage of the Antiquities Act of 1906. There were five new national parks, eighteen national monuments, more than fifty wildlife reservations, and 150 national forests created during his presidency. Though an avid hunter, Roosevelt advocated sustainable limits, not wasteful consumption, and a conservationist approach such as he advocated with logging in the National Forests. On a 1902 hunting trip in Mississippi, he famously refused to kill a bear cub that had been tied to a tree. When news of the incident was reported, the name "Roosevelt Bear," and later "Teddy Bear," came into use to describe children's plush bear toys.

As for consumer protection, in 1906, Roosevelt signed the Pure Food and Drug Act and the Meat Inspection Act. To curb corporate misdeeds, among other initiatives, he strengthened the Interstate Commerce Commission and initiated "trust-busting," antitrust suits to break up monopolies such as Standard Oil. In 1903, he created the Department of Commerce and Labor (divided into two departments in 1913). He also initiated arbitration in the coal strike of 1902. At home, he led a crusade against child labor, while in the newly acquired Philippines, he abolished slavery and involuntary servitude.

In foreign policy, Roosevelt was an activist. In the Western Hemisphere, he promulgated the "Roosevelt

FROM THEODORE ROOSEVELT'S SQUARE DEAL SPEECH
April 5, 1905

We must act upon the motto of all for each and each for all. There must be ever present in our minds the fundamental truth that in a republic such as ours the only safety is to stand neither for nor against any man because he is rich or because he is poor, because he is engaged in one occupation or another, because he works with his brains or because he works with his hands. We must treat each man on his worth and merits as a man. We must see that each is given a square deal, because he is entitled to no more and should receive no less. Finally, we must keep ever in mind that a republic such as ours can exist only by virtue of the orderly liberty which comes through the equal domination of the law over all men alike, and through its administration in such resolute and fearless fashion as shall teach all that no man is above it and no man below it.

VICE PRESIDENT
CHARLES W. FAIRBANKS

Having assumed the presidency after the death of William McKinley, Theodore Roosevelt had no vice president until after the 1904 election, when Charles Warren Fairbanks was elected. Born on May 11, 1852, in Delaware, Ohio, Fairbanks was admitted to the Ohio Bar in 1874 but moved to Indianapolis, Indiana, soon after. For a time he was a protégé of the millionaire railroad financier Jay Gould, but he took an interest in Republican politics. He was elected to the US Senate from Indiana in 1896 and was an advisor to William McKinley. In 1904, Roosevelt favored Robert Hitt of Illinois as a running mate, but the Republican Convention chose Fairbanks. He was seen as more of a traditional Republican who could balance reform-minded Roosevelt and keep the party united.

After an uneventful vice presidency, Fairbanks was not chosen to run in 1908 with William Howard Taft, Roosevelt's handpicked successor, so he returned to private practice. Fairbanks backed Taft against Roosevelt in 1912. Four years later, when the Republican Party united around Supreme Court Justice Charles Evans Hughes as their presidential candidate, Fairbanks was picked as his running mate. After they lost, Fairbanks returned to Indianapolis, where he died on June 4, 1918.

Vice President
Charles Warren Fairbanks.
Library of Congress

Members of the Roosevelt-Rondon Scientific Expedition that explored Brazil's Rio da Dúvida (River of Doubt) in 1913-1914 included, from the left, Father John Augustine Zahm, Brazilian explorer Cândido Mariano da Silva Rondon, Kermit Roosevelt, ornithologist George Cherrie, Leo Miller, four unidentified Brazilians, Theodore Roosevelt, and Anthony Fiala. Only Roosevelt, Kermit, Cherrie, Rondon, and the Brazilians would descend the river. According to the Library of Congress, at the end of the expedition, Roosevelt, "suffering from illness and injuries incurred during his long journey, returned from Manaos (Manaus) to New York." The river has since been renamed Rio Roosevelt. *Library of Congress*

FROM THEODORE ROOSEVELT'S CITIZENSHIP IN A REPUBLIC SPEECH
April 23, 1910

It is not the critic who counts; not the man who points out how the strong man stumbles, or where the doer of deeds could have done them better. The credit belongs to the man who is actually in the arena, whose face is marred by dust and sweat and blood; who strives valiantly; who errs, who comes short again and again, because there is no effort without error and shortcoming; but who does actually strive to do the deeds; who knows great enthusiasms, the great devotions; who spends himself in a worthy cause; who at the best knows in the end the triumph of high achievement, and who at the worst, if he fails, at least fails while daring greatly, so that his place shall never be with those cold and timid souls who neither know victory nor defeat.

Corollary" to the Monroe Doctrine, under which the United States would intervene to resolve disputes between European and Latin American countries. Meanwhile, in 1903, he negotiated a deal with newly independent Panama to build the Panama Canal. He mediated the 1905 Treaty of Portsmouth to end the Russo-Japanese War, for which he earned the Nobel Peace Prize. He built up the US Navy, sending sixteen of its battleships, nicknamed the "Great White Fleet," on a fourteen-month round-the-world tour in 1907 to 1909.

He courted the media with frequent press conferences and established a White House briefing room because he knew that this conduit to the electorate was a key to maintaining his popularity.

Roosevelt had promised in 1904 that he would not to run in 1908 and he spent the ensuing years grooming William Howard Taft as his handpicked successor. After Taft won the election and began to govern in his own right, Roosevelt became so displeased that he began speaking out against him.

In 1912, Roosevelt decided to run against Taft for the presidential nomination. It was the first time that some of the delegates to the Republican Convention were chosen by state primaries, and Roosevelt won 9 of 12, including Taft's home state of Ohio. Roosevelt came to the convention with 278 delegates to Taft's 48, but at the convention, where the majority of delegates were chosen, there was an immense battle for votes, which Taft won. This, in turn, split the Republican Party, and a sizable majority split off to form the short-lived Progressive Party as a vehicle for running Roosevelt for president. When Roosevelt announced that he was optimistic, feeling as strong as a bull moose, the party was quickly nicknamed as the "Bull Moose Party."

His strength was demonstrated in October 1912, when Roosevelt became the third of the past six presidents to have a bullet fired into his body. John Fleming Schrank shot Roosevelt as he prepared to give a speech in Milwaukee. In typical Roosevelt style, he ascertained that the bullet in his chest had not penetrated his lung, so the "bull moose" proceeded to deliver his ninety-minute speech. Afterward, he was treated for his injury. He survived, but the bullet, slowed by impacting papers and a glasses case in Roosevelt's pocket, was never removed. Schrank died in the state mental hospital in 1943.

In the 1912 general election, Roosevelt became the only third-party candidate in American history to come in ahead of a major party. Unfortunately for him, he came in second. Woodrow Wilson, the Democratic nominee, won with 435 electoral votes, Roosevelt received 88, and Taft was a distant third with only eight.

After leaving office, Roosevelt devoted himself to scientific expeditions to remote parts of the world. From 1909 to 1910, under the auspices of the Smithsonian Institution, he led an expedition into central Africa to collect more than ten thousand specimens of animals. He was later criticized for this, given that "collect" meant "kill" and many of these were species such as elephants and white rhinos. The dead animals were, however, preserved and mounted and still exist in many natural history museums around the United States.

In 1913–1914, under the sponsorship of the American Museum of Natural History, Roosevelt led an expedition into the Amazon jungle over 625 uncharted miles of the Rio da Dúvida (River of Doubt). During this trip, a minor leg injury became infected, almost killed him, and left him with lifelong health issues.

During World War I, he became an outspoken critic of atrocities committed by German troops in Belgium and by German submarines on the high seas. He proposed raising an army of volunteers analogous to the Rough Riders of 1898 to go to Europe

above: A photograph of Theodore Roosevelt as a former president, taken at the Washington, DC, studio of Harris & Ewing. The studio was owned and operated by George W. Harris and Martha Ewing. *Library of Congress*

inset: A Roosevelt commemorative gold coin from the 2013 Presidential One-Dollar Coin Program. *US Mint Pressroom Image Library*

to fight the Germans, but the idea was rejected by President Woodrow Wilson.

When his youngest son, Quentin, was killed in action while flying with the US Army Air Service, Roosevelt was deeply saddened. He died less than six months later on January 5, 1919. He was buried at Youngs Memorial Cemetery, near his home in Oyster Bay, New York.

27

1909–1913

William H. Taft

REPUBLICAN PARTY

The first president to throw a ceremonial first pitch in major league baseball, William Howard Taft was the only man to serve as both president of the United States and chief justice of the Supreme Court, though he had yearned for the latter post for most of his career. Taft was also the largest president. Though he lost weight in later years, he weighed around 335 pounds while in office. Stories persist that he once became stuck in a White House bathtub and had to be extracted, but this is unproven. He was also prone to dozing off during meetings and dinners and was diagnosed with extremely high blood pressure.

Taft was born on September 15, 1857, near Cincinnati, Ohio, the son of Louisa Torrey Taft and Alphonso Taft, who served as attorney general and secretary of war under President Ulysses S. Grant. He graduated from Yale College (now Yale University) in 1878, and from Cincinnati Law School in 1880. He married Helen Herron in 1886.

Taft was appointed as an assistant county prosecutor in 1882, and later worked as a tax collector before being appointed as a superior court judge in Cincinnati in 1887. After two years in Washington, DC, as President Benjamin Harrison's solicitor general, Taft was named to the Sixth District of the US Court of Appeals in Cincinnati in 1892.

In 1900, in the wake of the Spanish-American War, President William McKinley appointed Taft to organize a civilian government for the Philippines, where he served as a locally popular governor general from 1901 to 1904. Taft served as secretary of war under Theodore Roosevelt, though he spent much of his time in the Philippines or elsewhere in the Far East. Throughout the Roosevelt years, Taft was torn between his desire for a seat on the Supreme Court and his fondness for the Philippines. Indeed, Roosevelt offered him the Supreme Court job more than once and Taft declined. Between 1906 and 1909, when the US Army occupied Cuba to restore order, Roosevelt sent Taft to function as governor. Taft also traveled to Panama to supervise the progress of the

above: The Taft Family at home in Manila while the future president served as the first civilian governor-general of the Philippines between 1901 and 1904. To Taft's left are son, Charles; daughter, Helen; and wife, Nellie. Taft was very popular with Filipinos who remembered the hardships of Spanish rule. *H. L. Knight*

top: An official engraving of William Howard Taft. *Bureau of Engraving and Printing*

This photograph of William Howard Taft, taken in 1908, was part of a famous series of photos which were called "The Evolution of a Smile." Photographer George W. Harris and Taft had just finished a formal portrait sitting when the phone rang. It was a call from President Theodore Roosevelt informing Taft that he had just been nominated as the Republican candidate for president. As the Library of Congress notes, Harris kept shooting, capturing Taft's reaction on film "at a time when candid pictures were almost unknown." The negatives from the Harris & Ewing Studio collection were many years later donated to the Library of Congress. *Library of Congress*

William H. Taft **131**

William H. Taft with billionaire philanthropist Andrew Carnegie (to the immediate left of Taft, with a white beard), Secretary of State Elihu Root (second to the right of Taft) and Cardinal James Gibbons (to the right of Root), among others, at the Pan American Union Building, Washington, DC. At various times, Root served as president or chairman of the Carnegie Endowment for International Peace, the Carnegie Institution of Washington, and the Carnegie Corporation of New York. *Library of Congress*

Panama Canal. By now, Roosevelt had decided to groom Taft as his successor and he often filled in while Roosevelt was out of Washington.

In 1908, according to Roosevelt's plan, Taft was nominated as the presidential nominee of the Republican Party. The Democrats, meanwhile, nominated their defeated candidate of 1896 and 1900, the still-popular William Jennings Bryan. As in the previous elections, Bryan came up short, losing to Taft 321 to 162 in the Electoral College, while Taft took 51.57 percent of the popular vote.

In office, Taft's agenda continued Roosevelt's trust busting and Civil Service strengthening measures and championed passage of the Sixteenth Amendment which paved the way for a federal income tax. Meanwhile, he opposed the Eighteenth Amendment, calling for Prohibition of alcoholic beverages in the United States.

Whereas Roosevelt pushed his agenda from a "bully pulpit," Taft was reticent to use his power. He did file more antitrust suits than Roosevelt, including one against US Steel, but he

FIRST LADY
HELEN LOUISE "NELLIE" TAFT

Born in Cincinnati on June 2, 1861, Helen Louise "Nellie" Herron was the daughter of Harriet Collins and John Williamson Herron, a law partner of Rutherford B. Hayes and later a judge. She graduated from the Cincinnati College of Music and was a teacher. She had known William Howard Taft for seven years when they were married on June 19, 1886. After a three-month trip to Europe, they settled in Cincinnati, where their three children were born. She encouraged her husband's political career and accompanied him on his lengthy tour of duty in the Philippines and Asia.

Nellie Taft suffered a stroke shortly after becoming first lady, from which she recovered well enough for minimal entertaining. She is perhaps best remembered for promoting the planting of Japanese cherry trees around the Washington Tidal Basin, which was done in 1912. She died on May 22, 1943, and is interred next to her husband at Arlington National Cemetery.

The Children of William Howard Taft and Nellie Taft
Robert Alphonso Taft (1889–1953)
Helen Taft Manning (1891–1987)
Charles Phelps Taft II (1897–1983)

The official portrait of First Lady Helen Taft, painted in 1910 by Karl Bror Albert Kronstrand. *White House*

President William H. Taft speaking to the crowd at the unveiling of the George Armstrong Custer Equestrian Monument in Monroe, Michigan, in 1910. Elizabeth Bacon "Libbie" Custer, pictured below Taft and looking away sourly, was her late husband's most tireless champion. *Unknown photographer*

lacked Roosevelt's charisma and creativity, and never had a good rapport with the press. In trying to placate all wings of his party, Taft fell below Roosevelt's expectations. So too did Taft's determination to defer tough decisions to the courts.

Early in 1912, on Taft's watch, the last two states of the contiguous forty-eight, Arizona and New Mexico, were admitted to the Union. As the year wore on, the presidential campaign heated up. Roosevelt returned to the political arena to challenge his successor for the Republican nomination. Roosevelt scored major wins in the first-ever Republican primaries and went to the 1912 Republican Convention feeling confident. However, the presence of Republican US Senator Robert "Fighting Bob" La Follette of Wisconsin divided the opposition to Taft, and Taft won the nomination. This propelled Roosevelt's supporters to launch a third-party challenge under the banner of the Progressive "Bull Moose" Party.

In the general election, Taft came in at a disappointing third place, with only eight electoral votes and 23.17 percent of the popular vote. The division within the Republican Party resulted in the election of Woodrow

VICE PRESIDENT

JAMES S. SHERMAN

Born in Utica, New York, on October 24, 1855, James Schoolcraft Sherman was a distant cousin of Roger Sherman, a Declaration of Independence signatory, and of Gen. William Tecumseh Sherman. Admitted to the New York Bar in 1880, he was elected to the US House of Representatives in 1886, where he served until 1891 and again from 1893 to 1909. At the 1908 Republican Convention, Sherman, who was a New York conservative, was chosen to balance the ticket with Taft, who was a Midwestern moderate. As vice president, Sherman served the Taft Administration by his work on Capitol Hill moving legislation through Congress. In 1912, he became the first vice president to be renominated since John C. Calhoun in 1828. When Sherman died of kidney trouble on October 30, 1912, a few days before the election, Nicholas Murray Butler was designated as Taft's running mate, but Taft lost the election.

James Schoolcraft "Sunny Jim" Sherman. *Library of Congress*

above: William Howard Taft, as Chief Justice of the United States Supreme Court, with President Warren G. Harding and former Secretary of War Robert Todd Lincoln at the dedication of the Lincoln Memorial on May 30, 1922. *Library of Congress*

left: Though Taft had been Theodore Roosevelt's hand-picked successor, the two became estranged after Taft took office and their relationship became acrimonious. This 1912 cartoon by Leonard Raven-Hill for the British satirical magazine *Punch* shows the two in a barroom brawl. Taft is trying to knife Roosevelt, the former president is trying to shoot his former friend, and Uncle Sam looks on. *Library of Congress*

Wilson, the first Democratic president since Grover Cleveland and only the second since Andrew Johnson.

In 1921, eight years after leaving the White House, Taft's fondest wish was finally granted when the post of Chief Justice of the Supreme Court became vacant, and President Warren G. Harding nominated him. Taft served until 1930, the year of his death, during which time he administered the oath of office to two subsequent presidents. He died on March 8, 1930, of cardiovascular disease and is one of two former presidents (the other being Kennedy) buried at Arlington National Cemetery.

His son, Robert Alphonso Taft, represented Ohio in the US Senate from 1939 to 1953 and unsuccessfully sought the Republican nomination for president in 1940, 1948, and 1952.

The official portrait of William Howard Taft, painted in 1911 by Anders Leonard Zorn. *White House*

William H. Taft 135

28

1913–1921

Woodrow Wilson

DEMOCRATIC PARTY

Woodrow Wilson was the first president of the United States to actively promote the notion of an American leadership role in the global community of nations. He saw the United States as a force for good in the world, energetically promoting democracy in the wake of the collapse of major, long-standing empires during World War I. He conceived of the idea of the League of Nations and

actively promoted it, although ironically, the US Senate never ratified membership for the United States.

Born on December 28, 1856, in Staunton, Virginia, he was the son of Presbyterian Pastor Joseph Ruggles Wilson and British-born Jessie Janet Woodrow. The elder Wilson later served as a Confederate Army chaplain, and still later as professor at the Columbia Theological Seminary. Woodrow attended Davidson College in North Carolina before transferring to Princeton University in New Jersey, from which he graduated in 1879. He attended law school at the University of Virginia and earned his PhD in history and political science from Johns Hopkins University in Baltimore in 1886.

In the meantime, while in Georgia handling his uncle's estate, Wilson married Ellen Louise Axson, a childhood acquaintance, in 1885.

Wilson entered academia, teaching at Cornell University in Ithaca, New York, and later at Bryn Mawr College in Pennsylvania. In 1888, he broke his contract with the latter school to move to Wesleyan University in Connecticut. In 1890, he settled at his alma mater, Princeton University,

top: A portrait photograph of Woodrow Wilson. *Library of Congress*

left: President Woodrow Wilson and his daughter Eleanor enjoy good seats at a baseball game. At the time, the Senators of the American League were Washington's professional team. *Library of Congress*

The official presidential portrait of Woodrow Wilson, painted in 1913 by Frank Graham Cootes. *White House*

A hand-colored photograph of President Woodrow Wilson asking a joint session of Congress for a declaration against Germany on April 2, 1917. This marked the United States' entry into the World War I. *Library of Congress*

where he remained for two decades, becoming president of the school in 1902.

Also elected president of the American Political Science Association, Wilson was growing increasingly interested in Democratic Party politics. In 1910, he left his post at Princeton to accept the party's nomination for governor of New Jersey and was elected. Having promised reforms, he sought to limit the influence of bosses and machines in New Jersey politics. Less than two years into his new career, Wilson attracted the attention of Democrats at the national level.

At the 1912 Democratic Convention there was no clear favorite as there had been when William Jennings Bryan was the standard-bearer. James Beaumont "Champ" Clark of Missouri, the Speaker of the US House of Representatives, was the front-runner, but Wilson polled a close second. And so it went for twenty-nine ballots until Wilson pulled ahead. After forty-six ballots, Wilson finally had the necessary majority. In the general election, Roosevelt and Taft split the Republican vote, though Wilson won 435 electoral votes to a cumulative 96 for the two of them. In the popular vote, Wilson took 41.84 percent to a cumulative 50.57 percent for his top two challengers.

Wilson came into office with an agenda to lower tariffs and make up for the lost revenue through federal income tax, made possible under the Sixteenth Amendment, adopted in 1913. He also promoted passage of the Federal Reserve Act of 1913, which established a network of a dozen regional banks to issue Federal Reserve Notes—aka US Dollars— which remain as the legal currency of the United States.

When it came to the "trustbusting" of his predecessors, Wilson pressed for the Federal Trade Commission Act of 1914, which created a regulatory commission to reduce unfair trade practices. That same year, he earned praise from organized labor and the animosity of corporate interests, by sending troops to protect striking miners in Colorado and compel collective bargaining.

On the personal side, Ellen Wilson died of kidney failure in 1914, but the president bounced back, marrying Edith Bolling Galt in 1915. This was a distraction for Wilson just as the world was tumbling into a global war with serious long-term implications for the United States.

World War I began in August 1914 with a round of declarations of war that involved all of the major powers of Europe and the Middle East—Britain, France, and Russia on one side, opposed by Germany, Austria-Hungary, and the Ottoman Empire on the other. Even before the conflict mushroomed into a war on an unprecedented scale, American public opinion, as well as that of Wilson himself, was firmly opposed to becoming involved. However, when German submarines began sinking American ships in the Atlantic, this resolve was strained. Meanwhile, in 1916, Wilson was distracted by attacks by Mexican bandits along the southern border, and he mobilized the US Army to cross the border to hunt them down.

The war in Europe, which was consuming lives by the hundreds of thousands, was the backdrop against which the 1916 presidential election occurred. Wilson was renominated, while the Republicans nominated US Supreme Court Justice Charles Evans Hughes, who had previously been governor of New York. Politically, the two candidates were so close that Theodore Roosevelt quipped that the only difference between Wilson and the bearded Hughes was a shave. The general election was also so close that the winner was not known for several days. Wilson won 277 to 254 in the Electoral College while taking 49.24 percent of the popular vote.

Though Wilson had campaigned on the slogan "He kept us out of war," the submarine attacks, combined with the revelation of a German scheme to involve Mexico against

The "Big Four" of Allied leaders meet at the Paris peace conference after World War I on May 27, 1919. From left to right, they are British Prime Minister David Lloyd George, Italian Premier Vittorio Orlando, French Premier Georges Clemenceau, and President Woodrow Wilson. *US Army Signal Corps*

VICE PRESIDENT

THOMAS R. MARSHALL

Born on March 14, 1854, in North Manchester, Indiana, Thomas Riley Marshall was the son of Daniel Marshall and Martha Patterson. His only sibling, a sister, died in infancy. When Thomas was a young boy, Daniel took him to see the Lincoln-Douglas debates and to introduce him to both men. He later recounted this story while campaigning. Thomas Marshall graduated from Wabash College in Crawfordsville, Indiana, in 1873 and was admitted to the bar in 1875. He opened a law practice in Columbia City, specializing in criminal cases and discovering his gift for oratory while arguing for his clients in the courtroom.

Marshall began drinking heavily after the death of his fiancée, Kate Hooper, on the eve of their wedding day, but after he met and married Lois Kimsey thirteen years later, she straightened him out and turned him into a prohibitionist.

Already active in Democratic Party politics, Marshall was elected governor of Indiana in 1908, where he opposed child labor and capital punishment, and perrsonally participated in writing a new state constitution which would have extended the state's regulatory reach if it had been adopted.

At the 1912 Democratic Convention, Marshall was chosen as the vice presidential nominee to balance Woodrow Wilson's roots in the East and

Thomas Riley Marshall in 1912. Library of Congress

South. Presiding over the US Senate, Marshall had a feisty reputation, issuing gag orders and pushing for a rule to break filibusters with a two-thirds vote. There was a move to drop Marshall from the ticket in 1916, but Wilson kept him in the interest of unity. During World War I, Wilson sent Marshall on a cross-country speaking tour to keep support for the war running strong. When Wilson was incapacitated, Edith Wilson and other White House insiders kept the details from Marshall, fearing that he would attempt to assume the presidency.

Marshall returned to Indiana after his term, but died of a heart attack while visiting Washington on June 1, 1925.

FIRST LADY
ELLEN AXSON WILSON

Like her future husband, Ellen Axson was the child of a Presbyterian clergyman. The first wife of Woodrow Wilson was born on May 15, 1860, in Savannah, Georgia, the daughter of the Reverend Samuel Edward Axson and Margaret Jane Hoyt Axson. Though they had known one another as children, their courtship did not begin until 1883. They were married on June 24, 1885, with his father and her grandfather jointly officiating. They had three daughters, with the first two being born in the South at their mother's insistence. Eleanor was born in Connecticut.

Ellen divided her time between the duties of a university professor's wife and her amateur painting. After becoming first lady, she set up a studio in the White House. The Wilsons did not hold an inaugural ball, but they did host the White House weddings of their two youngest daughters in 1913 and 1914. Ellen died of kidney disease on August 6, 1914, three months after Eleanor's wedding, and was buried in her family's plot in Rome, Georgia. After Ellen's death, her unmarried daughter Margaret acted as White House hostess until her father's second marriage in 1915.

The Children of Woodrow Wilson and Ellen Axson Wilson
Margaret Woodrow Wilson (1886–1944)
Jessie Woodrow Wilson Sayre (1887–1933)
Eleanor Randolph Wilson McAdoo (1889–1967)

FIRST LADY
EDITH BOLLING WILSON

Woodrow Wilson's second wife was born of October 15, 1872, in Wytheville, Virginia, the daughter of Sarah "Sallie" Spears White and Judge William Holcombe Bolling. Through William's line, Edith Bolling was a descendant of Pocahontas, the Powhatan woman who famously interacted with the English settlers at Jamestown in the early seventeenth century, and who later married John Rolfe. As she was growing up, Edith became an amateur folklorist, collecting and studying folk tales told locally. She studied at Martha Washington College in Virginia and at Powell's School for Girls in Richmond. In 1896, she married a Washington, DC, jeweler named Norman Galt, and they had a son who died in infancy in 1903.

Widowed in 1908, Edith was introduced to Woodrow Wilson in March 1915 at the White House by the president's cousin. Despite rumors that she had been having an affair with Wilson before his wife's death, they courted and finally married on December 18, 1915, at her home and not in the White House. During World War I, Edith famously abided by rationing protocols at the White House, and even allowed sheep to graze on the White House grounds.

After Woodrow's stoke left him partially paralyzed and bedridden in late 1919, Edith became the president's closest aide, screening all the documents that came to the White House for his attention and deciding what he should see. As such, she came close to functioning in the role of America's first female

inset: Woodrow Wilson and his wife Ellen in a garden at Princeton University, circa 1910. *Library of Congress*

above: Edith Bolling Wilson. *Library of Congress*

chief executive. Because of her thoroughness and competence, she was also able to obscure the extent of Wilson's disability.

Edith Wilson remained in Washington after her husband's death and died of heart failure on December 28, 1961. She was initially interred next to the president at Washington Cathedral, but was later relocated elsewhere in the building.

the United States, pushed the country into World War I. In April 1917, just a month after being sworn in for a second term, Wilson was at the US Capitol asking Congress for a Declaration of War.

Wilson now found himself a world leader, standing at the helm of an industrial superpower that possessed the strength to make a difference in the war—and as Wilson saw it, in the postwar world. In January 1918, he outlined his vision in his "Fourteen Points," which called for international cooperation, open agreements, free trade, self-determination, and a just and democratic world peace.

The war brought about a mobilization of both American military might and American industrial might unseen since the Civil War. Though the critical mass of American troops did not reach Europe until the summer of 1918, their arrival tipped the balance against Germany. The Armistice ending World War I was signed on November 11, 1918.

In 1919, an idealistic and optimistic Wilson traveled to Europe to attend the Paris Peace Conference and to promote his global vision and his idea for a League of Nations. For his trouble, Wilson received the 1919 Nobel Peace Prize.

Europe embraced the League of Nations, but the US Congress did not. As he set out on a nationwide speaking tour to sell his world view to the American people, Wilson suffered a series of strokes which left him an invalid. Unable to adequately lobby for his pet project, he watched it defeated. Largely incapacitated through the remainder of his term, he remained mainly in the seclusion of the White House without the true extent of his frailty known to the public.

After leaving office, he remained in Washington, DC, where he died of a stroke on February 3, 1924. He was interred at Washington National Cathedral, the only president whose final resting place is in the capital city.

above: Wilson, who had been crippled and partially paralyzed by a stroke in 1919, emerged from seclusion in August 1923 to attend the funeral of his successor, Warren G. Harding. Wilson died six months later. *Library of Congress*

right: One of Woodrow Wilson's personal typewriters is on display at the Woodrow Wilson House, the building at 2340 S Street NW in Washington, DC, where the former president lived after leaving office in 1921 and where he died in 1924. According to Wilson biographer John Milton Cooper, he bought his first typewriter, a Caligraph, in 1883 "and thereby jumped aboard the technological bandwagon." The one pictured is a portable Hammond Multiplex that Wilson used while traveling. *Photo from dctim1, licensed under the terms of the Creative Commons attribution share alike*

29

Warren G. Harding

REPUBLICAN PARTY

I f Woodrow Wilson embraced and projected the expansive role of the United States as a leading world power, Warren Gamaliel Harding was the opposite. He was elected having promised a "return to normalcy." He explained that "America's present need is not heroics, but healing; not nostrums, but normalcy; not revolution, but restoration; not agitation, but adjustment; not surgery, but serenity; not the dramatic, but the dispassionate; not experiment, but equipoise; not submergence in internationality, but sustainment in triumphant nationality."

Born on November 2, 1865, in Blooming Grove, Ohio, Warren Harding was the son of Dr. George Tryon Harding and Phoebe Elizabeth Dickerson Harding. The oldest of eight children, he grew up in Caledonia, Ohio, where his father owned a newspaper. He graduated from Ohio Central College in Iberia in 1882, and worked for a time selling insurance and teaching school before buying his own newspaper in Marion, Ohio, and turning it into a success. In 1891, Harding married Florence Kling, the divorced daughter of Amos Hall Kling, a bitter rival in the newspaper business.

In 1899, Harding was elected to the Ohio state legislature, where he created alliances with men such as Harry Daugherty in the Republican state machine. He served as lieutenant governor from 1904 to 1906 and ran unsuccessfully for governor in 1910. In 1914, he was elected to the US Senate in the first election after the passage of the Seventeenth Amendment, allowing senators to be elected directly rather than by state legislatures.

top: A portrait of Warren G. Harding. *Library of Congress*

above: Harding (right) receives a visit from General John J. Pershing on August 30, 1921. Pershing, who led the American Expeditionary Force to victory over Germany in World War I, was Chief of Staff of the US Army at the time. *Library of Congress*

In the Senate, he opposed Prohibition and the League of Nations.

At the 1920 Republican Convention, Gen. Leonard Wood of New Hampshire, a popular hero of the Spanish-American War, was the favorite of a large field of presidential candidates. Harding was on the list, but in the first ballot, he was not even in the top five. As voting progressed, the various factions would not budge, and in an all-night session in a smoke-filled room, Ohio Boss Harry Daugherty promoted Harding as the compromise candidate, and he was nominated on the tenth ballot.

On the campaign trail, Harding's newspaper background served him well in relations with the press, and he also made extensive use of radio. It was the first presidential election in which women could vote, and Harding was popular with women. After World War I, his "return to normalcy" message resonated with the electorate. Harding won by a landslide, defeating Ohio Governor James Middleton Cox 404 to 127 in the Electoral College while capturing 60.32 percent of the popular vote.

Some of his appointments are laudable. Charles Evans Hughes, late of the Supreme Court, became secretary of state, and future president Herbert Hoover became secretary of commerce. Other appointments were regrettable. The infamous boss Daugherty was rewarded with the post of attorney general, and he brought a cast of controversial characters known as the "Ohio Gang" to Washington.

Though his presidency is remembered today as a cavalcade of scandals, Harding remained popular with the electorate, if not the Congress. Harding favored lower taxes and a Veterans Bureau and pushed the Budget and Accounting Act of 1921, which created the Bureau of the Budget and the General Accounting Office. Thanks perhaps, at least in part, to Harding's "normalcy" the Roaring Twenties were a booming time in American history.

The official presidential portrait of Warren G. Harding by Edmund Hodgson Smart. *White House*

Warren G. Harding **143**

FLORENCE KLING HARDING

The first woman able to vote for her husband for president, Florence Mabel Kling was also the first First Lady to ride in an airplane, own a radio, and invite movie stars to the White House. She was known as "the Duchess," running the White House as the elegant, but well-oiled centerpiece of Washington society. Born in Marion, Ohio, on August 15, 1860, she was the daughter of Louisa Bouton Kling and Amos Hall Kling, a banker and newspaperman who was a future business rival of Warren G. Harding. She studied at the Cincinnati Conservatory of Music but dropped out in January 1880 to elope with her first husband, Henry Atherton "Pete" DeWolfe. Her only child, Marshall Eugene DeWolfe, was born in September 1880. Florence and Pete split up because of his heavy drinking, and they divorced in 1886.

Florence Mabel Kling Harding.
Library of Congress

Over the objections of her father, she married Warren G. Harding on July 8, 1891, and worked with him in the newspaper business, where by all accounts, she was the driving force of the business's success. When her husband became involved in a long-term affair with her friend, Carrie Phillips, Florence considered divorce. She reportedly hired a private detective to monitor Harding's affair with Nan Britton.

The Duchess took to her role as first lady with great enthusiasm, hosting some of the most popular parties on the social calendar, where drinks flowed as though there was no Prohibition in the land. She was also outspoken on subjects about which she took an interest.

Her decision not to ask for an autopsy after her husband's death will always provide fertile ground for conspiracy theorists who hold her responsible. After his death, the kidney problems that had nagged her in earlier years returned, and her general health declined. She died on November 21, 1924, only fifteen months after her husband, with whom she was laid to rest.

The Possible Child of Warren G. Harding and Nan Britton
Elizabeth Ann Britton Harding Blaesing (1919–2005)

The most notable political disgrace of the Harding administration was the Teapot Dome Scandal, named for the shape of a Wyoming mountain atop an underground petroleum reserve that was being maintained for the emergency use of the US Navy. Secretary of the Interior Albert Fall was found to be taking substantial bribes to allow surreptitious private access to the oil and became the first former cabinet secretary to go to jail. Daugherty, meanwhile, was widely accused of corruption, bribery, and drug trafficking. When Daugherty was later tried on corruption charges, he successfully blamed former aide Jess Smith, who had committed suicide.

It was on the personal side that the Harding scandals reached their most outrageous. One oft-repeated tale is that Harding lost the White House China in a poker game—in the White House. While this remains unconfirmed, extended poker games did run routinely, fueled by gallons of illicit alcohol. Though the Eighteenth Amendment had instituted Prohibition in the United States in 1920, banning alcohol for beverage use, it was not enforced in the executive mansion. Alice Roosevelt Longworth commented that Harding ran the White House like a speakeasy.

Harding was noted for his numerous extramarital affairs, especially a lengthy one with Carrie Fulton Phillips, which

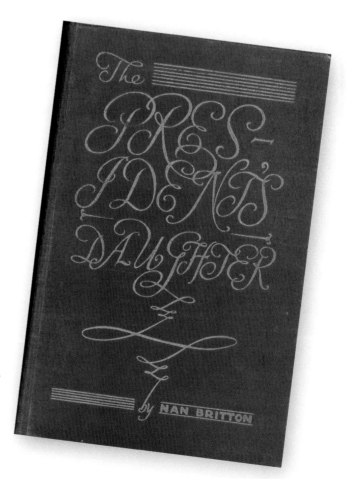

right: Published in 1928, *The President's Daughter* was a sensational account by Nan Britton of her alleged six-year affair with Warren G. Harding. Ms. Britton told of the birth of her daughter, Elizabeth Ann, asserting that the father was Harding. Unable to find a publisher, Nan Britton formed an organization called the Elizabeth Ann Guild and donated the proceeds to children born out of wedlock. The book was considered to be so scandalous that the New York Society for the Suppression of Vice asked the New York City police to seize the book at the bindery before release.
Author's collection

Warren G. Harding, Secretary of State Charles Evans Hughes, and their wives attend Opening Day of the 1922 baseball season at Washington's Griffith Stadium. Located near Georgia Avenue and Fifth Street and named for Washington Senators owner Clark Griffith, the field was home to the team from 1911 through 1960. *Library of Congress*

was ongoing before and during his time in the Senate. Their love letters still exist but remain sealed. Her attempts at extortion after he became president were a great embarrassment for Harding and his wife—and for the Republican Party.

Harding is widely believed to have also had an extended affair before and during his presidency with Nan Britton, who was twenty-four when he was elected. She had a daughter named Elizabeth Ann Harding, whom she claimed to have been fathered by Harding. Elizabeth Ann died in 2005, adamantly refusing a DNA test to confirm paternity. Harding's wife was aware of the multiple affairs, reacting with indignant resignation.

Warren G. Harding died in the presidential suite of the Palace Hotel in San Francisco on August 2, 1923, while returning from a visit to Alaska. The cause of death is unknown. A heart attack is considered most likely, though food poisoning was suggested at the time. His wife, who was with him when

he died, refused to allow an autopsy and burned many of his papers. This led to the widely repeated theory that she had killed him. He is interred in the grand Harding Memorial in Marion, Ohio.

VICE PRESIDENT

CALVIN COOLIDGE

At the 1920 Republican Convention, when it took ten ballots and an all-nighter in a smoke-filled room to reach a consensus on Warren G. Harding as the presidential nominee, Calvin Coolidge was picked as his running mate from a field of seven on the first ballot. More than two years later, he was visiting family in rural Vermont when a messenger arrived to tell him that he was the president of the United States. Coolidge and his own presidency are described in detail in the following chapter.

30

1923–1929

Calvin Coolidge

REPUBLICAN PARTY

The only president to date to have been born on the Fourth of July, John Calvin Coolidge Jr. came into the world in 1872 in Plymouth Notch, Vermont, but lived most of his life in Massachusetts. He was the son of Victoria Josephine Moor Coolidge and John Calvin Coolidge Sr., a farmer who was active in Vermont Republican politics and who served in the state legislature.

The younger Coolidge graduated from Amherst College in Massachusetts in 1895 and moved to Northampton, Massachusetts, to apprentice with a law firm. Admitted to the bar in 1897, he established his practice in Northampton a

year later. In 1905, he met and married Grace Goodhue, a fellow Vermont native.

Coolidge's political career began in 1898 with a successful run for Northampton City Council. After serving in several local offices, he was elected to the state legislature as a Republican in 1906. In 1910, he was elected as mayor of Northampton, but he returned to the state house in 1912, where he later served as president of the state senate. On the issues of the day, he favored fiscal responsibility and women's suffrage but opposed Prohibition. Beginning in 1915, Coolidge was elected to three successive one-year terms as lieutenant governor of Massachusetts as the running mate of Governor Samuel McCall. In 1918, when

above: Calvin Coolidge as president.
Library of Congress

left: Calvin Coolidge posing on the White House lawn with four unidentified members of the Osage tribe on June 2, 1924. On that date, Coolidge signed the Indian Citizenship Act of 1924, also known as the Snyder Act, which granted full citizenship to indigenous people who were previously considered to be citizens of sovereign Indian nations. *Library of Congress*

Calvin Coolidge standing next to a Buick sedan fitted out for his use with radio equipment. Note the loudspeaker on the running board. For AM band reception with the state of the art of the 1920s, a very long antenna was required. Technically, this was addressed by running a continuous wire back and forth across the roof of the vehicle. *Library of Congress*

McCall decided not to run, the Republican Party chose Coolidge as their standard-bearer.

As governor, Coolidge's defining moment came during the 1919 Boston Police Strike. When the disagreement over a police union was a labor issue, he deferred to local authorities, but when violence and chaos ensued and was exploited by criminal elements, Coolidge called in the National Guard to restore order. Afterward, he was elected to a second term.

At the 1920 Republican Convention, Coolidge was a surprise choice as a vice presidential candidate, picked by the delegates because he was decisive and not controlled by one of the political machines.

Having been elected as Warren G. Harding's vice president, Coolidge remained in the shadows, earning him the nickname "Silent Cal." Nevertheless, he was more involved than his public persona suggested, being the first vice

FIRST LADY
GRACE ANNA COOLIDGE

Born on January 3, 1879, in Burlington, Vermont, Grace Anna Goodhue was the only child of Andrew Issaclar Goodhue and Lemira Barrett Goodhue. She graduated from the University of Vermont in 1902, and was a teacher at the Clarke School for the Deaf in Northampton, Massachusetts when she met Calvin Coolidge. Though Coolidge did not—and never would—get along with Grace's mother, the couple were married on October 4, 1905, in her parents' home in Burlington.

She supported his political career and proved herself an asset because her infectious and outgoing cheerfulness balanced his shy reticence. As Coolidge famously described their relationship, "for almost a quarter of a century she has borne with my infirmities, and I have rejoiced in her graces."

In Washington, DC, as the wife of the vice president and later as first lady, she was extremely well liked and well respected on the social scene. One of the biggest events that she hosted in the White House was the reception honoring Charles Lindbergh after his nonstop flight across the Atlantic in 1927. According to the White House Historical Association, "in 1931 she was voted one of America's twelve greatest living women."

After her husband's death, she avoided the limelight but remained active in charity work on behalf of the deaf and the American Red Cross. She died on July 8, 1957, and is buried next to her husband.

The Children of Calvin Coolidge and Grace Anna Coolidge
John Coolidge (1906–2000)
Calvin Coolidge Jr. (1908–1924)

Grace Anna Goodhue Coolidge at the White House. *Library of Congress*

Calvin and Grace Coolidge owned many pets, of which the most famous was probably Rob Roy, their white collie, seen here playing with the couple at the White House. Other pets included another white collie named Prudence Prim, several other dogs and cats, a pair of canaries named Nip and Tuck, and raccoons named Rebecca and Reuben. *Library of Congress*

Calvin and Grace Coolidge shortly after taking up residence at the White House in 1923. The president wears a black arm band in memory of his recently deceased predecessor. *Library of Congress*

CHARLES G. DAWES

More famous for the Dawes Plan, which resolved an international crisis after World War I, than for being vice president, Charles Gates Dawes never held another major elective office. He was born in Marietta, Ohio, on August 27, 1865, the son of Gen. Rufus Dawes and Mary Beman Gates Dawes. A businessman, he specialized in investing in companies across the Upper Midwest that supplied gas for lighting cities. He was also a pianist and composer, noted for writing the music that was adapted with lyrics in 1958 as the pop song "It's All in the Game," recorded by artists from the Four Tops to Elton John to Van Morrison.

left: Charles Dawes. *Library of Congress*

Dawes's Republican Party political career began in 1896 when he helped manage William McKinley's White House bid. He was rewarded with a job as Comptroller of the Currency. In 1901, he left Washington to run for the US Senate. Having lost, he returned to the private sector as a banker. During World War I, he helped structure private loans to Britain and France. After the United States entered the war, Dawes was commissioned as a major in the Corps of Engineers. Eventually promoted to brigadier general, he served as a logistical manager with the US Army in France.

After the war, Dawes served as the first director of the Bureau of the Budget as well as being a member of the Allied Reparations Commission. While serving on the latter, he developed the Dawes Plan to help stabilize the German economy and avert a crisis. For this, he was awarded the Nobel Peace Prize.

At the 1924 Republican Convention, Illinois Governor Frank Lowden was nominated as the vice presidential candidate, but he declined to run. The delegates then turned to Dawes, who had been a distant third when Lowden was nominated. As vice president, Dawes was a frustration for Coolidge in his presiding over the Senate. One notable incident involved Dawes being caught napping when an important confirmation vote came up. Had Dawes been awake, he could have broken a tie and Coolidge's nominee would have been confirmed. In 1928, although he was not running for reelection, Coolidge insisted that Dawes not be renominated. He was not, but incoming President Herbert Hoover appointed Dawes as Ambassador to the United Kingdom.

As the Great Depression deepened, Hoover brought Dawes to Washington in 1932 to head the Reconstruction Finance Corporation, but Dawes resigned to return to the private sector as a banking executive. He died in Evanston, Illinois, on April 23, 1951.

president to routinely attend cabinet meetings. He was never implicated, however, in the scandals that plagued the Harding Administration.

When Harding died on August 2, 1923, Coolidge and his wife were visiting his family in Plymouth Notch. Because there was no telephone, a messenger delivered the news and Coolidge was sworn in as president of the United States by his father, who was then a justice of the peace. They then walked across the street to the general store and enjoyed a Moxie, Coolidge's favorite soft drink.

Coolidge initially retained the Harding cabinet in the interest of unity, but he later fired the mischief-plagued Harry Daugherty for not cooperating in a probe of the Teapot Dome Scandal.

At the 1924 Republican Convention, Coolidge was nominated on the first ballot, challenged by the perennial populist candidate Robert La Follette of Wisconsin, who came in a distant second. In turn, La Follette decided to run as a

The official presidential portrait of Calvin Coolidge was painted by Charles Sydney Hopkinson. *White House*

Calvin Coolidge congratulates Washington Senators pitcher Walter "Big Train" Johnson after the team defeated the New York Yankees for the 1924 American League pennant. The Senators went on to defeat the New York Giants in game seven, with Johnson on the mound pitching in extra innings, to win the nailbiter 1924 World Series. *Library of Congress*

third party candidate in the general election. As his vehicle, he chose to run under the banner of the "Progressive Party." It used the same name as the now-defunct party under which Theodore Roosevelt ran in 1912, and which La Follette had then opposed, but it was a different entity. When the votes were counted, Coolidge had been reelected with 54.04 percent of the popular vote. In the Electoral College, he received 382 votes to 136 for Democrat John Davis of West Virginia and just 13 for La Follette.

The campaign had taken place under the cloud of the death of Coolidge's younger son from blood poisoning, and this cloud also darkened the president's full term in office.

As the economy in the Roaring Twenties boomed, Coolidge pursued a generally non-interventionist policy. He disdained regulation, though he favored legislation that allowed for a reduced workweek and higher wages. He frequently spoke out in favor of the rights of Catholics and African-Americans, and he signed the Indian Citizenship Act, which granted American citizenship to people previously classed separately as citizens of indigenous Indian nations. He was criticized for vetoing farm price support legislation and for the slow federal response to the devastating Mississippi River floods of 1927.

In 1928, Coolidge made it known that he would not run for another term because ten years was "too long" and no other man had been president for more than eight. He retired to Northampton, where he wrote his memoirs and a syndicated newspaper column. He died of heart disease on January 5, 1933, and is buried at the Plymouth Notch Cemetery in Vermont.

31

1929–1933

Herbert Hoover

REPUBLICAN PARTY

The first president of the United States born west of the Mississippi, Herbert Hoover differed from most of his predecessors in that he was an engineer rather than a lawyer, and his only major elective office was the presidency.

Born in West Branch, Iowa, on August 10, 1874, he was the middle child of blacksmith Jesse Hoover and Canadian-born Hulda Randall Minthorn, both of whom were Quakers. After his parents died in 1880 and 1884 respectively, Hoover found himself an orphan at age nine. He lived with various relatives in Iowa before being sent to live with his mother's brother, Dr. John Minthorn in Oregon in 1885. Hoover attended Stanford University in California, working his way through school with jobs that included a stint with the US Geological Survey. He graduated with a geology degree in 1895 and went to work as a mining engineer.

Between 1897 and 1908, he worked overseas, mainly in Australia and China, and mainly with London-based Bewick, Moreing & Co., of which he eventually became a partner. In 1899, he married Lou Henry who he had first met at Stanford, and she traveled with him to his

overseas assignments. Having left Bewick, Moreing in 1908, Hoover became an independent consultant. Investments in mines all over the world made him a wealthy man.

As World War I began, Hoover, who was then living in London, led a successful volunteer effort to evacuate Americans from war-ravaged Europe. His organizational skills brought him international attention and his help was enlisted by the Commission for Relief in Belgium to help expedite aid to starving civilians in German-occupied Belgium. When the United States entered the war in 1917, President Woodrow Wilson put him in charge of the US Food Administration, a massive effort to manage food supplies and stabilize grain prices. As part of this, certain commodities were rationed, and Americans got used to the likes of "Meatless Mondays." After the war, Hoover continued his work in famine-stricken Europe as head of the American Relief Administration.

When he returned to the United States in 1919 as a high profile public figure, Hoover was approached by both political parties. He considered various options but wound up

above: President-elect Hoover and his wife aboard the USS *Utah* in 1928. This battleship was sunk at Pearl Harbor in 1941. *Department of Defense*

top: A portrait of President Herbert Hoover. *National Archives*

Herbert Hoover acquired his faithful companion, the shepherd named King Tut, while he was in Europe after World War I managing food relief for war-torn Belgium. During his presidential campaign in 1928, photographs of the two friends were widely circulated. The *New York Times* described the one seen here as "one of the happiest pictures ever made" of Hoover. King Tut died at the age of eight in late 1929. *Library of Congress*

above: A 1931 painting of Herbert Hoover's birthplace by artist Grant Wood. The birthplace is a two-room cottage built for Jesse Clark Hoover and his wife, Hulda, in the spring of 1871 in West Branch, Iowa. It is currently part of the Herbert Hoover National Historic Site, which also includes a reconstruction of Jesse's original blacksmith shop, the Herbert Hoover Presidential Library and Museum, and the final resting place of Herbert Hoover and his wife. An Iowa native, Wood is known for his work depicting the rural Midwest in the early twentieth century. His signature painting is *American Gothic*, one of the most famous American paintings of the century. *Public domain image from Wikimedia Commons*

accepting the post of secretary of commerce in the Harding Administration. He saw this low profile post as the potential driving wheel of economic growth and prosperity, and quickly became the most publicly visible of the cabinet secretaries. He brought an engineer's perspective to international trade promotion, industrial standardization, and highway planning, and worked with banking institutions to promote home ownership.

The Great Mississippi Flood of 1927 provided Hoover with his greatest moment as secretary of commerce. Though relief efforts were not then a federal responsibility, President Coolidge asked Hoover to organize and engineer a response as he had done in Europe in World War I. It was his success in this effort that catapulted him into the presidency.

Though Coolidge did not actively support him, Hoover won the Republican nomination on the first ballot, and won the general election with 58.21 percent of the popular vote.

Herbert Hoover and famed aviator Amelia Earhart at the White House in 1932 after she had become the first female pilot to fly solo across the Atlantic Ocean. Walking behind them is First Lady Lou Hoover. Mrs. Earhart's husband, author and publishing heir George Palmer Putnam, is second to the right of Mrs. Hoover. *Library of Congress*

VICE PRESIDENT

CHARLES CURTIS

The first vice president with American Indian ancestry, Charles Curtis was born on January 25, 1860, in Topeka, Kansas, at a time when Kansas was not yet a state. He was the son of Orren Curtis and Ellen Papin Curtis, who had one grandparent who was Osage and one who was Kaw. He spent his early years on the Kaw Reservation, living with the family of his mother, who died when he was three. He spent his teens with his father's parents in Topeka. He married Anna Elizabeth Baird in 1884 and had three children. She died in 1924, and he did not remarry.

Curtis studied law, was admitted to the Kansas Bar in 1881, and served as prosecuting attorney in Shawnee County from 1885 to 1889. In 1892, he was elected to the US House of Representatives as a Republican, where he served until 1907. He was the author of the Curtis Act of 1898 which limited the power of American Indian tribal governing institutions and paved the way toward the assimilation of Indian people into mainstream society. Curtis was an advocate of tribal land being divided among individuals rather than being controlled by tribal councils.

Between 1907 and 1913, Curtis was appointed to serve in the US Senate, and in 1915, after the Seventeenth Amendment permitted popular election of senators, he ran statewide and won. He remained in the Senate until 1929 when he became vice president. Beginning in 1925, he was Senate Majority Leader. At the 1928 Republican Convention, Curtis was nominated on the first ballot with scant opposition.

After his tenure as vice president, Curtis remained in Washington, DC, where he opened a private law practice. He died of a heart attack on February 6, 1936, and is buried next to his wife in Topeka.

right: A portrait of Charles Curtis. *Library of Congress*

FIRST LADY
LOU HENRY HOOVER

The only first lady who was conversant in Mandarin Chinese, Lou Henry Hoover was also the first to make regular national radio broadcasts. Born on March 29, 1874, in Waterloo, Iowa, she was the daughter of banker Charles Delano Henry and Florence Ida Weed Henry. She grew up in California, where she enjoyed time spent outdoors. Like her husband, she graduated from Stanford University with a degree in geology. After they were married on February 10, 1899, at her parents' home in Monterey, she traveled overseas with him, where they lived in Australia and China. It was while they were in Shanghai that she learned to speak Mandarin. During and after World War I, she worked with her husband on the relief projects that gained him worldwide notoriety.

While her husband was serving as secretary of commerce in the Harding Administration, Lou Hoover served as the national president of the Girl Scouts from 1922 to 1925, a position to which she returned between 1935 and 1937. She died of a heart attack in New York City on January 7, 1944. Originally interred in Palo Alto, California, she was later moved to her husband's side in West Branch, Iowa.

The Hoovers had two sons, both of whom graduated from Stanford. The oldest, Herbert Charles Hoover, served as an under secretary of state in the Eisenhower Administration.

The Children of Herbert Hoover and Lou Henry Hoover
Herbert Charles Hoover (1903-1969)
Allan Henry Hoover (1907-1993)

inset above: A formal portrait of Lou Henry Hoover. *National Archives*

He defeated Democratic candidate Alfred E. Smith by a margin of 444 to 87 in the Electoral College.

Hoover's presidency began on an optimistic note, with a general belief that the current wave of prosperity would continue indefinitely, and that the end of poverty was in sight. However, in October 1929, only seven months after Hoover took office, the Stock Market Crash tipped the United States economy into the Great Depression, the worst economic downturn in American history. He responded with limited federal works projects, but his philosophical disinclination toward government intervention and deficit spending limited what the federal government could or would do. Economists have debated ever since over the correct response at the beginning of the Great Depression, but there is no consensus. It was a challenge that Hoover's resume suggested he could handle, but one that history has recorded as his biggest failure.

Exhausted by his first term, Hoover only reluctantly agreed to run for a second, and was renominated on the first ballot at the 1932 Republican Convention. In the general election, however, Hoover was defeated in a landslide election by Franklin Delano Roosevelt, who took 57.41 percent of the popular vote and won 472 electoral votes to Hoover's 59.

Hoover and his wife retired to California, from which they took extended driving trips throughout the West. In 1936, Hoover was not the Republican nominee, but the Democrats continued to run against him as the symbol of a failed response to the Great Depression. During World War II, he advocated relief efforts for German-occupied Europe as he had done in World War I, but these were on a much smaller scale.

He kept out of the limelight in later years, though he was always invited to make ceremonial appearances at Republican conventions. He died of a massive internal hemorrhage in New York City on October 20, 1964, and is buried in West Branch, Iowa, adjacent to the Herbert Hoover Presidential Library and Museum.

above: Lou Henry Hoover served as the national president of the Girl Scouts from 1922 to 1925 and from 1935 to 1937 and was active in the interim. She is seen here on the left at a dinner held in her honor in December 1930. In the center is Girl Scout Audrey Kellogg, welcoming the First Lady. Also pictured is Mrs. Robert C. Mead, chairman of the federation. *National Archives*

right: A 1918 letter of thanks from Herbert Hoover in his capacity as head of the US Food Administration to Juliette Gordon Low, founder of the Girl Scouts of the USA. In 1912, Ms. Low formed the first American Girl Guide troop, based on the British model. In 1915, that organization became the Girl Scouts. *National Archives*

UNITED STATES FOOD ADMINISTRATION

WASHINGTON

IN REPLY REFER TO

June 13, 1918.

Mrs. Juliette Low,
1163 East 63rd Street,
New York City.

My dear Mrs. Low:

The work accomplished by the Girl Scouts last year in production of vegetables from home gardens, and in picking, canning, preserving and drying of fruit and vegetables, has been of material benefit in solving the problem of food distribution.

This year, with the increasingly larger problem of supplying food to our armies, and to the civilian populations of the Allies and America, I trust that the Girl Scouts will continue their efforts in production and conservation of foodstuffs. The organization affords an opportunity for its members to further their assistance in this problem, upon which the future of the war largely depends, by spreading the knowledge of how the food shortage can be met amongst their families and friends. If in doing this, all the Girl Scouts in the country could secure the co-operation of all the members of all their families, and of all the friends they can influence, there would be enough food saved to feed a large army.

Girl Scouts can be a big factor in assisting in the work of the Food Administration, and I am glad to take this opportunity of expressing my appreciation of their excellent work.

Faithfully yours,

Herbert Hoover

Franklin D. Roosevelt

DEMOCRATIC PARTY

The only president of the United States elected to both a third and fourth term, Franklin Roosevelt was in office during two of the most difficult and most defining episodes in the twentieth century, the Great Depression and World War II. In both cases, the United States weathered unprecedented adversity to emerge stronger. Whether this was in spite of Roosevelt or because of him has been debated, but history has favored the latter perspective. Though born into privilege, he became the iconic hero of common people. Though he led the most powerful nation in the world at the apogee of its strength relative to the rest of the world, polio had rendered him incapable of walking across the room. Though he was one of the most visible personalities in America, almost no one was cognizant of this disability.

Born on January 30, 1882, in Hyde Park, Dutchess County, New York, Franklin Roosevelt was a member of two wealthy intertwined families with deep roots in the Hudson River Valley going back to the time of the earliest Dutch and English settlers. He was the only child of businessman James Roosevelt and Sara Ann Delano, who was, by all accounts, a very overprotective mother. Franklin had a much older half brother, James Roosevelt "Rosey" Roosevelt by his father's first marriage to Rebecca Brien Howland. Rosey was actually several months older than his father's second wife. Franklin was a fifth cousin to Theodore Roosevelt. In 1905, Franklin married a fifth cousin once removed, Anna Eleanor Roosevelt,

top: President Franklin D. Roosevelt reviews the Pacific Fleet on San Francisco Bay, July 14, 1938. *FDR Library/National Archives*

above: New York State Senator Roosevelt in 1911. *National Archives*

facing page: An official campaign portrait of Franklin Roosevelt taken by Leon Perskie on August 21, 1944. *FDR Library/National Archives*

ANNA ELEANOR ROOSEVELT

The most visible first lady yet, Eleanor Roosevelt traveled tirelessly throughout the United States, promoting the agenda of her husband's administration as well as her own ideas. She became an outspoken advocate of civil rights, which placed her well ahead of her time. In 1939, when African-American concert singer Marian Anderson was locked out of performing at Constitution Hall, Eleanor famously arranged for her to sing on the steps of the Lincoln Memorial.

She was born in New York City on October 11, 1884, the daughter of the extremely wealthy Elliott Bulloch Roosevelt and Anna Rebecca Hall Roosevelt, both of whom were dead by the time she was ten. She was raised by her mother's mother, a distant and aloof individual who made Eleanor feel unwanted. In 1902, she became romantically involved with her fifth cousin once removed, Franklin D. Roosevelt, much to the consternation of his overprotective mother, Sara Delano. They were married on March 17, 1905, with her uncle, President Theodore Roosevelt giving her away.

Their daughter Anna was born in 1906, followed by five sons between 1907 and 1916. The Roosevelts had two sons named "Franklin." The oldest died in 1909 at the age of seven months, and Franklin Delano Roosevelt Jr., was born in 1914.

Eleanor Roosevelt had an unhappy marriage, especially in the early years. She was constantly berated and belittled by her mother-in-law, who lived next door, to the extent that she had a nervous breakdown. She did not like nor have empathy for small children, possibly because of her own experience with an alcoholic father and indifferent grandmother.

Then there was her husband's infidelity. In 1918, she became aware of Franklin's romance with her own secretary, Lucy Mercer (later Lucy Mercer Rutherford), that continued on and off until his death. Much has been written of infidelity on both sides of their open and businesslike marriage. In addition to Lucy Mercer, he had a romantic involvement with Marguerite "Missy" LeHand, who was Roosevelt's private secretary from 1920 until she was incapacitated by a stroke in 1941. Eleanor, too, has been linked romantically by various accounts to a number of people, both male and female, from reporter Lorena Hickock to her bodyguard, Sgt. Earl Miller.

When Roosevelt was governor, and later when he was in the White House, Eleanor spent a great deal of time making public appearances that he could not because of his paralysis. She made many speeches in support of her husband, the New Deal, and the war effort, and she was a much-sought public speaker in her own right, commanding substantial speaking fees which she donated to charity.

After her husband's death, she continued her work. Described by President Harry Truman as the "First Lady of the World," she was United States delegate to the United Nations General Assembly from 1946 to 1952, and she chaired the United Nations Commission on Human Rights from 1946 to 1951. She also chaired John F. Kennedy's presidential Commission on the Status of Women from 1961 to 1962. Eleanor Roosevelt died of heart failure in New York City on November 7, 1962, and was buried next to Franklin at Hyde Park.

The Children of Franklin D. Roosevelt and Eleanor Roosevelt

Anna Eleanor Roosevelt (1906–1975)
James Roosevelt II (1907–1991)
Franklin Roosevelt (1909–1909)
Elliott Roosevelt (1910–1990)
Franklin Delano Roosevelt Jr. (1914–1988)
John Aspinwall Roosevelt II (1916–1981)

left: Eleanor Roosevelt at age 18 in a school photograph. *National Archives*

below: A hand-colored photograph of Eleanor Roosevelt, circa 1936. *FDR Library/National Archives*

President and Mrs. Roosevelt with Postmaster General James Farley (left) and Secret Service Agent Thomas J. "Tommy" Qualters at the Jackson Day Dinner at the Mayflower Hotel in Washington, DC, on January 8, 1938. *FDR Library/National Archives*

who was destined to be one of the most activist first ladies in American history.

Franklin Roosevelt graduated from Harvard in 1903 and enrolled at the Columbia Law School. He was admitted to the New York Bar in 1907 without having finished at Columbia. He entered politics in 1910, running for the state legislature as a Democrat in heavily Republican Dutchess County and winning. In office, he was one of the Democrats who opposed the Tammany Hall Democratic machine, and he was an outspoken supporter of Woodrow Wilson in the 1912 election. The latter earned him an appointment in 1913 as assistant secretary of the navy, where he served until 1920. This greatly appealed to him because he was a yachtsman and an avid amateur naval historian.

In 1914, while serving in the Navy Department, Roosevelt attempted a run for the US Senate, but his opposition to Tammany Hall cost him the nomination. At the 1920 Democratic Convention, Roosevelt emerged as the unexpected nominee for vice president. He was picked for name

recognition, and to geographically balance the ticket with the presidential nominee, James Middleton Cox of Ohio. In November, they were buried by the Harding-Coolidge landslide, and Roosevelt went back to New York and his law practice.

FROM FRANKLIN D. ROOSEVELT'S FIRST INAUGURAL ADDRESS
March 4, 1933

So, first of all, let me assert my firm belief that the only thing we have to fear is fear itself—nameless, unreasoning, unjustified terror which paralyzes needed efforts to convert retreat into advance. In every dark hour of our national life a leadership of frankness and of vigor has met with that understanding and support of the people themselves which is essential to victory. And I am convinced that you will again give that support to leadership in these critical days. . . . These dark days will be worth all they cost us if they teach us that our true destiny is not to be ministered unto but to minister to ourselves and to our fellow men.

above: In August 1936 President Roosevelt made an extensive, 3,000-mile inspection tour of the Midwest, then suffering under the crippling drought that turned the region into the "Dust Bowl." He was photographed speaking from his train during a stop in Bismarck, North Dakota, by Arthur Rothstein for the Resettlement Administration. *National Archives*

right: The red, white, and blue button used in the 1940 presidential campaign. Voters picked Roosevelt for the job four times. *National Archives*

Franklin Roosevelt's life took a dramatic turn in 1921. While vacationing at Campobello Island in Canada, he contracted polio, which resulted in his being paralyzed from the waist down. He spent the rest of his life in denial, insisting that he was improving and would soon be cured. He purchased a spa in Warm Springs, Georgia, to which he often traveled for treatments. With the help of aides and the acquiescence of the press, he successfully obscured the fact that he could no longer walk. The media never pictured him in his wheelchair, nor did they mention that he could stand only with the use of heavy metal braces.

His political career went on, despite his disability. In 1928, he supported the presidential run by fellow New York Democrat Alfred E. Smith, and Smith encouraged Roosevelt to run for governor of New York that year. He ran, and was elected by a margin of one percent. Increasingly popular, he was reelected by a 14 percent margin in 1930.

By 1932, Roosevelt was the rising star in the Democratic Party. At the Democratic Convention, Roosevelt led on the first ballot for the presidential nomination, challenged by Al Smith, who wished to run again, and by Speaker of the House John Nance Garner of Texas. On the fourth ballot, Garner switched to support Roosevelt, who then had the votes for the nomination. In turn, Garner was nominated for vice president.

The 1932 election took place at the depths of the Great Depression amid 25 percent unemployment and great dissatisfaction with the way that Herbert Hoover was dealing with the crisis. Promising a completely different approach, which he described in his nomination acceptance speech as "a new deal for the American people," Roosevelt defeated Hoover 472 to 49 in the Electoral College, and won 57.41 percent of the popular vote.

The term "New Deal" came to characterize both his campaign promises and his presidential agenda. In his first inaugural address, Roosevelt told the American people that "the only thing we have to fear is fear itself," a statement that served to inspire confidence and set the tone for his presidency. He developed his rapport with the American people with folksy radio broadcasts that he called "Fireside Chats." In these, which he used throughout his presidency,

FROM FRANKLIN D. ROOSEVELT'S FIRESIDE CHAT ON SOCIAL SECURITY
April 28, 1935

We have survived all of the arduous burdens and the threatening dangers of a great economic calamity. We have in the darkest moments of our national trials retained our faith in our own ability to master or own destiny. Fear is vanishing. Confidence is growing on every side, renewed faith in the vast possibilities of human beings to improve their material and spiritual status through the instrumentality of the democratic form of government. That faith is receiving its just reward. For that we can be thankful to the God who watches over America.v

Franklin Roosevelt signing the landmark Social Security Act on August 14, 1935. He is surrounded, from left to right by Representative Robert Doughton (D-NC), an unknown person in the shadows, Senator Robert Wagner (D-NY), Representative John Dingell (D-MI), Representative Joshua Twing Brooks (D-PA), Secretary of Labor Frances Perkins, Senator Pat Harrison (D-MS), and Representative David Lewis (D-MD). *Library of Congress*

above: President Roosevelt delivering a Fireside Chat from the White House on September 30, 1934. *FDR Library/National Archives*

left: The ubiquitous blue eagle of the National Recovery Administration appeared in countless store windows and advertisements in 1933 to 1935. The controversial NRA was a New Deal program that sought to create "codes of fair competition" for business and labor. Unpopular with certain business interests, the NRA was successfully challenged in court and dissolved. *Author's collection*

he attempted to explain his agenda in concise terms and to convey the sense that he was speaking to his listeners as though he was in their homes.

He called immediately for a bank holiday to stave off a panic run on the banks and called a special session of Congress. He moved quickly, issuing executive orders and pushing New Deal legislation through Congress to create jobs and bring immediate relief. His "First Hundred Days" saw the passage of fifteen major bills, including the National Industrial Recovery Act. This created the Public Works Administration, which stimulated the economy with massive infrastructure projects, and the controversial National Recovery Administration (NRA), which imposed regulations and restrictions on business and industry.

Roosevelt consolidated relief programs under the Federal Emergency Relief Administration, expanded the Reconstruction Finance Corporation, and started the Agricultural Adjustment Administration. He made good on a promise to push for repeal of Prohibition, which was accomplished by ratification of the Twenty-first Amendment later in 1933. Among his most popular programs was the Civilian Conservation Corps, which created tens of thousands of infrastructure jobs. His

JOHN N. GARNER

Known as "Cactus Jack" for advocating the prickly pear as the Texas state flower, John Nance Garner was born near Detroit, Texas, on November 22, 1868, the son of John Garner III and Sarah Jane Guest Garner. He briefly attended Vanderbilt University in Tennessee before being admitted to the Texas Bar in 1890 and starting a law practice in Uvalde. In 1893, he ran as a Democrat for county judge against fellow Democrat Mariette Elizabeth "Ettie" Rheiner. He won, and in 1895, he and his electoral opponent were married. After serving two terms in the state legislature, Garner was elected to the first of his many terms in the US House of Representatives in 1902. In 1931, he became speaker of the house, which brought him to national prominence.

At the 1932 Democratic Convention, Garner was a dark horse presidential candidate but was selected to run for vice president as Franklin Roosevelt's running mate. As vice president, his role in the Roosevelt Administration was limited, but in his second term, his Texas conservatism and his connections to the oil industry led him to become more outspoken in his opposition to many New Deal programs, and to Roosevelt's attempt to "pack" the Supreme Court. Garner was replaced on the ticket in 1940 and returned to his ranch in Texas. Over the years, he was occasionally consulted as an elder statesman by Democratic politicians. He died on November 7, 1967.

John Nance Garner *National Archives*

HENRY A. WALLACE

A third-generation Iowa farmer and farm journal publisher, Wallace was born in Orient, Iowa, on October 7, 1888, the son of May Brodhead Wallace and Henry Cantwell "Harry" Wallace, who had served as secretary of agriculture in the Harding Administration—as Henry Agard would between 1933 and 1940 under Roosevelt. Henry Agard Wallace graduated from Iowa State College in 1910 with an interest in agronomy and breeding high-yield hybrid corn. Using his wife's inheritance, he started the Hi-Bred Corn Company, which is now part of DuPont. Though raised as a Presbyterian, Wallace flirted with Theosophy during the 1930s and was for several years a devotee and pen pal of Nicholas Roerich, a strange Russian mystic and self-styled spiritualist, who eventually became an embarrassment to Wallace as vice president.

Wallace embraced Roosevelt's New Deal social initiatives, and his loyalty as secretary of agriculture led to Roosevelt's picking him as a running mate in 1940. In 1942, he coined his signature axiom, as he called for a "Century of the Common Man" in which "the common man must learn to increase his productivity so that he and his children can eventually pay to the world community all that they have received." This reminded many commentators on both left and right of the ideas promulgated by Karl Marx in the nineteenth century as a basis of Marxism.

While Roosevelt had formed his "special relationship" with Winston Churchill, Wallace denounced Churchill as an imperialist, while becoming greatly enamored with the Soviet Union and socialism. By 1944, he had become an embarrassment to the Democratic Party and was replaced on the ticket by Harry Truman. After becoming president, Truman appointed Wallace as secretary of commerce, but his outspoken support for Soviet expansion in Eastern Europe led to Truman's letting him go.

In 1948, Wallace was nominated to run for president under the Progressive Party banner. He earned no electoral votes and only two percent of the popular vote. Thereafter, he returned to his agricultural interests. He died in Danbury, Connecticut on November 18, 1965.

Henry Agard Wallace. *Department of Agriculture*

HARRY S. TRUMAN

When Wallace was dropped as a potential running mate for Franklin Roosevelt in 1944, the Democratic Party turned to US Senator Harry S. Truman of Missouri, the chairman of the committee investigating waste and fraud in the arms manufacturing industry. As vice president, he rarely met with Roosevelt, and was never briefed on major programs, including the Manhattan Project that was developing nuclear weapons. Less than three months later, he was the president of the United States. Truman and his own presidency are described in detail in the following chapter.

Works Progress Administration created two million jobs, and the Tennessee Valley Authority created jobs while providing electricity to an underserved part of the country.

Among the elements of the New Deal that survive to this day are the Securities and Exchange Commission, the Federal Deposit Insurance Corporation, and Social Security.

In the 1936 presidential election, Roosevelt's popularity carried him to victory over Kansas Republican Governor Alfred Mossman "Alf" Landon by a landslide margin of 523 to 8 in the Electoral College and with 60.8 percent of the popular vote.

Roosevelt's second term began with a major defeat. In 1935 and 1936, the Supreme Court had ruled that a number of New Deal programs were unconstitutional. Roosevelt responded by promoting a controversial bill to "pack the court." The Judicial Procedures Reform Bill of 1937 would have allowed the president to appoint up to six additional

above: This 1931 Plymouth Phaeton was one of several cars that were specially designed and fitted with hand controls so that Roosevelt could drive without the use of his legs. *FDR Library/National Archives*

left: A candid photo of Franklin Roosevelt at an August 1940 picnic on "Sunset Hill" near Pine Plains, New York. His Scottish terrier Fala was one of the most famous of presidential pets ever. Fala was popular with the pubic and the media and became part of the Roosevelt image. The doll is a handmade Shaker doll made by Mary Garettson of Rhinebeck, New York. *FDR Library/National Archives*

justices to the Supreme Court, thus creating a majority that would support the New Deal. Debated for several months, the bill was not passed.

In 1940, Roosevelt made the controversial and unprecedented decision to run for a third term in the White House. World War II had begun in Europe. It was argued that the United States needed continuity in a time of international crisis. Though the United States economy had improved considerably, there was a sense that the New Deal was still a work in progress that needed Roosevelt's hand at the helm.

Roosevelt was renominated, albeit with some opposition from Vice President Garner, who was dropped from the ticket in favor of Secretary of Agriculture Henry Wallace. After hard-fought early ballots at their convention, the Republicans nominated New York businessman Wendell Willkie. He went on to lose 449 to 82 in the Electoral College, while Roosevelt took 54.74 percent of the popular vote.

A major issue in 1940 was keeping the United States out of what was seen as "Europe's War." Roosevelt had done so thus far, but he made no secret that he considered Adolf Hitler and Nazism as intrinsically evil and a threat to civilization. Between September 1939 and June 1940, Germany had conquered virtually all of Europe from Poland to France to Norway, and in September 1940, Germany had signed the Tripartite Pact formally creating a three-way Axis with Fascist Italy and Imperial Japan. Roosevelt was eager to support the United Kingdom as the last bastion of democracy in Europe that opposed Hitler. Though the Isolationists were still a strong force in public opinion polls, there was growing sympathy for the British.

In 1941, Roosevelt pushed through the Lend-Lease Act, which allowed him to supply arms to cash-strapped Britain. He also met with British Prime Minister Winston Churchill to draft the Atlantic Charter, calling for a mutual commitment to a peaceful postwar world "free of want and fear." It was a tacit understanding that the United States and the United Kingdom would one day be allied against the Axis in World War II.

On December 7, 1941, Japan provided the catalyst with their attack on the United States fleet at Pearl Harbor. Popular opinion now favored war. Roosevelt asked Congress for a declaration of war against Japan, Germany declared war on the United States, and the United States reciprocated.

Though the United States was ill-prepared for World War II, all aspects of American society came together to create an unprecedented mechanism for meeting the challenge. Within two years, the United States had the largest

above: President Roosevelt in his wheelchair on the porch at Top Cottage in Hyde Park, New York, with fellow polio victim Ruthie Bie and Fala in February 1941. This photograph, taken by his friend, Margaret "Daisy" Suckley, is one of only a tiny handful of images that show him in his wheelchair. *FDR Library/National Archives*

below: Franklin Roosevelt swimming in a pool in Warm Springs, Georgia. This activity allowed him to exercise without the use of his legs. *FDR Library/National Archives*

army in its history and the largest navy and air force in world history. Meanwhile, American industry stepped up with previously unimaginable levels of production.

Roosevelt and Churchill formed a "special relationship," integrating their respective armed forces into a close alliance led by a Combined Chiefs of Staff organization that shared command at every level. The two leaders met at ten major conferences after Pearl Harbor, and included the Soviet Union's Josef Stalin in two "Big Three" conferences.

During this time, Roosevelt, Churchill and their advisors were actively working on plans for a postwar international organization to replace the League of Nations. They called it the "United Nations" and saw their own cooperation against the Axis as the seamless precursor to such an entity.

As the United States and its allies halted the Axis advances in 1942 and slowly turned the tide in 1943, Roosevelt was in evidence through his Fireside Chats and public appearances

President Roosevelt and British Prime Minister Churchill aboard the HMS *Prince of Wales* during the Atlantic Conference in Placentia Bay, Newfoundland, on August 10, 1941. From this meeting came the landmark Atlantic Charter, which defined Allied goals for the postwar world. It inspired many future international agreements, as well as the United Nations. Among the goals were global cooperation to secure better economic and social conditions, and freedom from fear and want. *FDR Library/National Archives*

President Roosevelt riding in a jeep with future president Dwight Eisenhower at the Castelvetrano Airport in Sicily on December 14, 1943. Roosevelt was on an inspection tour of the area after its recent liberation from German occupation. Eisenhower, then a major general, was commander of British and American forces in the Mediterranean Theater of Operations and had led Operation Husky, the invasion of Sicily, as well as Operation Avalanche, the Allied invasion of the Italian mainland. In December 1943, it was announced that Eisenhower would be Supreme Allied Commander in Europe. *Library of Congress*

throughout the country, trying to be the voice of reassurance that he had been since his first inaugural address. By 1944, the Axis was on the defensive, and though the cost was steep, there was no doubt that victory was inevitable.

Through it all, the president was growing increasingly exhausted. His complexion grew ashen and his health declined. Nevertheless, he remained popular, and this spurred his decision to run for a fourth term as president in 1944. By now, there were people in their thirties who had never voted in a presidential election where he was not on the ballot.

He won 92 percent of the votes at the 1944 Democratic Convention, at which Henry Wallace was dropped as his vice presidential running mate. Wallace had grown controversial because of his erratic behavior, and he was replaced by

FROM FRANKLIN D. ROOSEVELT'S DAY OF INFAMY ADDRESS TO CONGRESS
December 8, 1941

Yesterday, December 7, 1941, a date which will live in infamy, the United States of America was suddenly and deliberately attacked by naval and air forces of the Empire of Japan. Always will our whole nation remember the character of the onslaught against us. No matter how long it may take us to overcome this, the American people in their righteous might will win—through to absolute victory. We will not only defend ourselves to the uttermost but will make it very certain that this form of treachery shall never again endanger us. With confidence in our armed forces—with the unbounding determination of our people—we will gain the inevitable triumph, so help us God!

On his last campaign, President Roosevelt delivers a campaign address at Fenway Park in Boston on November 4, 1944, three days before he was elected to an unprecedented fourth term. He was joined by Robert Emmet Hannegan, the former commissioner of Internal Revenue, who was now the chairman of the Democratic National Committee. *FDR Library/National Archives*

Missouri Senator Harry Truman, who had risen to national prominence by heading the committee investigating industrial waste and war profiteering. The Republicans, meanwhile, nominated New York Governor Thomas E. Dewey, whose own rise to national attention came when he was heralded "crime-buster" as New York City's District Attorney.

FROM FRANKLIN D. ROOSEVELT'S FOURTH INAUGURAL ADDRESS
January, 20 1945

We Americans of today, together with our allies, are passing through a period of supreme test. It is a test of our courage—of our resolve—of our wisdom—of our essential democracy. If we meet that test successfully and honorably we shall perform a service of historic importance which men and women and children will honor throughout all time. As I stand here today, having taken the solemn oath of office in the presence of my fellow countrymen in the presence of our God I know that it is America's purpose that we shall not fail.

For a fourth time, Roosevelt was elected president with over half the popular vote, this time with 53.39 percent, while defeating Dewey 432 to 99 in the Electoral College.

In February 1945, shortly after being inaugurated, Roosevelt traveled to Yalta in Crimea for his last Big Three conference with Churchill and Stalin. Despite indications that Stalin intended to install a puppet government in Poland, Roosevelt came home optimistic that the Big Three cooperation could be perpetuated into his vision for a postwar United Nations. However, time was running out. In March, he went to Warm Springs to rest up for his appearance at the United Nations Conference scheduled for late April.

On April 12, 1945, Roosevelt collapsed from a cerebral hemorrhage and died shortly thereafter. His body was brought back to Washington, DC, and then taken on to Hyde Park for interment. Franklin D. Roosevelt did not live to see the American victory in World War II nor the founding of the United Nations, but both occurred by the end of the year and on a timetable of which he was aware.

above: Franklin Roosevelt, looking alert and engaged, is flanked by Soviet Marshal Josef Stalin and British Prime Minister Winston Churchill at their first summit conference in Tehran in December 1943. When the "Big Three" met next at Yalta in February 1945, Roosevelt was exhausted and noticeably haggard. *National Archives*

left: The last photograph of Franklin Roosevelt was taken by Nicholas Robbins at the President's cottage at Warm Springs, Georgia, on April 11, 1945. *FDR Library/ National Archives*

FROM FRANKLIN D. ROOSEVELT'S ADDRESS TO CONGRESS AFTER THE YALTA CONFERENCE
March 1, 1945

I hope that you will pardon me for this unusual posture of sitting down during the presentation of what I want to say, but . . . it makes it a lot easier for me not to have to carry about ten pounds of steel around on the bottom of my legs . . . The Crimean Conference ought to spell the end of a system of unilateral action, the exclusive alliances, the spheres of influence, the balances of power, and all the other expedients that have been tried for centuries and have always failed. We propose to substitute for all these, a universal organization in which all peace loving nations will finally have a chance to join.

1945–1953

Harry S. Truman

DEMOCRATIC PARTY

Harry Truman was born in Lamar, Missouri, on May 8, 1884, the son of Martha Ellen Young Truman and John Anderson Truman, a rancher and cattle dealer. The family moved to Independence when Harry was six. He had no middle name, just the initial, which is sometimes seen without punctuation. He studied at the University of Missouri and took night classes at the Kansas City Law School, but completed neither. He was the only twentieth century American president not to have earned a college degree.

In 1905, he enlisted in the Missouri National Guard, and went overseas as a captain with the 129th Field Artillery, assigned to the 35th Infantry Division. He participated in the Meuse-Argonne Offensive in September 1918 as well as other actions.

After returning to the United States in 1919, he married Bess Wallace and started a short-lived haberdashery business. He was taken under the wing of Kansas City Democratic Party boss Tom Pendergast, with whose nephew Truman had served during the war—and groomed for public office. He was first elected to local office in 1922, and served in a number of low-level offices until 1933, when he received a key patronage appointment with the New Deal's Civil Works Administration. Though he had earmarked Truman for local political office, Pendergast found himself without a candidate for the US Senate in 1934, so he put Truman into that slot, and Truman won. In 1940, despite Pendergast's being in jail for tax evasion, Truman ran successfully for reelection.

top: President Truman smiling for photographers after a speech in January 1946. *National Archives*

above: President Truman in 1912 as a Missouri National Guardsman. *National Archives*

Harry S. Truman's official presidential portrait was painted in 1945 by Greta Kempton. The Capitol Building is in the background because Truman, who was a two-term senator and former vice president who presided over the US Senate, wanted to emphasize his legislative career. *Truman Library/National Archives*

FIRST LADY
ELIZABETH "BESS" WALLACE TRUMAN

Born in Independence, Missouri, on February 13, 1885, Bess Wallace was the oldest child of David Willock Wallace and Margaret Elizabeth Gates Wallace. She met Harry Truman when they were schoolchildren and they were married on June 28, 1919, after he returned from World War I. Their daughter, later a noted mystery writer, was born in 1924.

Unused to lavish entertaining before coming to the White House, neither Harry nor Bess were inclined to do so once they arrived, so this was kept to a minimum, and Bess was not part of the Washington social scene. For more than two years, while the White House was undergoing a massive renovation, the Trumans lived across Pennsylvania Avenue at Blair House. In 1953, they returned to Independence, where they lived until his death in 1972, and where she remained until she passed away from congestive heart failure on October 18, 1982. At age ninety-seven, she was the longest living first lady in history. She is interred next to her husband at the Harry S. Truman Library.

The Daughter of Harry S. Truman and Bess Truman
Mary Margaret Truman Daniel (1924–2008)

Bess Truman and daughter, Margaret, in December 1948 at Blair House, across Pennsylvania Avenue from the White House. The Trumans lived here while the executive mansion underwent extensive renovations. *National Archives*

President Truman and Prime Minister Churchill standing on the rear platform of a special Baltimore & Ohio train in March 1946 as Churchill embarked for Fulton, Missouri, to deliver his landmark "Iron Curtain" Speech. Truman's military aide, General Harry Vaughan, is seated nearby. *National Archives*

In 1941, accusations of waste, fraud and profiteering in arms manufacturing led to the creation of the Senate Special Committee to Investigate Contracts Under the National Defense Program, with Truman picked to chair it. Whereas the Roosevelt Administration lobbied to pack the committee with New Deal Democrats, Truman earned high marks from across the aisle for making it a bipartisan effort. The Truman Committee, as it came to be known, continued to do business, holding hearings and visiting defense contractors, throughout the war.

In 1944, Democratic Party leaders who felt that Henry Wallace was a liability, convinced Franklin Roosevelt that he should be replaced on the ticket for the November election, and they settled on Truman because of his reputation for honesty and integrity while chairing the commission. At the Democratic Convention, Wallace led on the first ballot, with Truman as a close second. By the third ballot, after considerable maneuvering, the nomination went to Truman.

After the inauguration, Truman saw little of Roosevelt. On April 12, 1945, he was summoned to the White House by Eleanor Roosevelt, who told him that he was president. When he asked whether there was anything he could do, she famously replied "Is there anything we can do for you? You are the one in trouble now!"

His immediate trouble was his being in the dark with regard to the strategic direction of World War II, and that no one had told him about the American nuclear weapons

VICE PRESIDENT

ALBEN W. BARKLEY

Having had no vice president during his first three and a half years in office, Harry Truman picked longtime US Senator Alben William Barkley as his running mate for the 1948 election. He was born Willie Alben Barkley on November 24, 1877, in Wheel, Kentucky, the son of tenant farmers John Wilson Barkley and Electa Eliza Smith Barkley. He worked his way through Marvin College in Clinton, graduating in 1897 and later returning to the faculty. In 1898, he moved to Paducah,

Alben Barkley in his office. *Library of Congress*

where he apprenticed to an attorney, studied law, and was admitted to the bar in 1901. He married Dorothy Brower in 1903, and they had three children.

Barkley entered politics in 1905 with the first of several successful runs for local office. In 1912, he won a contentious race for the US House of Representatives, where he would remain until 1927. In Washington, he supported the Wilson Administration's programs, from the Federal Reserve to the League of Nations, learning the value and rewards of party loyalty. In 1923, while still in the house, he mounted an exhausting campaign for governor of Kentucky, not because he wanted the job, but because he wanted a pretext to establish statewide recognition to support a run for the US Senate. In 1926, when he ran, his preparatory work paid off. He was elected, and went on to serve for twenty-two continuous years, and for most of those as one of the most powerful men in Washington. Between 1937 and 1947, when the Democrats were in power, he was the Senate majority leader. From 1947 to 1949, he was Senate minority leader. At the 1948 Democratic Convention, he was nominated by acclamation and went on to be the oldest man ever elected vice president. In 1952, there was a move to draft Barkley for the presidential nomination, but he was deemed too old. In 1954, he ran once again for the US Senate and was elected. He died on April 30, 1956, while giving a speech in Lexington, Virginia.

program. When briefed on the casualties anticipated in the invasion of Japan that was planned for later in the year, Truman decided to use the weapons to save American lives and end the war sooner rather than later. In May and August respectively, Truman was able to announce the end of World War II against Germany and Japan. In the meantime, he participated in the last Big Three Allied summit conference of the war, which took place in Potsdam, Germany, in July.

above: President Truman in February 1951 receiving a report on the accomplishments of the Boy Scouts from a delegation of Eagle Scouts who are giving him the Boy Scout salute. *National Archives*

right: President Truman at his desk in the White House signing a proclamation declaring a national emergency in the wake of the Chinese intervention in the Korean War in December 1950. *Defense Department*

After the war, Truman embraced the United States' role in the world as Wilson and Roosevelt had done, activity supporting the United Nations, and making the United States the first country to recognize Israel. He also continued the spirit of the New Deal by embracing civil rights as an issue. Among other things, he began desegregation of the Armed Forces. He also facilitated the independence of the US Air Force from the US Army, and consolidated the War Department and Navy Department into a single cabinet office that became the Department of Defense.

As mobilization for war had presented challenges, so too did demobilization, which Truman wished to do quickly in order to reduce expenditures. Meanwhile, pent up demand for consumer goods put a strain on the economy, and labor issues, which had not been raised in wartime, boiled over in the form of massive strikes in the steel and coal industries.

As Truman's popularity sank, the Republicans took control of Congress in the 1946 midterm election. This led the conventional wisdom to predict a Republican victory in the 1948 presidential election as well. The Republican field included popular Ohio Senator Robert Taft, son of President William Howard Taft, who had led Senate opposition to the New Deal. However, it was 1944 presidential candidate Thomas E. Dewey who carried the convention and took the nomination.

Meanwhile, foundering approval was the least of Truman's worries. The Democrats renominated him, though not without opposition, only to have the party split three ways. On Truman's left, former Democratic Vice President Henry Wallace defected to accept the candidacy of the Progressive Party, while on the right, Southern Democrats representing the states of the former Confederacy walked out of the Democratic Convention to endorse Governor Strom Thurmond of South Carolina to run for president under the standard of the States Rights Democratic, or "Dixiecrat," Party.

Even as he cloaked himself in the mantle of the once-popular New Deal, Truman realized that the old coalition was no more. Conventional wisdom and all of the polls—including all nine Gallup Polls—had Dewey heading for a landslide victory.

In what has been called the biggest upset in the history of presidential elections, Truman won. It was by a razor-thin margin in many states, but the electoral votes counted up to 303 for Truman, 189 for Dewey and 39 for Thurmond. Truman took 49.55 percent of the popular vote.

Truman's full term in office was dominated by international crises in which the Soviet Union took advantage of American demobilization to flex its muscles. First came the Berlin Blockade of 1948 to 1949, an effort to drive Britain, France, and the United States out of Berlin, which was successfully overflown by transport aircraft in the Berlin Airlift. Next came the Soviet-sponsored North Korean invasion of South Korea that was later actively supported by Communist China, and which resulted in a stalemate that still prevails. At home, Truman controversially intervened to block a 1952 steel strike on the grounds of wartime necessity, but the Supreme Court reversed his order.

After the 1948 election, Truman moved out of the White House for two years as the crumbling mansion was gutted in the biggest renovation in its history. In November 1950, while he was living across the street at Blair House, Puerto Rican separatists made an attempt on his life, but the Secret Service prevented them from reaching him. A 1952 plebiscite on Puerto Rican independence favored the status quo by over 80 percent.

The Twenty-second Amendment, ratified in 1951, precluded presidents from running for more than two terms, but did not apply to Truman as the incumbent at the time. Nevertheless, he chose not to run in 1952.

After leaving office, Truman and his wife returned to Independence, where they found themselves in financial difficulty. In 1957, Congress intervened and Truman was the first man ever to receive a pension for serving as president of the United States. His Presidential Library in Independence was also the first one to be federally financed under the 1955 Presidential Libraries Act.

Truman died of pneumonia on December 26, 1972, and is interred with his wife on the grounds of the Truman Library and Museum.

above: Former President Harry S. Truman called on President Lyndon B. Johnson at the White House on November 23, 1963, the day after the Kennedy assassination. *National Archives*

below: A first day cover showcasing the Harry S. Truman stamp that was issued on May 8, 1973. *US Postal Service*

Dwight D. Eisenhower

REPUBLICAN PARTY

A celebrated general during World War II, Dwight Eisenhower was the only president to serve in the US Army during both world wars. He is remembered for presiding over an era of unprecedented prosperity in the United States but largely forgotten as the catalyst behind the remarkable and ubiquitous Interstate Highway System.

Born in Denison, Texas, on October 14, 1890, he was the last president of the United States born in the nineteenth century. He was the third of seven boys, all of them nicknamed "Ike," an abbreviation for their surname, plus an adjective. Dwight was "Little Ike," though in later years, his friends knew him simply as "Ike." In 1892, his parents, David Jacob Eisenhower and Ida Elizabeth Stover Eisenhower, moved the family to Abilene, Kansas, where the young Ike grew up. He passed entrance exams for both service academies, but was too old for Annapolis, so he chose West Point.

He graduated with the Class of 1915, known later as "the class the stars fell on" because fifty-nine of his classmates became generals. Eisenhower was one of two five-star generals in the class.

He served at a variety of US Army posts in the United States and was preparing to ship out for France in 1918 when the Armistice ending World War I was signed. In 1919,

top: A Nicodemus Hufford portrait of Gen. Dwight Eisenhower as chief of staff. *US Army*

right: Mamie and Lt. Dwight Eisenhower at St. Mary's University in San Antonio, Texas, in 1916. *National Archives*

The official presidential portrait of Dwight D. Eisenhower was painted by James Anthony Wills. *National Archives*

At about 8:30 p.m. on June 5, 1944, Gen. Dwight Eisenhower met with the men who would be the tip of the spear of the Normandy Invasion. Company E, 502nd Parachute Infantry Regiment of the 101st Airborne Division was then at Greenham Common Airfield in England, preparing to jump into enemy-held territory that night. His order of the day was "Full victory—nothing less." Lieutenant Wallace Strobel, seen here wearing number 23, recalled that he was talking about fly fishing with his men, as he always did before a stressful operation. *US Army*

GENERAL DWIGHT EISENHOWER'S MESSAGE ON THE EVE OF D-DAY
June 2, 1944

Soldiers, Sailors and Airmen of the Allied Expeditionary Force! You are about to embark upon the Great Crusade, toward which we have striven these many months. The eyes of the world are upon you. The hopes and prayers of liberty loving people everywhere march with you. In company with our brave Allies and brothers in arms on other Fronts, you will bring about the destruction of the German war machine, the elimination of Nazi tyranny over the oppressed peoples of Europe, and security for ourselves in a free world. Your task will not be an easy one. Your enemy is well trained, well equipped and battle hardened. He will fight savagely . . . I have full confidence in your courage and devotion to duty and skill in battle. We will accept nothing less than full Victory! Good luck! And let us beseech the blessing of Almighty God upon this great and noble undertaking.

FROM GEN. DWIGHT EISENHOWER'S LONDON GUILDHALL ADDRESS
June 12, 1945

Humility must always be the portion of any man who receives acclaim earned in blood of his followers and sacrifices of his friends. Conceivably a commander may have been professionally superior. He may have given everything of his heart and mind to meet the spiritual and physical needs of his comrades. He may have written a chapter that will glow forever in the pages of military history. Still, even such a man, if he existed, would sadly face the fact that his honors cannot hide in his memories the crosses marking the resting places of the dead. They cannot soothe the anguish of the widow or the orphan whose husband or whose father will not return. The only attitude in which a commander may with satisfaction receive the tributes of his friends is a humble acknowledgement that, no matter how unworthy he may be, his position is a symbol of great human forces that have labored arduously and successfully for a righteous cause.

AN NATIONAL CONVENTION

Scenes from the 1952 Republican National Convention in Chicago, Illinois, include Dwight Eisenhower accepting the nomination for president on the convention floor (above) and he and his wife watching the proceedings on television (below) in their hotel room. *Library of Congress*

he was part of a transcontinental US Army convoy that was undertaken to demonstrate the need for good roads at a time when there was no paved highway across the United States. This influenced his later advocacy of Interstate Highways. During the interwar period, his experience included service in the Philippines and as chief of staff to Gen. Douglas MacArthur when he headed the US Army.

In 1942, after the United States entered World War II, Brigadier General Eisenhower was sent to the United Kingdom as US Commanding General for the European Theater of Operations. Late in the year, he became Supreme Commander, Allied Expeditionary Force for the invasion of Axis-controlled Northwest Africa. In February 1943, now a four-star general, Eisenhower became commander of Allied forces in the Mediterranean. In December, he went back to the United Kingdom to head the Supreme Headquarters, Allied Expeditionary Force, making him the Supreme Allied Commander for the invasion of Europe which took place on June 6, 1944. In December 1944, he became one of only five US Army generals ever elevated to five-star rank. In November 1945, having led United States forces to victory in Europe, Eisenhower came home to serve as chief of staff of the US Army. In 1948, Eisenhower left the service to become president of Columbia University, but he went back into uniform in 1950 as Supreme Commander of the North Atlantic Treaty Organization (NATO).

Though he had resisted earlier calls, he allowed himself to be convinced to run for the Republican presidential nomination in 1952. As in 1948, Robert A. Taft was a leading candidate, and he and Eisenhower closely split

MAMIE GENEVA DOUD EISENHOWER

Born in Boone, Iowa, on November 14, 1896, Mamie Geneva Doud was the daughter of businessman John Sheldon Doud and Elivera Mathilde Carlson Doud. She and her three sisters were raised in Iowa and Colorado, wintering in San Antonio, Texas. It was here that she met Dwight Eisenhower in 1915, while he was stationed at Fort Sam Houston. They were married on July 1, 1916, at her parents' home in Denver. Thereafter, she accompanied him to his various postings as a military officer in the United States and overseas, though she remained in Washington, DC, during World War II.

The Eisenhowers had two children Doud, known as "Icky," who died of scarlet fever at age three, and John, who was born after his brother's death and who later became a military historian.

Beginning in 1948, the Eisenhowers made their home at a farm near Gettysburg, Pennsylvania, except for their years at the White House, and during his short tenure with NATO, when they lived in France. Mamie Eisenhower is recalled as having been a gracious hostess, although she was reportedly rude to Jacqueline Kennedy while giving her a tour on the eve of the Kennedys moving into the White House.

Mamie Eisenhower at the White House on May 30, 1954.
National Archives

After her husband's death, Mamie Eisenhower remained at their home in Gettysburg until she passed away at Walter Reed Army Medical Center on November 1, 1979, after suffering a stroke. She was interred next to her husband and first son on the grounds of the Eisenhower Presidential Library in Abilene, Kansas.

The Children of Dwight and Mamie Eisenhower
Doud Dwight "Icky" Eisenhower (1917–1921)
John Sheldon Doud Eisenhower (1922–2013)

President Dwight Eisenhower sat for an official portrait session at the White House on May 29, 1959, midway through his second and final term in office. *National Archives*

a contentious first ballot at the Republican Convention before delegate shifts gave the nomination to Eisenhower. In the general election, Eisenhower defeated Democratic challenger Adlai Stevenson of Illinois (grandson of Grover Cleveland's second vice president) by a margin of 442 to 89 in the Electoral College and took 55.18 percent of the popular vote.

As president, Eisenhower's domestic policy included maintaining the few surviving New Deal programs, such as Social Security, rolling much of these activities into a new cabinet-level Department of Health, Education and Welfare. He completed Truman's program to desegregate the armed forces and established a Civil Rights Commission within the Justice Department. He promoted the 1956 Federal Highway Act, which kickstarted the Interstate Highway program.

Internationally, he traveled to Korea as president-elect and spurred the resolution of the Korean War through a ceasefire. He sought to counter the Soviet and Chinese Cold War adventurism with a parity in strategic nuclear systems. He also entered into military alliances such as the Southeast Asia Treaty Organization, which led to involvement in Vietnam.

Eisenhower was a popular president, who held more press conferences than his predecessors and utilized the new medium of television.

Because of health problems, including a 1955 heart attack, he had not originally planned to run for reelection in 1956, but changed his mind. Nominated unanimously at the Republican Convention, he faced Adlai Stevenson in a rematch of the 1952 contest. Eisenhower defeated his opponent by a greater margin than before, 457 to 73 in the Electoral College, and with 57.37 percent of the popular vote.

Toward the end of his presidency, he authorized U-2 surveillance flights over the Soviet Union to monitor missile and

VICE PRESIDENT

RICHARD NIXON

When Dwight Eisenhower was nominated at the 1952 Republican Convention, the party chose energetic young California Senator Richard Milhous Nixon as a unity candidate because his outspoken opposition to Communism was seen as appealing to the conservative wing of the party. He would run for president in 1960 as Eisenhower's heir apparent, but would be defeated. In his second try in 1968, he was successful. Nixon and his own presidency are described in detail in a later chapter.

FROM DWIGHT EISENHOWER'S MESSAGE TO CONGRESS

March 13, 1959

We cannot safely confine government programs to our own domestic progress and our own military power. We could be the wealthiest and the most mighty nation and still lose the battle of the world if we do not help our world neighbors protect their freedom and advance their social and economic progress. It is not the goal of the American people that the United States should be the richest nation in the graveyard of history.

above: Chief Justice Earl Warren administering the oath of office to Dwight Eisenhower on the east portico of the US Capitol in January 1957. *Library of Congress*

below: On August 30, 1954, Eisenhower signed the Atomic Energy Act of 1954, amending the Atomic Energy Act of 1946 to provide more support for a civilian nuclear industry. Eisenhower coined the slogan "Atoms for Peace" in a speech to the UN General Assembly on December 8, 1953. The notable people on hand included nuclear power advocate Lewis L. Strauss seated at far right, and physicist Henry DeWolf Smyth of the US Atomic Energy Commission standing second from left. *National Archives*

Former President Eisenhower and President John F. Kennedy arrive at Camp David, Maryland, on April 22, 1961, with their military aides for a series of discussions. Both appear to be in a congenial mood, despite the disastrous failure of the CIA-sponsored Bay of Pigs invasion of Cuba, which occurred less than a week earlier. *National Archives*

FROM DWIGHT EISENHOWER'S FAREWELL ADDRESS TO THE NATION
January 17, 1961

We now stand ten years past the midpoint of a century that has witnessed four major wars among great nations. Three of these involved our own country. Despite these holocausts, America is today the strongest, the most influential, and most productive nation in the world. Understandably proud of this pre eminence, we yet realize that America's leadership and prestige depend, not merely upon our unmatched material progress, riches and military strength, but on how we use our power in the interests of world peace and human betterment.

Throughout America's adventure in free government, our basic purposes have been to keep the peace, to foster progress in human achievement, and to enhance liberty, dignity and integrity among peoples and among nations. To strive for less would be unworthy of a free and religious people. Any failure traceable to arrogance or our lack of comprehension or readiness to sacrifice would inflict upon us grievous hurt, both at home and abroad.

A vital element in keeping the peace is our military establishment. Our arms must be mighty, ready for instant action, so that no potential aggressor may be tempted to risk his own destruction. This conjunction of an immense military establishment and a large arms industry is new in the American experience. The total influence—economic, political, even spiritual—is felt in every city, every statehouse, every office of the federal government. We recognize the imperative need for this development. Yet we must not fail to comprehend its grave implications. Our toil, resources and livelihood are all involved; so is the very structure of our society. In the councils of government, we must guard against the acquisition of unwarranted influence, whether sought or unsought, by the military-industrial complex. The potential for the disastrous rise of misplaced power exists, and will persist. We must never let the weight of this combination endanger our liberties or democratic processes. We should take nothing for granted. Only an alert and knowledgeable citizenry can compel the proper meshing of the huge industrial and military machinery of defense with our peaceful methods and goals so that security and liberty may prosper together.

nuclear programs. A U-2 aircraft shot down in May 1960 proved a great embarrassment and resulted in the collapse of a summit conference being held with the leaders of Britain, France, and the Soviet Union.

In 1959, on Eisenhower's watch, Alaska and Hawaii were admitted to the Union, the first non-contiguous states, and the last states admitted to date.

After leaving office, Eisenhower and his wife retired to their home in Gettysburg, Pennsylvania, and made few public appearances. He died on March 28, 1969, of congestive heart failure and is buried in the chapel at the Eisenhower Presidential Library in Abilene, Kansas.

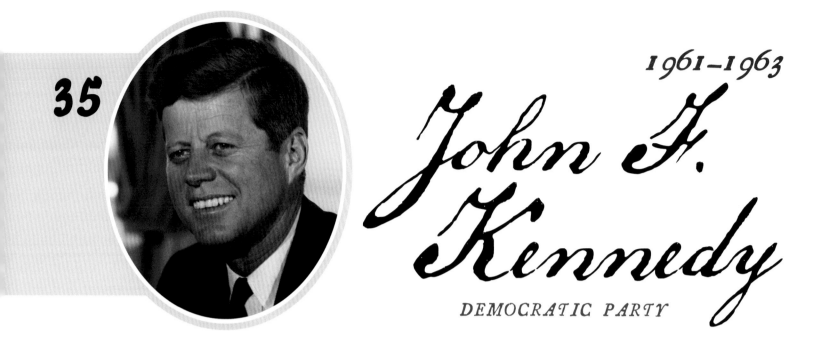

35

1961–1963

John F. Kennedy

DEMOCRATIC PARTY

Charismatic in life and highly memorialized in death, John Fitzgerald Kennedy is perhaps best remembered for his eloquence as a public speaker and his skillful deftness in the use of television as a medium of communication. "JFK," as he is often known, is to date the only president of the United States to have earned a Pulitzer Prize, and the only Roman Catholic. Assassinated while riding in a motorcade in Dallas, his funeral became a global media event.

Among his accomplishments were the creation of the Peace Corps and his advocacy of the Apollo Program, which culminated in six successful American expeditions to the moon. Often forgotten by future generations were his 1962 tax cut measures, which turned around a stagnating economy.

Personally, he suffered throughout his life from Addison's Disease, a chronic endocrine system disorder, as well as from the effects chronic back pain and of the drugs he took to combat it.

Born in Brookline, Massachusetts, on May 29, 1917, Kennedy was the son of Joseph Patrick "Joe" Kennedy and Rose Elizabeth Fitzgerald Kennedy, both of whom were members of politically influential Boston families. Joseph Kennedy was a businessman and successful liquor importer—during as well as after Prohibition—and was a major figure in the Democratic Party machine. In 1934, he was the first chairman of the Securities and Exchange Commission and served as Franklin Roosevelt's ambassador to the United Kingdom from 1938 to 1940.

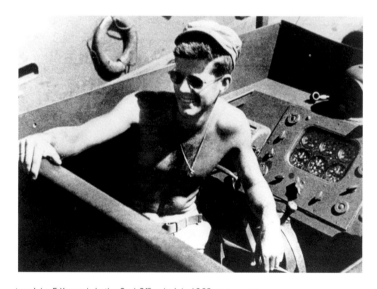

top: John F. Kennedy in the Oval Office in July 1963. *National Archives*

above: Lieutenant Junior Grade Kennedy aboard PT-109 in the South Pacific in 1943. *JFK Library/National Archives*

John F. "Jack" Kennedy enrolled at Harvard in 1936, but left in 1937 to tour Europe. In 1938, he joined his family in London, where his father was ambassador, but returned to the United States when World War II began in 1939. He graduated from Harvard in 1940 with a degree in international affairs. His thesis, describing events in England leading up to the war was later commercially published as *Why England Slept* and became a bestseller.

above: During his speech at Rice University on September 12, 1962, John F. Kennedy discussed the space program, which interested him greatly. He told his audience that "We set sail on this new sea because there is new knowledge to be gained, and new rights to be won, and they must be won and used for the progress of all people . . . as we set sail we ask God's blessing on the most hazardous and dangerous and greatest adventure on which man has ever embarked. . . . We choose to go to the moon in this decade and do the other things, not because they are easy, but because they are hard, because that goal will serve to organize and measure the best of our energies and skills, because that challenge is one that we are willing to accept, one we are unwilling to postpone, and one which we intend to win, and the others, too." *NASA*

Kennedy joined the US Navy on the eve of the United States entry into World War II, and volunteered for service aboard patrol torpedo boats. In 1943, he was sent to the Pacific Theater and put in command of PT-109 on patrol duty in the Solomon Islands. On the night of August 2, 1943, when PT-109 was rammed by a Japanese destroyer, Kennedy led his men to safety on an island. As he swam, he pulled one injured man by clinching the man's life jacket strap in his teeth. After they were rescued, Kennedy returned to duty in command of

PT-59. In 1944, he was sent home because of problems with his injured back.

John Kennedy's father had previously groomed his oldest son, Joe Kennedy Jr., for a future life in Democratic Party politics, but when young Joe was killed in action in the war, Jack stepped in. He was elected to the US House of Representatives in 1946, and served for three terms. In 1952, he ran to represent Massachusetts in the US Senate, defeating

FIRST LADY
JACQUELINE BOUVIER "JACKIE" KENNEDY

Well-read and articulate as well as personable and photogenic, Jacqueline Lee "Jackie" Bouvier Kennedy brought a level of style and sophistication to the White House that captured the public imagination. She was so attractive and so popular that even her husband was overshadowed. On a visit to Europe in 1961, he famously told reporters that "I am the man who accompanied Jacqueline Kennedy to Paris—and I have enjoyed it!"

Born on July 28, 1929, in Southampton, New York, Jacqueline Bouvier was the older of two daughters of wealthy Wall Street broker John Vernou "Black Jack" Bouvier III and Janet Norton Lee Bouvier. As she was growing up, the family divided their time between New York City and a compound at East Hampton on Long Island, but after their parents' divorce and their mother's 1942 remarriage to Hugh Auchincloss, Jacqueline and her sister, Lee, lived at his estate in McLean, Virginia.

In 1951, Jacqueline graduated from George Washington University with a degree in French literature, and worked as a newspaper photographer. In 1952, she met Kennedy, then a Congressman. They were married on September 12, 1953, in a well-attended society wedding in Newport, Rhode Island. Their first daughter, Arabella, was stillborn in 1956, and a second daughter, Caroline, was born in 1957.

During Kennedy's presidential campaign, Jacqueline did not accompany him on the campaign trail because she was pregnant and had a history of problem

President Kennedy and Mrs. Kennedy in a formal portrait in the Yellow Oval Room of the White House on March 28, 1963. National Archives

pregnancies, but she did support him by taping television spots and doing interviews. Their son, John F. Kennedy Jr., was born shortly after the election.

As had been the case for Edith Roosevelt in 1901, who found the White House "dark" and "musty," Jacqueline Kennedy described it as "cold and dreary," despite the major renovation a decade earlier. She then undertook a major internal facelift, the effects of which are still visible. She created a fine arts committee to administer the restoration process and brought in early American furniture expert Henry du Pont as a consultant. In 1962, when the work was completed, she hosted a televised tour with Charles Collingwood of CBS. She also hosted events with leading figures from the scientific, artistic and literary communities.

Her life was darkened in August 1963 by the death of her second son, Patrick Bouvier Kennedy, who was born prematurely and who died of respiratory distress syndrome two days later.

Three months later, on November 22, she was with her husband when two bullets mortally wounded him. Jacqueline Kennedy oversaw the details of the state funeral and lit the eternal flame that she asked be installed at his grave. It was in an interview a few days later that she compared her brief time in the White House to King Arthur's legendary Camelot, and this term came to be used as a synonym for the Kennedy presidency.

On October 20, 1968, four months after the assassination of her brother-in-law, Robert Kennedy, she married Greek shipping magnate Aristotle Onassis on his private island. Many in the media expressed disappointment with the woman they now nicknamed, "Jackie O." After Onassis died in 1975, she became a respected book editor, first at Viking Press, and later at Doubleday, where she worked for the rest of her life. She died of lymphoma on May 18, 1994, and was buried next to John F. Kennedy.

The Children of John F. Kennedy and Jacqueline Kennedy
Arabella Kennedy (1956–1956)
Caroline Kennedy Schlossberg (1957–)
John F. Kennedy Jr. (1960–1999)
Patrick Bouvier Kennedy (1963–1963)

The Kennedy family at Hyannis Port in August 1962. From left to right, John F. Kennedy Jr., Jacqueline Kennedy, Caroline Kennedy, and the president. JFK Library/National Archives

above: A poster from the 1960 election campaign. *LBJ Library/National Archives*

above, left: President Kennedy aboard the United States Coast Guard yacht *Manitou* in Narragansett Bay, Newport, Rhode Island. The president sailed on the yacht during his vacation at Hammersmith Farm in Newport. *JFK Library/National Archives*

incumbent Henry Cabot Lodge, who had first been elected in 1936.

In 1953, he married Jacqueline Bouvier, who went on to become one of America's best-remembered first ladies.

While serving in the US Senate, Kennedy underwent a series of delicate and painful spinal operations, during which he almost died. In 1956, as he was recovering, he wrote the book *Profiles in Courage*, vignettes of eight US Senators whom he admired, which earned him the Pulitzer Prize in 1957.

At the 1956 Democratic Convention, Kennedy made a strong showing in the voting for a vice presidential running mate for Adlai Stevenson but lost out to Estes Kefauver of Tennessee. Given that the ticket was doomed by Eisenhower's popularity, this was seen as a lucky loss for Kennedy's future presidential ambitions. In 1958, Kennedy won reelection to the US Senate, which positioned him for a presidential run in 1960.

In 1960, Kennedy's strategy was to actively run in the Democratic primaries as a mechanism for developing momentum ahead of the convention.

Party primaries had been used in the selection of convention delegates for half a century, but fewer than a third of the states held them and few candidates considered them in their campaign plans. Kennedy wanted to demonstrate that he had popularity outside his home turf and to offset the criticism that his being a Roman Catholic would be a problem in a nationwide campaign. He met his

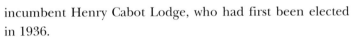

VICE PRESIDENT

LYNDON B. JOHNSON

The influential Senate majority leader, Lyndon Baines Johnson went to the 1960 Democratic Convention hoping to be nominated for president, but the momentum developed in the primaries by John F. Kennedy proved insurmountable. Kennedy, to everyone's surprise, then invited Johnson to be his running mate. With Johnson on the ticket to assure southern votes, Kennedy swept to victory. As vice president, Johnson found himself marginalized. The man who was used to casting shadows found himself in one. Then, he accompanied Kennedy to Dallas, and returned to Washington as president of the United States. Johnson and his own presidency are described in detail in the following chapter.

FROM JOHN F. KENNEDY'S
INAUGURAL ADDRESS
January 20, 1961

Let the word go forth from this time and place, to friend and foe alike, that the torch has been passed to a new generation of Americans—born in this century, tempered by war, disciplined by a hard and bitter peace, proud of our ancient heritage—and unwilling to witness or permit the slow undoing of those human rights to which this Nation has always been committed, and to which we are committed today at home and around the world.

Let every nation know, whether it wishes us well or ill, that we shall pay any price, bear any burden, meet any hardship, support any friend, oppose any foe to assure the survival and the success of liberty.

Now the trumpet summons us again—not as a call to bear arms, though arms we need; not as a call to battle, though embattled we are—but a call to bear the burden of a long twilight struggle, year in and year out, "rejoicing in hope, patient in tribulation," a struggle against the common enemies of man: tyranny, poverty, disease, and war itself.

The energy, the faith, the devotion which we bring to this endeavor will light our country and all who serve it—and the glow from that fire can truly light the world.

And so, my fellow Americans: ask not what your country can do for you—ask what you can do for your country.

John F. Kennedy delivering his inaugural address. Seated in the front row from left to right are former First Lady Mamie Eisenhower, Lady Bird Johnson, Jacqueline Kennedy, former President Dwight Eisenhower, Vice President Lyndon Johnson, and former Vice President Richard Nixon. *US Army*

above: John F. Kennedy speaking in front of Springwood, Franklin D. Roosevelt's home in Hyde Park, New York, on August 14, 1960, during his presidential campaign. *FDR Library/ National Archives*

principal primary challenger, Senator Hubert Humphrey of Minnesota, in neighboring Wisconsin and won. Of the sixteen states holding primaries, Kennedy won in ten, while Humphrey took one plus the District of Columbia.

At the Democratic Convention, Kennedy faced the opposition of two men who had not entered the primaries. They were Adlai Stevenson, who decided to make a third try for the White House, and Lyndon B. Johnson of Texas, the powerful Senate Majority Leader. Kennedy won on the first ballot, but Johnson made a substantial showing among southern Democrats, so Kennedy picked him—despite Johnson's derogatory personal jabs at Kennedy—as his vice presidential running mate to unify the party.

The Republicans nominated Vice President Richard Nixon as their presidential candidate, and polls showed him in the lead until the first-ever presidential debates held in October seemed to favor Kennedy. The election itself was close, with the popular vote margin being narrower than a single percentage point, but Kennedy won with 49.72 percent, while beating Nixon 303 to 219 in the Electoral College.

In his inaugural address, Kennedy delineated his presidency with the phrase ". . . ask not what your country can do for you—ask what you can do for your country," which underscored the volunteerism component of Kennedy's "New Frontier" social agenda. Loosely based on Roosevelt's New Deal, it emphasized economic aid programs and civil rights. Robert Francis Kennedy, the president's brother, whom he named as his attorney general, became a close advisor on domestic issues, especially on civil rights.

John F. Kennedy hoped for the New Frontier to be his central focus, but international events quickly dominated his agenda. The April 1961 invasion of Cuba at the Bay of Pigs by exiled Cubans opposed to strongman Fidel Castro and aided by the CIA, was a fiasco and failure that made Kennedy appear weak and indecisive. In June 1961, he appeared ill at ease at a summit conference with Soviet leader Nikita Khrushchev, which also damaged his credibility. He understood that the Cold War between the United States and the Soviet Union was going to be a central focus of his presidency, but initially he seemed to be on the retreat.

Reacting to Kennedy's apparent weakness, Khrushchev first ordered the construction of the Berlin Wall in August 1961. When Kennedy did not interfere, he audaciously placed nuclear weapons into Cuba, assuming Kennedy would accept it as a *fait accompli*. Instead, in October

above: President Kennedy and his brothers, Attorney General Robert F. Kennedy and Senator Edward M. Kennedy, outside the Oval Office on August 28, 1963. *JFK Library/National Archives*

FROM JOHN F. KENNEDY'S ADDRESS TO CONGRESS ON THE SPACE PROGRAM
May 25, 1961

I believe that this nation should commit itself to achieving the goal, before this decade is out, of landing a man on the moon and returning him safely to the earth. No single space project in this period will be more impressive to mankind, or more important for the long range exploration of space . . . explorations which are particularly important for one purpose which this nation will never overlook: the survival of the man who first makes this daring flight. But in a very real sense, it will not be one man going to the moon—if we make this judgment affirmatively, it will be an entire nation. For all of us must work to put him there.

left: John F. Kennedy delivering his historic message on the space program to a joint session of Congress on May 25, 1961. Vice President Lyndon Johnson is on the left, Speaker of the House Sam Rayburn is on the right. *NASA*

above: President Kennedy signs the Proclamation for Interdiction of the Delivery of Offensive Weapons to Cuba in the Oval Office at the White House on October 23, 1962. *JFK Library/National Archives*

opposite page, main: The posthumous official presidential portrait of John F. Kennedy by Aaron Shikler that was commissioned by Mrs. Kennedy. *White House*

opposite page, inset: The Kennedy half dollar was first minted in 1964 and is still in production. Use of existing work by US Mint sculptors Gilroy Roberts and Frank Gasparro allowed dies to be made and striking to began in January 1964. *US Mint*

1962, Kennedy demanded that they be removed, ordered a naval blockade and put the United States armed forces on alert for a possible invasion. Khrushchev backed down, a nuclear war was averted, and Kennedy had his defining moment of foreign policy decisiveness.

This was followed by a Nuclear Test Ban Treaty in 1963. During that year, Kennedy also made a visit to West Berlin to eloquently denounce the Berlin Wall.

In 1963, Kennedy turned to his domestic agenda, outlining the ideas that would become the Civil Rights Act of 1964 in a speech he gave on the same day that he federalized the Alabama National Guard to assure the right of two black students to enter the University of Alabama.

In November 1963, anticipating the need to assure southern votes and Democratic Party unity in the 1964 election campaign, Kennedy and Vice President Johnson embarked on a speaking tour of Texas. At 12:30 p.m. on November 22, as the president's motorcade was passing through Dallas, Kennedy was struck by two bullets. He died a half hour later at Parkland Hospital. Jacqueline Kennedy was present when he was hit. Johnson and his wife were in another car. Kennedy's body, as well as the Johnsons and Mrs. Kennedy were all taken to Air Force One, the presidential aircraft, where Johnson was sworn in as president of the United States aboard the aircraft at 2:38 p.m.

Lee Harvey Oswald was arrested and charged with the assassination that same day, but he was murdered two days later. As there was no trial, Chief Justice Earl Warren was tasked with leading an exhaustive investigation of the killing. The Warren Commission concluded in the massive report published in 1964 that Oswald, shooting from the Texas School Book Depository where he worked, was the only gunman involved. This was met with a great deal of skepticism, which still continues. In 1979, the House Select Committee on Assassinations concluded that Kennedy was "probably assassinated as the result of a conspiracy," but this conclusion was also received skeptically. It is a mystery that may never be resolved.

A state funeral, attended by dignitaries from around the world, was held in Washington, DC, on November 25, 1963, and Kennedy's body was transported across the Potomac River to Arlington National Cemetery. Numerous buildings, streets, and other features in cities around the world were named for Kennedy in the months following. In the United States, two of the most prominent are New York City's international airport, and the Kennedy Space Center in Florida.

FROM JOHN F. KENNEDY'S ADDRESS AT THE BERLIN WALL
June 26, 1963

There are many people in the world who really don't understand, or say they don't, what is the great issue between the free world and the Communist world. Let them come to Berlin. There are some who say that communism is the wave of the future. Let them come to Berlin. And there are some who say in Europe and elsewhere we can work with the Communists. Let them come to Berlin. And there are even a few who say that it is true that communism is an evil system, but it permits us to make economic progress. *Lass' sie nach Berlin kommen*. Let them come to Berlin.

Freedom is indivisible, and when one man is enslaved, all are not free. When all are free, then we can look forward to that day when this city will be joined as one and this country and this great Continent of Europe in a peaceful and hopeful globe. When that day finally comes, as it will, the people of West Berlin can take sober satisfaction in the fact that they were in the front lines for almost two decades.

All free men, wherever they may live, are citizens of Berlin, and, therefore, as a free man, I take pride in the words "*Ich bin ein Berliner*" ["I am a Berliner"].

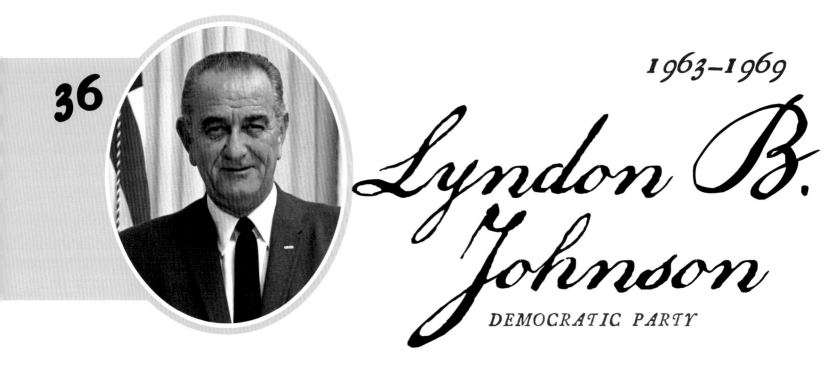

36

1963–1969

Lyndon B. Johnson

DEMOCRATIC PARTY

An admirer and briefly a confidant of Franklin D. Roosevelt, Lyndon B. Johnson imagined that his own presidential legacy would include the greatest transformation of American domestic society since the New Deal. He grouped his many social engineering initiatives under the banner of what he called the "Great Society." However, like Roosevelt, his best-laid plans were interrupted by a war. Unlike Roosevelt in World War II, though, Johnson found himself chained to a war that he could not win. Unlike World War II, which had united American domestic society, the Vietnam War tore it apart and became an unanticipated darkening of Johnson's legacy.

Born in a farmhouse in Stonewall, Texas, on August 27, 1908, Lyndon was the oldest child of Samuel Ealy Johnson Jr. and Rebekah Baines Johnson. He graduated from Southwest Texas State Teachers' College (now Texas State University) in 1930 and worked briefly as a teacher before pursing a fascination for politics. His work as a Democratic Party campaign aide brought him to Washington, DC, as a Congressional aide. In Washington in 1934, he met and married fellow Texan Claudia Alta "Lady Bird" Taylor. In 1935, Johnson returned to Texas as state director of the New Deal's National Youth Administration, which gave him the opportunity to build a constituency for a successful run for the US House of Representatives in 1936.

Known professionally by his initials "LBJ," he would remain in the House for a dozen years, becoming an increasingly important part of the Texas delegation. He also came to the

above: Young Lyndon Johnson in Johnson City, Texas, circa 1915. *LBJ Library*

top: President Lyndon B. Johnson in the Oval Office. *LBJ Library*

attention of President Roosevelt, who used Johnson as his eyes and ears in the House. When the United States entered World War II, Johnson joined the US Navy Reserve. In 1942, Roosevelt asked Congressman/Lieutenant Commander Johnson to undertake a fact-finding trip to the South West

A White House photo taken on January 17, 1968, showing Lyndon B. Johnson on the telephone in the Oval Office. *LBJ Library*

FIRST LADY
CLAUDIA ALTA "LADY BIRD" JOHNSON

An astute businesswoman in her early twenties, Claudia Alta Taylor made the investments that helped to finance her husband's fledgling political career. She was born on December 22, 1912, in Karnack, Texas, the youngest of three children and first daughter of Minnie Lee Pattillo Taylor and Thomas Jefferson Taylor, a self-made wealthy businessman and landowner. Reportedly, it was her nanny who nicknamed her "Lady Bird," and her husband typically called her "Bird." She was fond of the outdoors as a child and an advocate of highway beautification as first lady.

She graduated from the University of Texas in Austin in 1933, and added a second degree in journalism a year later, planning for a newspaper career. Shortly thereafter, she met Lyndon Johnson, and they were married on November 17, 1934, in San Antonio. They had two daughters, Lynda Bird and Lucy (later Luci) Baines. All four members of the family shared the initials "LBJ."

A portrait photograph of Lady Bird Johnson taken on the south lawn of the White House. *National Archives*

Beginning in 1943, Lady Bird Johnson began using money inherited from her family to buy radio and television stations in Texas which were held by the LBJ Holding Company and which made a substantial profit for the Johnsons.

As Jacqueline Kennedy's priority as first lady was White House beautification, Lady Bird Johnson's was in the outdoors, first with the founding of the Society for a More Beautiful National Capital and its flower-planting campaign, and vlater with a program to plant wildflowers along highways. She was an advocate of the 1965 Highway Beautification Act that called for limits on billboards and eyesores such as junkyards along interstate highways. She was the first first lady to have a press secretary and a White House staff.

When they left the White House, she and her husband retired to Texas, where they both wrote their memoirs. After his death in 1973, she remained active in beautification and other projects around the United States. She was awarded the presidential Medal of Freedom in 1977 and the Congressional Gold Medal in 1988.

She suffered two serious strokes in 1993 and 2002, and gradually lost her eyesight from macular degeneration. She passed away on July 11, 2007, and was interred next to her husband.

The Children of Lyndon Johnson and Lady Bird Johnson
Lynda Bird Johnson Robb (1944–)
Luci Baines Johnson Nugent Turpin (1947–)

above: Lyndon B. Johnson was sworn in as president aboard Air Force One on November 22, 1963, by Judge Sarah T. Hughes, shortly after John F. Kennedy was killed. He is flanked on his right by Lady Bird Johnson and on his left by Jacqueline Kennedy. *National Archives*

Pacific Theater. He reported to Roosevelt on the poor conditions for American troops, which accelerated improvements and brought Johnson the chairmanship of the House Naval Affairs Committee.

In 1948, Johnson was elected to the US Senate, becoming Minority Leader in 1953, and with the Democrats now in control, he became Senate Majority Leader in 1955. His personal style of interacting with fellow senators, which ranged from humor to flattery to reproach—often in the same conversation—usually bore his desired results and led to his being one of the most effective Senate leaders ever.

In 1960, he entered the race for the Democratic presidential nomination after Kennedy had developed unstoppable momentum, and found himself in second place at the convention and on the ticket. There was a great deal of animosity between Johnson and the Kennedy brothers—the president and Robert Kennedy, the attorney general—because of derogatory comments made by Johnson over the years about the Kennedy family. It was a marriage of convenience. As vice president, the man used to being in charge, found himself shut out of the decision making by Kennedy's tightly wound inner circle.

Assuming the presidency after Kennedy's assassination, Johnson embraced many aspects of Kennedy's agenda, from civil rights to the space program, but began to promote his Great Society, a name he coined in anticipation of his 1964

presidential bid. By the summer of 1964, the Civil Rights Act and the Economic Opportunity Act had passed Congress and were signed by Johnson. Under the latter, Johnson announced his "War on Poverty," a basket of initiatives that included such elements as the Job Corps and the Food Stamp program.

In August 1964, a shootout between the US Navy and North Vietnamese patrol boats in the Gulf of Tonkin resulted in Johnson ordering retaliatory air strikes. This marked the beginning of the gradual slide into the Vietnam War.

In the 1964 campaign, Johnson presented himself as the inheritor of the Kennedy legacy, much to the chagrin of Robert Kennedy, and this strategy worked. Having faced minimal opposition to his nomination, Johnson chose Minnesota Senator Hubert Humphrey as his running mate. In the general election, Johnson easily defeated Republican candidate Barry Goldwater of Arizona 486 to 52 in the Electoral College and captured 61.05 percent of the popular vote, the best showing since James Monroe's uncontested reelection in 1820.

With a popular mandate and a strong and prosperous economy, Johnson pressed forward. In 1965, Medicare and Medicaid were added to the Social Security program. Johnson sat down with civil rights leaders such as the Reverend Martin

above: Johnson reacts to bad news in a July 17, 1965, phone call. *LBJ Library*

below: Secretary of State Dean Rusk, President Lyndon B. Johnson and Secretary of Defense Robert McNamara discuss the Vietnam War on February 9, 1968, nine days after North Vietnam and the Viet Cong launched their Tet Offensive in South Vietnam. *Defense Department*

Luther King and planned an agenda that included a second civil rights bill enacted as the Voting Rights Act of 1965. Despite this, a wave of civil unrest swept the United States over the next several years, including major riots in Watts in Los Angeles in 1965, and in Newark and Detroit in 1967, doing serious and permanent damage.

The Vietnam War also became an issue. Johnson felt himself walking a tightrope between not wanting to be seen as weak and not wanting to have the United States embroiled in a foreign war while he was building his Great Society. Thus he flooded troops and materiel into Southeast Asia to protect South Vietnam, but chose to limit the actions that American personnel could attack in North Vietnam. It was a dangerous stalemate of his own making, that he hoped to resolve by sending more American troops—mostly draftees— into South Vietnam. As American casualties soared in the pursuit of ambiguous goals, a wave of anger and alienation, especially among draft age youth, swept the nation.

It had long been anticipated that Johnson would run for reelection in 1968, which he was permitted to do under the Twenty-second Amendment because he had served less than two years of Kennedy's term. In March, he entered the New Hampshire Primary, where he was nearly beaten by anti-war Democratic Senator Eugene McCarthy of Minnesota. In turn,

Robert Kennedy, who also opposed the war, announced his candidacy and polls favored him over Johnson in upcoming primaries. Faced with a disintegrating party and a struggle for renomination, Johnson announced on the last day of March that he would not be a candidate for renomination in 1968.

What ensued was a dark period for the Johnson presidency and a fractured Democratic Party. Adding to the disruption caused by antiwar rallies spreading across the United States was a wave of urban unrest that followed the assassination of Martin Luther King on April 4. Vice President Hubert Humphrey announced his candidacy with the support of party insiders, but on the primary trail, it was a duel between McCarthy and Kennedy. However, on June 5, just after winning the California Primary, Kennedy was assassinated. A fragmented party staggered into the Democratic Convention in Chicago as massive riots raged in the streets outside. Humphrey was nominated and Alabama Governor George Wallace led a defection of southern Democrats to run for president under the banner of the American Independent Party. The Republicans, meanwhile, nominated former Vice President Richard Nixon, who won the election.

Lyndon Johnson retired to his Texas ranch to write his memoirs. Having suffered heart attacks in 1970 and 1972, he died on January 22, 1973. He is interred in the family cemetery at the ranch, which is about 60 miles west of the Lyndon Baines Johnson Library and Museum.

Lady Bird Johnson provides some last-minute suggestions ahead of her husband's March 31, 1968, national address announcing a bombing halt in Vietnam and his intention not to run for reelection. *LBJ Library*

VICE PRESIDENT

HUBERT H. HUMPHREY

Known as the "Happy Warrior" for his sunny disposition even in the face of adversary, Hubert Horatio Humphrey was, for most of his career, a leading force in the national Democratic Party and *the* leading force in the Democratic Farmer-Labor Party (the Minnesota affiliate of the Democratic Party). His many unsuccessful bids for the presidency spanned the years from 1952 to 1972, but only in 1968 was he nominated by his party to run.

Hubert Humphrey. *National Archives*

Humphrey was born in Wallace, South Dakota, on May 27, 1911, the son of druggist Hubert Humphrey Sr. and Norway-born Ragnild Kristine Sannes Humphrey. He grew up working in his father's drug store, where the two also concocted patent medicines. In 1934, the younger Humphrey met and married Muriel Buck of Huron, South Dakota. In 1937, he left the family business to return to the University of Minnesota, from which he had dropped out in 1931, and graduated in 1939. He found employment with a series of New Deal agencies, as a college professor from 1943 to 1944, and later as a radio commentator. Having taken an interest in politics, he ran for mayor of Minneapolis and served from 1945 to 1948.

He won national prominence at the 1948 Democratic Convention by successfully championing a civil rights plank in the platform. Also in 1948, he was elected to the US Senate from Minnesota, the first Democrat in the job since before the Civil War. Reelected twice, he became Majority Whip in 1961 and was critical to the passage of civil rights legislation. Having tried several times for the Democratic nomination for president, he was picked in 1964 as Lyndon Johnson's running mate.

As vice president, Humphrey was unflinchingly loyal to Johnson, his civil rights programs, and his Great Society. Humphrey continued to support Johnson as his escalation of the Vietnam War fell out of step with Democratic liberals, and the Happy Warrior incurred their wrath. When Johnson dramatically took himself out of the running in 1968, Humphrey became an heir apparent in a deeply divided party, which he sought to unite. At the troubled Democratic Convention, Humphrey received the nomination, picked Edmund Muskie of Maine as his running mate, and set out to face the Republicans. They lost, and Humphrey returned to Minnesota and a short-lived career as a university professor.

In 1970, Humphrey ran again for the US Senate, was elected, and remained in that office for the rest of his life. In 1972, he did try again for the Democratic presidential nomination, but despite support from the party insiders, his association with Johnson and the still-ongoing Vietnam War tainted him and he lost to anti-war candidate George McGovern, who in turn lost to Richard Nixon in the general election.

Hubert Humphrey died at his home in Waverly, Minnesota, on January 13, 1978, and is buried at Lakewood Cemetery in Minneapolis.

37

1969–1974

Richard M. Nixon

REPUBLICAN PARTY

Best remembered today for being the only man to resign the presidency, Richard Milhous "Dick" Nixon was previously elected twice to the vice presidency and was elected twice to the presidency. He was also the first president of the United States to visit all fifty states, and to visit China while in office.

Nixon was born in Yorba Linda, California, on January 9, 1913, the second of the five sons of rancher Francis Anthony "Frank" Nixon and Hannah Milhous Nixon, whom Dick later described as a "Quaker Saint." When Dick was nine, the ranch went bust and the family moved to nearby Whittier. Dick graduated from Whittier College, a Quaker school, in 1934 and received a scholarship to the Duke University School of Law, from which he graduated in 1937. He returned to Whittier, was accepted to the bar and hired by a law firm. In 1940, he met and married Thelma "Pat" Ryan. Their two daughters were born after World War II. The Nixons relocated to Washington, DC, in 1942 so that Dick could take a job with the wartime rationing component of the Office of Price Administration.

Nixon joined the US Navy, completed Officer Candidate School, requested a combat assignment, and was sent to the South Pacific as a supply officer. In 1945, he returned stateside to serve in the war contract termination department at Bureau of Aeronautics.

His political career began in 1946 after a college friend invited him to return to Whittier to run as a Republican for the US House of Representatives. Reelected in 1948, Nixon became known as an anti-Communist for his role in hearings

above: This campaign leaflet from Nixon's 1950 US Senate campaign reminded voters that he helped bring down Alger Hiss. *Nixon Library*

top: A 1971 official portrait of Richard Nixon. *National Archives*

of the House Un-American Activities Committee. In 1950, he won a race for an open US Senate seat by reportedly using smear tactics against Democratic Congresswoman Helen Gahagan Douglas.

In 1952, the Republican Party nominated Gen. Dwight Eisenhower for president, and picked Nixon as his running mate because he was young, he was an outspoken

anti-Communist, and because he had won a statewide election in California, an increasingly important state. During the campaign, Nixon was accused of taking money—legally but suspiciously—from a Republican campaign fund. He responded with a nationally televised speech in which he asserted that he was an unpretentious man with an unpretentious wife who wore not a mink coat, but a "respectable Republican cloth coat." He added that the only gift had been a cocker spaniel named "Checkers" that was given to his daughter Tricia. The "Checkers Speech" is considered one of Nixon's most masterful moments. Eisenhower and Nixon won in 1952 and were reelected in 1956.

Nixon was perhaps the most involved vice president to date, not only attending cabinet meetings, but chairing them in Eisenhower's absence. However, he made no effort to take over the reins of government when Eisenhower was down

Richard Nixon's greatest summit conferences, both from the historical and pop cultural perspectives, were his meetings with the leaders of the People's Republic of China and with the King of Rock and Roll. At the top, he toasts Chinese Premier Zhou Enlai in Beijing on February 25, 1972. Above, he receives an unannounced visit at the White House from Elvis Presley on December 21, 1970. *National Archives, both*

PATRICIA "PAT" NIXON

Born on March 16, 1912, in Ely, Nevada, Thelma Catherine "Pat" Ryan was the daughter of Katherine Halberstadt Ryan and William M. Ryan Sr., a farmer and gold prospector. When she was two, the family moved to Southern California, settling on a farm in that part of Artesia that later became Cerritos. She attended Fullerton Junior College and graduated from the University of Southern California in 1937. Pat Ryan met and married young attorney Richard Nixon in 1940. Their daughters, Patricia, known as "Tricia," and Julie were born in 1946 and 1948 respectively. Julie later married David Eisenhower, the grandson of Dwight Eisenhower. Though she was lukewarm to politics, Pat helped her husband campaign for public office from the late 1940s to 1972. In 1972, she became the only first lady up to that time since Eleanor Roosevelt to address a national party convention.

An official 1970 portrait of Patricia Nixon. *National Archives*

While her husband was vice president and later president, she accompanied him on his many trips, both domestically and around the world, becoming the most widely traveled first lady until Hillary Clinton. Her trips included a visit to a combat zone in South Vietnam. She is remembered for bringing more historical furnishings and objects into the White House collection than Jacqueline Kennedy had, and making antiques on display accessible and touchable for blind visitors to the White House.

She was unaware of her husband's role in the Watergate Scandal until the end, and found the experience of his resignation "heartbreaking."

She suffered a severe stroke in 1976, recovered completely, but experienced another in 1983. After two years in New York City, the Nixons settled in New Jersey 1981 to be near their children. Pat Nixon died on June 22, 1993, ten months before her husband.

The Children of Richard Nixon and Patricia Ryan Nixon
Patricia "Tricia" Nixon Cox (1946–)
Julie Nixon Eisenhower (1948–)

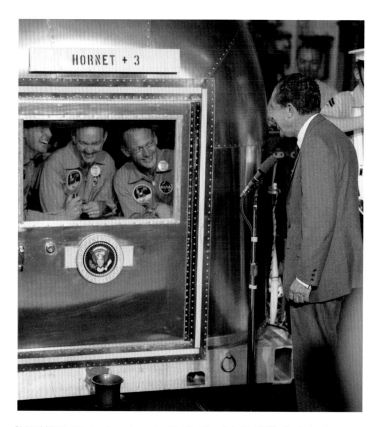

Richard Nixon welcomes the astronauts of Apollo 11 on July 24, 1969 after their return to earth from the first manned expedition to the moon. Neil Armstrong, Michael Collins, and Edwin E. "Buzz" Aldrin were inside a mobile quarantine facility aboard the USS *Hornet*. NASA

after his heart attacks. Nixon also made overseas goodwill visits to the Far East and Latin America, where his motorcade was attacked by demonstrators. On a 1959 trip to the Soviet Union, he found himself in an impromptu discussion with Nikita Khrushchev in the kitchen of a replica American home at the American National Exhibition in Moscow. Known as the "Kitchen Debate," the exchange was broadcast nationally in the United States earning Nixon praise for his calm assurance and articulate defense of American values.

In 1960, Nixon was easily nominated for president at the Republican Convention, picking Henry Cabot Lodge of Massachusetts as his running mate. A close election, which followed close polling throughout the campaign, gave the win to Kennedy.

In 1962, Nixon ran unsuccessfully for governor of California against Edmund "Pat" Brown, after which he told the media "You won't have Nixon to kick around anymore because, gentlemen, this is my last press conference." It wasn't. With the Democratic Party torn apart in 1968, Nixon ran for the Republican nomination, with his chief rival being Nelson Rockefeller of New York. Having been nominated, he chose Maryland Governor Spiro Agnew as his running mate. He

defeated Hubert Humphrey by a margin of 301 to 191 in the Electoral College and with 43.42 percent of the popular vote.

His first term was marked by his working toward what became a series of foreign policy triumphs, all of which were achieved at the end of that term. The Strategic Arms Reduction Treaty (SALT I) and the Anti-Ballistic Missile Treaty with the Soviet Union were both signed in 1972. In Southeast Asia, he widened the war into Cambodia and undertook more aggressive operations against North Vietnam. A ceasefire ended the Vietnam War in January 1973. Nixon's biggest first term foreign policy success was the effort toward normalization of relations with the People's Republic of China, which culminated in Nixon's visit to Beijing in February 1972.

The long effort to send American astronauts to the moon succeeded on Nixon's watch. Beginning with Apollo 11

above: Richard Nixon, the man who founded his political career on opposition to Communism, is seen here conversing with the leaders of the Soviet Union. Above, Nixon is seen in a discussion with Leonid Brezhnev on June 19, 1973, during the Soviet Leader's visit to the United States, a year after the two negotiated the SALT I, the first arms limitation pact between their countries. *National Archives*

below: Then–Vice President Nixon is seen in his famous "Kitchen Debate," an impromptu exchange with Soviet Premier Nikita Khrushchev on July 24, 1959, at the American National Exhibition at Sokolniki Park in Moscow. Nixon insisted that average Americans had kitchens such as the one that was displayed, but Khrushchev wasn't so sure. *National Archives*

in July 1969, and ending with Apollo 17 in December 1972, six American expeditions successfully landed on the lunar surface, an accomplishment that has yet to be repeated.

In the 1972 presidential election, Nixon easily defeated Democratic Challenger Senator George McGovern of South Dakota by a margin of 520 to 17 in the Electoral College and won 60.67 percent of the popular vote.

In his second term, the successes that had studded his first term were superseded by humiliating crises. In October 1973, when Israel was attacked by its neighbors in the Yom Kippur War, Nixon ordered emergency military aid. Unexpectedly, Arab oil producers in the Middle East declared a six-month Oil Embargo on the United States and Western Europe that upset the global economy. When oil supplies resumed in 1974, it was at substantially increased prices, resulting in permanent changes to the global economy.

above, Richard Nixon says farewell to his staff hours before his resignation became effective on August 9, 1974. His daughter Tricia and her husband Edward Cox are seen in the background. *National Archives*

top: Richard Nixon at a moment of triumph and at a moment of disgrace. At the top, he flashes his trademark "victory" sign while in Philadelphia during his successful 1968 campaign for the presidency.

Nixon's worst crisis began with a June 1972 break-in at the Democratic Party Headquarters at the Watergate office complex in Washington, DC. The burglars were apprehended and later shown to have had ties to Nixon's reelection campaign. During 1973 and 1974, investigations, including one by a Senate Select Committee, gradually traced the conspiracy up the White House chain of command, culminating in taped evidence showing that Nixon himself had ordered a cover-up of Administration involvement. In August 1974, the House of Representatives voted articles of impeachment against Nixon. In a nationally televised address on August 8, Nixon announced his resignation, effective the following day. He still faced criminal charges, but was pardoned by incoming president Gerald Ford on September 8.

Nixon returned to California, where he helped his wife recover from a debilitating stroke in 1976. After several years in seclusion, Nixon published his memoirs and began making limited public appearances, though he never shed the taint of the Watergate Scandal. He died in New York City on April 22, 1994, after suffering a stroke. He and his wife were interred on the grounds of the Nixon Presidential Library and Museum in Yorba Linda, California.

VICE PRESIDENTS

SPIRO T. AGNEW

The first vice president to resign since John C. Calhoun, Spiro Theodore Agnew did so under the shadow of criminal charges to which he pleaded "no contest." Agnew was born on November 9, 1918, in Baltimore, Maryland, the son of Margaret Marian Akers Pollard Agnew and Theodore Spiros Anagnostopoulos, who had changed his name after emigrating from Greece. Spiro Agnew attended Johns Hopkins University for three years before being drafted into in the US Army during World War II. He served in the European Theater and was awarded the Bronze Star. In 1947, he graduated from the University of Maryland School of Law and was admitted to the bar in 1949.

After serving in a variety of local government offices, including Baltimore County Executive, he was elected as governor of Maryland in 1966 as a Republican. In 1968, his being a governor of a traditionally Democratic state earned him the notice of Richard Nixon and a place as his running mate on the Republican ticket.

Running for vice president in 1968, a year of great internal strife, Agnew made "law and order" his campaign theme and carried it into office, where he was widely used by the Nixon Administration to denounce its critics. A master of alliteration and colorful characterization, he described the opposition media as being comprised of "nattering nabobs of negativism" or "hopeless, hysterical hypochondriacs of history," while opponents of the Vietnam War were "an effete corps of impudent snobs who characterize themselves as intellectuals." Having been reelected in 1972, Agnew came under investigation by the Maryland attorney general in 1973 for extortion, bribery, conspiracy, and tax fraud in his having accepted bribes while in state office. An embarrassment to Nixon in the midst of the Watergate affair, he resigned on October 10, 1973. He was fined and given a three-year suspended sentence. He eventually repaid what he had accepted in bribes. He later claimed that some of the charges against him were an attempt by Nixon to divert attention away from Watergate. Agnew died in Berlin, Maryland, on September 17, 1996, after being diagnosed with leukemia.

Vice President Spiro Agnew resigned in disgrace, pleading no contest to criminal tax evasion for bribes he took as Maryland's governor. *National Archives*

GERALD R. FORD

Between 1812 and 1963, eight Presidents and seven vice presidents had died in office and one vice president had resigned. In each case, the office of vice president remained vacant for the remainder of the term, which in several cases was more than three years. Numerous proposals had been made for a mechanism to appoint a vice president, but this was not finally done until the adoption of the Twenty-fifth Amendment in February 1967. It called for a vice president to be appointed with the consent of a two-thirds majority of both houses of Congress. When Agnew resigned, Richard Nixon nominated House Minority Leader Gerald Rudolph Ford. On December 6, 1973, after approval by Congress, Ford was sworn in as the first vice president under the Twenty-fifth Amendment. Eight months later, he became President. He and his own presidency are described in detail in the following chapter.

Gerald R. Ford

REPUBLICAN PARTY

A popular and long-serving leader in the US House of Representatives, Gerald Ford is perhaps best remembered as the only president of the United States never elected to that office, nor to the office of vice president. An Eagle Scout, he also worked as a ranger in Yellowstone National Park. When president, he survived two unrelated assassination attempts in the space of seventeen days in 1975.

Born Leslie Lynch King Jr. in Omaha, Nebraska, on July 14, 1913, he was the son of Martha Alicia Porter King and Leslie Lynch King Sr. His parents were divorced immediately after his birth, and in 1916, his mother married Gerald Rudolf Ford. The boy grew up in Grand Rapids, Michigan, informally known by the same name as his stepfather. In 1935, he legally adopted the name Gerald Rudolph Ford with the slightly different spelling.

Ford graduated from the University of Michigan in 1935, where he had been a star football player. He turned down contracts from the Detroit Lions and the Green Bay Packers to attend Yale Law School, from which he graduated in 1941. Having been admitted to the Michigan Bar in 1941, Ford joined the US Navy and served aboard the USS *Monterey* in the Pacific Theater in 1943 and 1944.

After World War II, Ford returned to Grand Rapids, where in 1948, he married Elizabeth Bloomer "Betty" Warren while in the midst of running for the US House of Representatives. Having been elected, he was reelected a dozen times. During his tenure in the House, Ford served on the Warren Commission investigating the assassination

above: Gerald Ford on the gridiron field at the University of Michigan in 1933. *Ford Library*

top: The 1974 official portrait of President Gerald Ford. *Ford Library*

of John F. Kennedy. Though he complained privately about secret CIA documents that were denied to the commission, he supported the conclusion that Lee Harvey Oswald had acted alone.

Ford rose to national prominence after being named House Minority Leader in 1965. He became an outspoken critic of Lyndon Johnson's Great Society and his handling of the Vietnam War. Ford and Illinois Republican Senator Everett Dirksen spoke out in regularly scheduled, televised press conferences proposing alternatives to Johnson's policies.

The official 1976 presidential portrait of Gerald R. Ford. *Ford Library*

Gerald R. Ford **207**

above: This campaign button from the 1976 election cycle speaks to Mrs. Ford's popularity. *Ford Library*

left: A 1974 photograph of President Gerald Ford and First Lady Betty Ford in the back seat of the presidential limousine. *Ford Library*

FIRST LADY
ELIZABETH "BETTY" BLOOMER FORD

Born in Chicago, Illinois, on April 8, 1918, Elizabeth Ann "Betty" Bloomer was the daughter of Hortense Neahr Bloomer and traveling salesman William Stephenson Bloomer Sr., who died when she was sixteen. The family moved to Denver, and later to Grand Rapids, Michigan, by the time Betty was in high school. She attended the Bennington School of Dance in Vermont, became a student of choreographer Martha Graham, and lived in New York City where she worked as a model. At her mother's insistence, she later returned to Grand Rapids, where she wed salesman and longtime acquaintance William Warren in 1942.

In 1948, after her divorce from Warren, she met Gerald Ford, whom she married on October 15, 1948. When Gerald was elected to Congress the same year, they moved to Virginia, where they lived for the next quarter century, and where they raised their four children, who were born between 1950 and 1957.

The month after becoming first lady, she underwent a mastectomy for breast cancer, which she willingly discussed in the media because she wanted "no cover-up in the Ford administration." The response, which raised breast cancer awareness, was positive. As first lady, she also spoke openly about such previously taboo issues as abortion, premarital sex, and drug use, which brought a mixed response from the media and the public. She actively supported the Equal Rights Amendment, which failed to achieve ratification.

What she did not mention was her own problems with substance abuse, which led to her being forced into rehabilitation by her family in 1978. Having recovered, she lent her name to the founding of the Betty Ford Clinic (later Betty Ford Center), a chemical dependency rehabilitation facility in Rancho Mirage, California.

In 1991, she received the presidential Medal of Freedom, followed by a Congressional Gold Medal in 1999 and the Woodrow Wilson Award in 2003. She passed away on July 8, 2011, in Rancho Mirage and was interred with her husband at the Gerald R. Ford Presidential Museum at Grand Rapids.

The Children of Gerald Ford and Betty Ford
Michael Gerald Ford (1950–)
John Gardner "Jack" Ford (1952–)
Steven Meigs "Steve" Ford (1956–)
Susan Elizabeth Ford Vance Bales (1957–)

The official portrait of Betty Ford. *Ford Library*

above: President Ford in the Oval Office. *Ford Library*

right: Whip Inflation Now (WIN) was an often-lampooned 1974 initiative by the Ford Administration to promote thrift and personal savings to address the inflation that was rampant at the time. Supporters of the program were encouraged to wear "WIN" buttons. *Ford Library*

below: President Ford and Secretary of State Henry Kissinger, conversing, on the grounds of the White House on August 16, 1974. *Ford Library*

Approved by Congress after the resignation of Spiro Agnew, Ford was sworn in as vice president on December 6, 1973. Shortly thereafter, he was briefed of evidence of Nixon's complicity in the Watergate cover-up. On August 9, 1974, Ford was sworn in as president of the United States, and on August 20, he nominated New York Governor Nelson Rockefeller for his vice president.

On September 8, 1974, Ford issued a full presidential pardon to Richard Nixon. He said it was in the interest of national unity, but many from both parties believed that it was part of a secret deal, and the controversial pardon hurt Ford and the Republican Party politically.

Ford's potential legislative agenda was limited by a weak economy and a strong Democratic majority in both houses of Congress, which increased in the 1974 midterm election. In December 1974, when there was a massive invasion of South Vietnam by North Vietnam, Ford proposed an aid initiative that was denied by Congress, and the invaders successfully occupied the south and unified the country under their rule by April 1975.

On September 5, 1975, Lynette "Squeaky" Fromme, a member of the notorious Charles Manson "family" attempted unsuccessfully to shoot Ford in Sacramento, California. Shortly after, on September 22, Sara Jane Moore tried to shoot the

above: President Ford confers with Secretary of Defense Donald Rumsfeld and White House Chief of Staff (and future vice president) Dick Cheney in April 1975. *Ford Library*

below: For the 1976 presidential campaign, Gerald Ford's running mate was Senator Bob Dole. *Ford Library*

opposite page: President Gerald Ford with his golden retriever Liberty in the Oval Office. *Ford Library*

president in San Francisco. Both were arrested and convicted, but were paroled in 2009 and 2007 respectively.

In 1976, Ford was renominated for president at the Republican Convention, but only after he had narrowly staved off a strong challenge from Ronald Reagan. The convention did not nominate incumbent Vice President Rockefeller to run for vice president, but instead chose Kansas Senator Robert Dole. Ford himself called his dumping of Rockefeller as "cowardly," but Rockefeller had shown little enthusiasm. Ford went on to lose a close election to Jimmy Carter by a margin of 297 to 240 in the Electoral College.

After the election, Ford retired to Southern California and remained active with public speaking and service on various corporate boards. He became a good personal friend of Carter, though the two retained policy differences. Ford was widely mentioned as a 1980 Republican presidential candidate, but did not actively pursue a candidacy.

He was in generally good health until late in life, but this declined after he suffered two minor strokes in 2000. When he died at his home in Rancho Mirage, California, of cerebrovascular disease on December 26, 2006, at age ninety-three, he had lived longer than any other president of the United States. He was interred at the Gerald R. Ford Presidential Museum in Grand Rapids.

MY 2 FAVORITE
FORD DOLE
4-LETTER WORDS

NELSON A. ROCKEFELLER

The grandson of the one-time richest man in the world, Nelson Aldrich Rockefeller once asserted that he did not want to be "vice president of anything," but he became the second man to be appointed as vice president of the United States under the Twenty-fifth Amendment. Though part of a family of incredibly wealthy businessmen, Rockefeller eschewed business for politics and served fifteen years as governor of New York while trying several times for the Republican presidential nomination.

Born in Bar Harbor, Maine, July 8, 1908, Nelson was the son of Abigail Greene "Abby" Aldrich Rockefeller and John Davidson Rockefeller Jr. His grandfather, John Davidson Rockefeller Sr., had co-founded the Standard Oil Company in 1870 and had become the world's richest man and America's first billionaire. Nelson Rockefeller graduated from Dartmouth College in New Hampshire in 1930, and worked for many of the family businesses, including several oil

Nelson Rockefeller. *LBJ Library*

companies, the family philanthropic organization, and Chase National (later Chase Manhattan) Bank.

In 1944, he served in the Roosevelt Administration as assistant secretary of state for American Republic Affairs, and in 1945 as a delegate to the United Nations Conference. Rockefeller later served in other appointed posts within the Truman and Eisenhower Administrations. In 1958, he was elected governor of New York, beating incumbent Democrat Averell Harriman, a fellow multimillionaire whose fortune also traced back to the nineteenth century. As governor, he expanded the State University of New York and undertook a massive transportation upgrade in the New York City area.

Running as a Republican moderate, he unsuccessfully sought the presidential nomination in 1960, 1964, and 1968, but remained a leader in the party's "Eastern Establishment." In 1974, Ford brought him in as vice president because of his party roots, his executive experience, and the perception that he would be an asset to the ticket in 1976. However, being a moderate led to his being dropped by the party that year.

Returning to private life, Rockefeller concentrated on philanthropy projects and the family art collection. He died of a heart attack on January 26, 1979, and was cremated.

39

James E. Carter

1977–1981

DEMOCRATIC PARTY

peanut farmer and former Georgia governor named James Earl "Jimmy" Carter was the first president of the United States elected from the South since Zachary Taylor, before whom, most presidents had been from southern states. Carter was also the third president, after Theodore Roosevelt and Woodrow Wilson, to be awarded the Nobel Peace Prize, though it was after his presidency.

The first president to be born in a hospital, he came into the world on October 1, 1924, in Plains, Georgia, the town where he would reside for most of his life. He was the oldest of the three children of businessman and merchant James Earl Carter Sr. and Bessie Lillian Gordy Carter. He initially attended Georgia Southwestern College in Americus, but was later appointed to the US Naval Academy in Annapolis, from which he graduated in 1946. He married Rosalynn Smith in that same year.

As a naval officer, Carter was assigned to the US Navy's nuclear submarine program, then in its formative years, but never commanded a submarine. In 1953, Carter resigned his commission and returned to Plains after the death of his father to help run the family business, the Golden Peanut Company. Because of debts owed by the business, Carter and his family lived in federally subsidized housing until he could turn the business around.

Carter won a seat in the state legislature as a Democrat in 1962 and was reelected in 1964. He gradually became a supporter of the civil rights movement, but this was unpopular among southern Democrats, so he tempered his views in 1966

Images from the 1976 presidential campaign include a Carter-Mondale button (author's collection) and the debate between Carter and Gerald Ford at the Walnut Street Theater in Philadelphia on September 23. *Ford Library*

top: An official White House photo of Jimmy Carter *National Archives*

when he ran unsuccessfully for the Democratic nomination for governor. In 1970, he made a second run for governor, still backing away from his earlier commitment to civil rights. Having been elected, though, he once again embraced desegregation and appointed a number of African-Americans to important posts.

The official presidential portrait of James Earl "Jimmy" Carter was painted by Tyler Robert Mabe. *White House*

FIRST LADY
ROSALYNN SMITH CARTER

Born in Plains, Georgia, on August 18, 1927, Eleanor Rosalynn Smith was the oldest of four children of Allethea "Allie" Murray Smith and Wilburn Edgar Smith, a farmer and mechanic who died of leukemia when Rosalynn was thirteen. She attended Georgia Southwestern College, and planned to attend Georgia State College for Women, until she got married. She wed Jimmy Carter, then enrolled at the US Naval Academy, on July 7, 1946. They had three sons born between 1947 and 1952 and a daughter born in 1967.

Rosalynn helped manage the Golden Peanut Company while Jimmy was on deployment, and when he went into politics, she readily became involved. While he was governor of Georgia, she served on the Commission to Improve Services for the Mentally and Emotionally Handicapped and as honorary chairperson for the Georgia Special Olympics, these issues becoming an important part of her own agenda.

When Carter ran for president, Rosalynn campaigned in forty-one states, often having to explain who the obscure candidate from Georgia was. When he was inaugurated, they made headlines by walking from the Capitol to the White House, rather than riding in a car. When she showed an interest in what was going on within the Administration, he invited her to sit in at cabinet meetings. She joined with Betty Ford in supporting the Equal Rights Amendment, and she testified in Congress—only the second First Lady, after Eleanor Roosevelt, to do so—in support of the Mental Health System Act in 1980.

An official White House portrait of Rosalynn Carter. *National Archives*

After leaving the White House, she was active, along with her husband, in the Carter Center and Habitat for Humanity, as well as with the Rosalynn Carter Institute for Caregiving at Georgia Southwestern State University.

The Children of Jimmy Carter and Rosalynn Smith Carter
John William "Jack" Carter (1947–)
James Earl "Chip" Carter III (1950–)
Donnel Jeffrey "Jeff" Carter (1952–)
Amy Lynn Carter (married to James Gregory Wentzel) (1967–)

President Jimmy Carter signs up for the monthly purchase of a savings bond in the White House Oval Office on April 9, 1980. Defense Secretary Harold Brown, left, served as chairman of the government-wide Savings Bond campaign, and baseball star Pete Rose of the Cincinnati Reds, center, was the honorary chairman. A decade later, Rose was discredited in a sports betting scandal. *Department of Defense*

In 1976, he entered the race for the Democratic presidential nomination with virtually no name recognition. However, in the wake of Watergate, his status as a Washington outsider was resonant and he made a strong early showing in the primaries. He became popular with the national media and younger voters, and went to the Democratic Convention having won twenty-seven primaries. Once nominated, he picked Minnesota Governor Walter Mondale as his running mate.

In the campaign, he faced Republican Gerald Ford in the first presidential election debates since 1960, and only the second debate series in the history of presidential elections. Ford was seen to have won the first of three but lost the second and thereafter slipped from the lead he had in the

President Jimmy Carter tours the TMI-2 Control Room at the Three Mile Island nuclear reactor in Dauphin County, Pennsylvania, on April 1, 1979. This was during the crisis following a partial nuclear meltdown which had occurred at the site on March 28, 1979. It was the worst accident in American commercial nuclear power plant history and one of the most serious domestic crises with which Carter had to cope as president. With him from right to left are Pennsylvania Governor Richard Thornburgh and Nuclear Regulatory Commission Director Harold Denton. *Carter Library*

polls. It was a close election, but Carter won 297 to 240 in the Electoral College and took 50.08 percent of the popular vote.

Carter came into office in the midst of a recession combined with high inflation and scrambled for solutions. He earned the antagonism of the left by bailing out the Chrysler Corporation, and of the right by abrogating the 1903 Hay-Bunau-Varill Treaty and giving the Panama Canal to Panama. In 1977, amid the ongoing effects of higher energy prices, Carter famously called the energy crisis the "Moral Equivalent of War," in an effort to rally the American people, but he offered no specific solution around which to rally.

In 1979, Carter's judgment and decisiveness was further called into question when he invited the deposed Shah of Iran to the United States for medical treatment. The Islamists who had previously seized control of the Iranian government responded with an oil embargo that rivaled that of 1973 to 1974. In turn, Iranian militants seized the United States embassy and held fifty-two American diplomats and citizens hostage for 444 days, until the end of Carter's presidency. Carter responded by going into seclusion for more than three months. A rescue mission was scrubbed when a rescue helicopter crashed into a refueling plane.

In 1980, when the Soviet Union invaded Afghanistan, Carter's response was the controversial move to lead an international boycott of the Moscow Olympic Games.

The 1980 election campaign took place amid the ongoing Energy Crisis and with American hostages still held in Tehran. Carter won the Democratic nomination, but only after fending off an energetic challenge from Edward Kennedy, the youngest brother of John F. Kennedy, who won a dozen

The signature foreign policy triumph of the Carter presidency were the Camp David Accords that were signed by Egyptian President Anwar El Sadat and Israeli Prime Minister Menachem Begin on September 17, 1978. The agreement followed twelve days of secret negotiations at Camp David that were initiated and hosted by President Carter. In the photo below, Carter is obviously delighted to see Begin and Sadat reach to shake hands. The Accords included a "Framework for the Conclusion of a Peace Treaty between Egypt and Israel," which led directly to the 1979 Egypt-Israel Peace Treaty for which Sadat and Begin received the Nobel Peace Prize. The photo at the right shows Carter, Sadat, and Begin at the signing of this peace treaty on March 27, 1979. *Carter Library, both*

In June 2015, Rosalynn and Jimmy Carter teamed up with the US Fish and Wildlife Service to help conserve habitat for the declining monarch butterfly population by donating to expand the Rosalynn Carter Butterfly Trail. Standing next to the former president is Cynthia Dohner, the USFWS Southeast Regional Director. *Carter Center*

primaries, including New York and California. In the general election, Carter faced Republican nominee Ronald Reagan and Republican maverick Congressman John Anderson, running as an independent. Carter lost by a margin of 489 to 49 in the Electoral College.

After leaving the White House, Carter returned to Georgia, led the peanut business, and turned to writing books and lecturing at Emory University. In 1982, he established the Carter Center on the Emory campus, a non-profit, non-governmental institution aimed at promoting human rights and fighting disease worldwide. He and his wife also became active in Habitat for Humanity, a Georgia-based organization dedicated to building affordable housing in disadvantaged locations around the world. Carter himself has been seen swinging a hammer on the group's projects. His efforts since leaving office led to his being awarded the 2002 Nobel Peace Prize.

VICE PRESIDENT

WALTER F. MONDALE

Born in Ceylon, Minnesota, on January 5, 1928, Walter Frederick "Fritz" Mondale was the son of Claribel Hope Cowan Mondale and Reverend Theodore Sigvaard Mondale, a Methodist minister. He graduated from the University of Minnesota in 1951, served as an enlisted man in the US Army during the Korean War and graduated from the University of Minnesota Law School in 1956. He married Joan Adams in 1956, and they had three children.

He worked on Democratic political campaigns beginning with Hubert Humphrey's senatorial campaign in 1948 and was appointed as Minnesota attorney general in 1960. In 1964, he was appointed to the US Senate seat vacated by Hubert Humphrey when he became vice president. Mondale was, in turn, elected to that seat in his own right in 1966. He declined a 1972 invitation to be George McGovern's running mate in order to remain in the Senate. While in the Senate, he served on the committee chaired by Senator Frank Church of Idaho that investigated abuses by the CIA and FBI.

Walter Mondale. *Library of Congress*

In 1976, he accepted Jimmy Carter's invitation to run for vice president, and once in office, he became the first vice president to have an office in the White House. He also functioned actively as the president's trouble-shooter.

Defeated for reelection as vice president in 1980, Mondale ran for the Democratic presidential nomination in 1984. He faced a strong primary challenge from Colorado Senator Gary Hart, who won twenty-six primaries, including most of the Western states, to only nineteen for Mondale. However, Hart's candidacy was derailed by a sex scandal and Mondale defeated him for the nomination at the Democratic Convention by a nearly two-to-one margin. Mondale made history by inviting New York Congresswoman Geraldine Ferraro onto the ticket as his running mate. She was the first woman ever to appear on a major party presidential ticket. In the general election, however, Mondale and Ferraro won only one state, Minnesota, losing to the Reagan-Bush Republican ticket by a margin of 525 to 13 in the Electoral College.

After the 1984 presidential election, Mondale returned to his private law practice, but from 1993 to 1996, during the Clinton Administration, he served as United States Ambassador to Japan. In 2002, when Senator Paul Wellstone of Minnesota was killed in a plane crash while running for reelection, Mondale was asked to take his place on the ballot, where he was narrowly defeated by Republican Norm Coleman.

40

1981–1989

Ronald W. Reagan

REPUBLICAN PARTY

Ronald Wilson Reagan is recalled best by his supporters for having been the driving force behind the end of the Cold War that had been a vexation for his predecessors in the office for four decades. Like John F. Kennedy, he brought an engaging personality, a good sense of humor, an eloquent public speaking style, and a near-photographic memory to the job. In contrast to Kennedy, who was the youngest person elected to the presidency, Reagan, at the age of sixty-nine, was the oldest. A sportscaster turned actor, he was the only president to have been a member of a trade union, the Screen Actors Guild, of which he was president from 1947 to 1952 and from 1959 to 1960.

Born on February 6, 1911, in Tampico, Illinois, Reagan was the second son of salesman John Edward "Jack" Reagan and Nelle Clyde Wilson Reagan. Though of Irish and English lineage, he was known as "Dutch," reportedly for the "Dutch boy" haircut he wore as a small child. He graduated in 1932 from Eureka College in Eureka, Illinois, where he was a member of the football team, captain of the swim team, and student body president. After graduation, he worked as a popular sportscaster on radio stations in Davenport and Des Moines in Iowa.

In 1937, while following the Chicago Cubs on a tour of California, Reagan took a screen test at Warner Brothers and was signed to a seven-year contract. He appeared in thirty films between 1937 and 1941. His most memorable was perhaps *Knute Rockne, All American* (1940). In it, he played George "The Gipper" Gipp and uttered the famous

above: Ronald Reagan as an announcer at WHO Radio in Des Moines, Iowa, circa 1934 to 1937. *Reagan Library*

top: A 1981 official presidential photo of Ronald Reagan. *National Archives*

line "win one for the Gipper." Thereafter, Reagan was often referred to as the "Gipper." The 1942 film *King's Row* made him a star, but World War II intervened and Reagan, a US Army reservist, was ordered to active duty. He volunteered for combat duty with the US Army Air Forces, but his poor eyesight kept him from flying, and he was assigned to the First Motion Picture Unit in California, which produced documentaries and training films. After the war, he starred in another two dozen films, mainly Westerns and action films,

President Ronald Reagan speaking at a campaign rally for Senator David Durenberger in Minneapolis, Minnesota, in 1982. *National Archives*

but is best known for hosting television programs such as the *General Electric Theater* and *Death Valley Days*.

He was married to actress Jane Wyman between 1940 and 1947, but they were divorced, and he married Nancy Davis in 1948.

Originally a Democrat, Reagan supported Dwight Eisenhower, became a Republican, and was a supporter of Barry Goldwater for president in 1964. Reagan's well-received speech at the Republican Convention that year led to his being urged to run for California governor. He defeated two-term Democratic Governor Edmund "Pat" Brown in 1966, and was reelected in 1970. In 1976, he mounted a strong, but unsuccessful, challenge to incumbent President Gerald Ford for the Republican presidential nomination.

In 1980, having established himself as a conservative radio commentator, Reagan again sought the Republican nomination. He won forty-four Republican primaries to only six for his leading challenger, George H. W. Bush. At the convention, he invited Bush onto the ticket as his vice presidential running mate. In the ensuing campaign, they initially trailed the Democratic ticket headed by incumbent President Jimmy Carter but narrowed the gap by focusing on the sluggish economy. In his debate with Carter less than week before the election, Reagan told the electorate "Next Tuesday all of you will go to the polls. You'll stand there in the polling place and make a decision. I think when you make that decision it might be well if you would ask yourself: Are you better off than

JANE WYMAN

The first wife of Ronald Reagan was born Sarah Jane Mayfield on January 15, 1917, in Saint Joseph, Missouri. Actress Jane Wyman was the daughter of Manning Jeffries Mayfield and Gladys Hope Christian Mayfield. Having made her acting debut in 1936, she met Reagan at Warner Brothers, and they were married on January 26, 1940. They had two children of their own, Christine, who lived for only one day, and Maureen. They also adopted John Flaugher, the son of an unwed couple, who became Michael Reagan. Though they were divorced in 1949, Jane Wyman voted for Reagan for president in 1980 and 1984. She continued to act in television roles into the 1990s. She died on September 10, 2007.

FIRST LADY
NANCY DAVIS REAGAN

Born Anne Frances Robbins in New York City on July 6, 1921, she was the daughter of salesman Kenneth Seymour Robbins and actress Edith Luckett Robbins. Known as "Nancy" throughout her life, she was adopted by Dr. Loyal Davis, who became her mother's second husband in 1929, whereupon she officially became Nancy Davis. After graduating from Smith College in Massachusetts in 1943, she began her acting career on Broadway. Relocating to Hollywood, she signed a seven-year contract with Metro-Goldwyn-Mayer Studios in 1949 and went on to appear in supporting roles in eleven feature films. She met Ronald Reagan in 1949, and they were married on March 4, 1952. She continued to act, appearing with her husband in only one film, *Hellcats of the Navy* (1957). She retired from acting in 1962.

Nancy Reagan had a close relationship with her husband throughout their marriage, but her relationship with her children, Patti and Ron, was strained as their political opposition to their father often became personal. She was never close to her husband's children from his first marriage.

She played an active but understated role in her husband's campaigns for governor of California in 1966 and 1970, for the presidential nomination in 1976, and for president of the United States in 1980 and 1984.

As with previous first ladies, she took an interest in White House renovations and in putting her own stamp on the executive mansion, raising money for extensive redecorating, and acquisition of new White House dishware. As a former actress, she demonstrated a style that won high marks from fashion editors and comparisons to Jacqueline Kennedy. Nancy Reagan is also remembered as first lady for her "Just Say No" drug awareness campaign which began in 1982. Pursuing this initiative, she traveled extensively and made frequent media appearances. She was deeply concerned for her husband's safety after the 1981 assassination attempt and became overly protective, which often found her at odds with his staff. Her own troubles during her time as first lady included a diagnosis of breast cancer which led to her mastectomy in 1987.

After leaving the White House, she and her husband retired to California. When he was diagnosed with Alzheimer's disease, she became his chief caregiver and was active with the National Alzheimer's Association. In 2002, Nancy Reagan was awarded the Presidential Medal of Freedom, and she and her husband were jointly awarded the Congressional Gold Medal.

After Ronald Reagan's death, Nancy remained active in projects associated with the Ronald Reagan Presidential Library, including her hosting of a 2012 Republican Presidential Debate.

The Children of Ronald Reagan and Jane Wyman

Maureen Elizabeth Reagan (1941–2001)
Michael Reagan (adopted son, born John Flaugher) (1945–)
Christine Reagan (1947–1947)

The Children of Ronald Reagan and Nancy Davis Reagan

Patti Davis (name legally changed from Patricia Ann Reagan) (1952–)
Ronald Prescott "Ron" Reagan (1958–)

left: The official White House portrait of Nancy Reagan. *National Archives*

you were four years ago?" In the general election, Reagan defeated Carter by 489 to 49 in the Electoral College, while taking 50.75 percent of the popular vote.

Reagan's economic agenda, nicknamed "Reaganomics" by its detractors, focused on a free market and tax reduction through the Economic Recovery Tax Act of 1981. According to the Bureau of Labor Statistics, the rate of growth in American Gross Domestic Product went from a 0.3 percent decline in 1980 to 4.1 percent growth in 1988, averaging 7.91 percent annual growth in current dollars during Reagan's presidency. Meanwhile, the unemployment rate declined from 7.1 percent in 1980 to 5.5 percent in 1988, while the inflation rate declined from 13.5 percent in 1980 to 4.1 percent in 1988. Despite his tax cuts and the Tax Reform Act of 1986, federal receipts grew at an annual average of 8.2 percent according to the Office of Management and Budget.

On national defense, Reagan had advocated a hard line that contrasted with Carter's cautious and conciliatory approach. The effect of this on the global perception of the United States is best illustrated by the fact that the American hostages who had been kept captive for 444 days of Carter's term were released within minutes of Reagan being sworn into office.

His approach to national defense and the Cold War differed markedly from that of his predecessors who had pursued a policy of parity with the Soviet Union and preventing nuclear war only through the perpetual threat of nuclear war. Reagan instead pursued an end to the Cold War through a policy of "peace through strength" that involved a substantial increase in defense spending and expanding the American armed forces. He went on to formulate the "Reagan Doctrine," under which the United States actively and militarily supported anti-communist and anti-Soviet resistance movements throughout the world through both overt

Ronald Reagan riding his Arabian horse El Alamein at his California Ranch, Rancho del Cielo. According to the National Archives, "El Alamein was given to Reagan in 1981 by Mexican President José López Portillo. . . . Though many reports call the horse 'white,' it is actually a gray." Reagan was an accomplished horseman. *National Archives*

FROM RONALD REAGAN'S
FIRST INAUGURAL ADDRESS
January 20, 1981

These United States are confronted with an economic affliction of great proportions. We suffer from the longest and one of the worst sustained inflations in our national history. It distorts our economic decisions, penalizes thrift, and crushes the struggling young and the fixed income elderly alike. It threatens to shatter the lives of millions of our people. Idle industries have cast workers into unemployment, human misery and personal indignity.

In this present crisis, government is not the solution to our problem; government is the problem. From time to time we've been tempted to believe that society has become too complex to be managed by self rule, that government by an elite group is superior to government for, by, and of the people. But if no one among us is capable of governing himself, then who among us has the capacity to govern someone else?

We are a nation that has a government—not the other way around. And this makes us special among the nations of the earth. Our Government has no power except that granted it by the people. It is time to check and reverse the growth of government which shows signs of having grown beyond the consent of the governed.

It is my intention to curb the size and influence of the Federal establishment and to demand recognition of the distinction between the powers granted to the Federal Government and those reserved to the states or to the people.

All of us—all of us need to be reminded that the Federal Government did not create the states; the states created the Federal Government.

To those neighbors and allies who share our freedom, we will strengthen our historic ties and assure them of our support and firm commitment. We will match loyalty with loyalty. We will strive for mutually beneficial relations. We will not use our friendship to impose on their sovereignty, for our own sovereignty is not for sale.

As for the enemies of freedom, those who are potential adversaries, they will be reminded that peace is the highest aspiration of the American people. We will negotiate for it, sacrifice for it; we will not surrender for it—now or ever. Our forbearance should never be misunderstood. Our reluctance for conflict should not be misjudged as a failure of will. When action is required to preserve our national security, we will act. We will maintain sufficient strength to prevail if need be, knowing that if we do so, we have the best chance of never having to use that strength.

Above all we must realize that no arsenal or no weapon in the arsenals of the world is so formidable as the will and moral courage of free men and women. It is a weapon our adversaries in today's world do not have. It is a weapon that we as Americans do have. Let that be understood by those who practice terrorism and prey upon their neighbors.

Ronald Reagan prepares to give a speech at the recommissioning ceremony for the battleship USS *New Jersey* at the Long Beach Naval Shipyard in California in May 1986. *US Navy*

and covert actions. Among other actions, Reagan sent United States troops to the island of Grenada in 1983 to remove a Marxist government imposed by a coup and to rescue several hundred Americans.

In a June 8, 1982, speech to the British Parliament, Reagan correctly predicted that "the forward march of freedom and democracy will leave Marxism-Leninism on the ash heap of history." He goaded the Soviet Union, describing it on March 8, 1983, as an "evil empire."

Also in March 1983, Reagan announced the Strategic Defense Initiative, a development program aimed at exploring ground- and space-based technology for defending against attacks by Soviet nuclear-armed missiles. Detractors in the United States nicknamed it "Star Wars," insisting that it could not work. However, the Soviets took it seriously. This and other Reagan Administration defense initiatives convinced the Soviet leadership to rethink their own nuclear ambitions. Negotiating from a position of strength, Reagan met four times with Soviet leader Mikhail Gorbachev, gradually unwinding Cold War tensions.

On March 30, 1981, less than four months into his presidency, Reagan became the first sitting president to survive a

above: President and Mrs. Reagan waving from the limousine during the Inaugural Parade in Washington, DC, on Inauguration Day, 1981. *National Archives*

below: Ronald Reagan delivering the 1983 State of the Union address. *Reagan Library*

bullet wound in an assassination attempt. He and three others were hit by bullets fired by would-be assassin John Hinckley as they exited the Hilton Hotel in Washington, DC, after the president delivered a speech. Reagan was taken to George Washington University Hospital, where he was stabilized and successfully recovered. At trial, Hinckley was found not guilty by reason of insanity, but placed under institutional psychiatric care.

At the 1984 Republican Convention, President Reagan and Vice President Bush were easily renominated, and went on to face the Democratic nominees, former Vice President Walter Mondale and New York Congresswoman Geraldine Ferraro.

When Mondale made an issue of Reagan's age, the president replied with the promise "I will not make age an issue of this campaign. I am not going to exploit, for political purposes, my opponent's youth and inexperience." In the general election, Reagan won 525 electoral votes to 13 for Mondale, and received 58.77 percent of the popular vote.

In his second term, Reagan faced the biggest foreign policy embarrassment of his presidency, the so-called

On June 12, 1987 President Reagan gave a speech at the Berlin Wall, in which he challenged Soviet leader Mikhail Gorbachev to "tear down this wall!" *National Archives*

Iran-Contra Scandal. It was an extraordinarily complicated scheme undertaken by members of the Administration, without, as they later insisted, the full knowledge of the president. At one end of the intrigue were several Americans held hostage in Lebanon by terrorists with links to the leaders of Iran. On the other end was a desire by Reagan and his Administration to support the Contra insurgent movement that was attempting to overthrow the pro-Communist Sandinista government of Nicaragua. Because direct aid to the Contras was prohibited by Congress, members of Reagan's national security team hatched a scheme to acquire the money elsewhere. The idea was to sell arms—using Israel as an intermediary—to a moderate opposition faction within the Iranian government with the hope that it could influence both a change of Iranian leadership and the release of the hostages. The profits of the sale would go to the Contras. The arms were delivered, and some of

the hostages were released, but the scheme was exposed before it fully evolved. A number of Administration officials, including Secretary of Defense Caspar Weinberger and National Security Advisor Robert McFarlane, were indicted for wrongdoing. They and others were later pardoned by President George H. W. Bush.

Reagan's second term was dominated by his ongoing efforts to achieve a drawdown of nuclear weapons and an end to the Cold War. A turning point came during his visit to the Berlin Wall on June 12, 1987. In his speech there. Reagan issued a challenge to Gorbachev, explaining "if you seek peace, if you seek prosperity for the Soviet Union and Eastern Europe, if you seek liberalization, come here to this gate! Mr. Gorbachev, open this gate! Mr. Gorbachev, tear down this wall!"

The Soviet leader let it be known that he was willing to make a deal. In December 1987, Reagan and Gorbachev

President Reagan and Soviet General Secretary Gorbachev enjoy a lighter moment during their first summit conference, held in Geneva, Switzerland in 1985. *Reagan Library*

FROM RONALD REAGAN'S FAREWELL ADDRESS
January 11, 1989

The lesson of all this was, of course, that because we're a great nation, our challenges seem complex. It will always be this way. But as long as we remember our first principles and believe in ourselves, the future will always be ours. And something else we learned: Once you begin a great movement, there's no telling where it will end. We meant to change a nation, and instead, we changed a world. . . .

"We the people" tell the government what to do, it doesn't tell us. "We the people" are the driver, the government is the car. And we decide where it should go, and by what route, and how fast. Almost all the world's constitutions are documents in which governments tell the people what their privileges are. Our Constitution is a document in which "We the people" tell the government what it is allowed to do. "We the people" are free. . . .

I hope we once again have reminded people that man is not free unless government is limited. There's a clear cause and effect here that is as neat and predictable as a law of physics: As government expands, liberty contracts. . . .

I've spoken of the shining city all my political life . . . it was a tall, proud city built on rocks stronger than oceans, windswept, God blessed, and teeming with people of all kinds living in harmony and peace; a city with free ports that hummed with commerce and creativity. And if there had to be city walls, the walls had doors and the doors were open to anyone with the will and the heart to get here. That's how I saw it, and see it still.

And how stands the city on this winter night? More prosperous, more secure, and happier than it was eight years ago. But more than that: After two hundred years, two centuries, she still stands strong and true on the granite ridge, and her glow has held steady no matter what storm. And she's still a beacon, still a magnet for all who must have freedom, for all the pilgrims from all the lost places who are hurtling through the darkness, toward home.

met in Washington to sign the Intermediate Range Nuclear Forces Treaty, and they agreed to ongoing Strategic Arms Reduction Talks. When Reagan visited Gorbachev in Moscow in 1988, he conceded that the Evil Empire of which he had spoken in 1983 was a thing of the past.

Within a year of Reagan leaving office, the Berlin Wall had been torn down and Marxism-Leninism was in the final stages of unraveling. Though his approval rating dipped below 50 percent in the wake of the Iran-Contra Affair, Reagan's popularity remained generally high throughout his presidency. When he left office, Gallup reported him with a 64 percent approval rating, the highest yet recorded for an outgoing president.

After leaving the White House, Reagan and his wife divided their time between a home in Bel Air, California, and their ranch in Santa Barbara County which had served as the "Western White House" during the presidential years. His last major public appearance was at the funeral of former President Richard Nixon in 1994. A few months later, he was diagnosed with Alzheimer's disease. In his final statement, he said "I now begin the journey that will lead me into the sunset of my life. I know that for America there will always be a bright dawn ahead."

After breaking his hip in a fall in 2001, his health deteriorated, and he died on June 5, 2004. Following a state funeral in Washington, DC, Ronald Reagan was interred on the grounds of the Ronald Reagan Presidential Library in Simi Valley, California.

VICE PRESIDENT
GEORGE H. W. BUSH

In the 1980 Republican Presidential primaries, Ronald Reagan's principal opponent was former Congressman George Herbert Walker Bush, who developed an early lead in the delegate count prior to the New Hampshire Primary, but slipped behind Reagan. At the Republican Convention, Reagan picked Bush as his running mate. After four years in the White House, Bush would remain for four more years in the top job. Bush and his own presidency are described in detail in the following chapter.

41

1989–1993

George H. W. Bush

REPUBLICAN PARTY

George H. W. Bush came to office having compiled one of the most extensive and varied résumés in American presidential history. Successful in business, he went on to serve in the US House of Representatives, as a diplomat, as chairman of the Republican Party, as the director of the Central Intelligence Agency, and as the first sitting vice president of the United States since Martin Van Buren to progress directly into the presidency. He also had two sons who were governors, one of whom became president of the United States.

Born in Milton, Massachusetts, on June 12, 1924, he was the son of wealthy and well-connected businessman Prescott Sheldon Bush and Dorothy Walker Bush, whose father was George Herbert Walker. George Bush graduated from the Phillips Academy in Andover, Massachusetts, in 1942, shortly after the United States entered World War II and enlisted in the US Navy as an aviator. He served as a torpedo bomber pilot aboard the USS *San Jacinto*, flying fifty-eight combat missions in a series of battles in the western Pacific during 1944. He was shot down once but was rescued by a US Navy submarine and returned to duty. In 1945, having returned to the United States to help train torpedo bomber pilots, Bush married Barbara Pierce, the daughter of a New York publisher.

After his discharge from the US Navy, Bush enrolled at Yale University, from which he graduated in 1948. He and Barbara then moved with their family to Texas, where George

above: George Bush, Yale baseball team captain, receives Babe Ruth's autobiography manuscript. *National Archives*

top: A 1989 official portrait of President George H. W. Bush. *National Archives*

President Bush hiked on the Kaibab Trail at the Grand Canyon in Arizona on September 18, 1991. *George Bush Library/The National Archives*

started out in the oil business, first as an employee of Dresser Industries, where his father had connections, and later as a partner in several start-ups. Having become wealthy and successful in his own right, Bush developed an interest in politics. In 1964, he failed in a bid for the US Senate, but he was elected to the US House of Representatives in 1966 and reelected in 1968. In 1970, President Richard Nixon convinced Bush to run again for the US Senate, but he lost. In turn, Nixon named him as the US Ambassador to the United Nations in 1971. Two years later, amid the Watergate Scandal, Nixon asked Bush to take over as chairman of the Republican Party. In this role, Bush advised Nixon to resign for the good of the party.

In 1974, after Nixon's resignation, President Gerald Ford named Bush to serve as the head of the US Liaison Office to the People's Republic of China. At the time, the United States was in the process of winding down its long-standing recognition of the Republic of China on Taiwan and transferring its recognition to mainland China, so the Liaison Office was a precursor to the eventual embassy and Bush's role was that of the de facto ambassador. In January 1976, Ford brought Bush back to Washington, DC, to head the Central Intelligence Agency at a time that it was being exposed for a myriad of wrongdoings, and morale was hitting rock bottom. Bush remained on the job for a year until the Democrats took the White House, and he then returned to the private sector.

In 1980, having launched his own bid for the White House, Bush did well at the start of the campaign, optimistically characterizing his momentum as the "Big Mo." Soon, however, the bigger "Mo" belonged to Reagan. At the Republican

FIRST LADY
BARBARA PIERCE BUSH

Born in the New York City Borough of Queens on June 8, 1925, Barbara Pierce was the third child and second daughter of Pauline Robinson Pierce and publisher Marvin Pierce, later the president of McCall Corporation. She was also a distant cousin of President Franklin Pierce. She grew up in Rye, New York, and met George H. W. Bush when they were both students at Phillips Academy in Massachusetts. They were married on January 6, 1945, after Bush returned from World War II. They had six children, all of whom lived into the twenty-first century, except Robin Bush, who died of leukemia at the age of three. This deeply tormented Barbara, whose hair turned from brown to white shortly thereafter.

During her husband's early political career, she was active on various political and charitable activities, but during his time at the CIA, he was not allowed to discuss his day-to-day activities with her, which she found deeply depressing. She spoke at the 1988 Republican Convention and found her niche as first lady as an outspoken advocate of literacy. She founded the Barbara Bush Foundation, a non-profit organization that is still active.

An official 1989 portrait of Barbara Bush. *National Archives*

The Children of George and Barbara Bush

George Walker Bush (1946–)
Pauline Robinson "Robin" Bush (1949–1953)
John Ellis "Jeb" Bush (1953–)
Neil Mallon Bush (1955–)
Marvin Pierce Bush (1956–)
Dorothy Bush Koch (1959–)

President and Mrs. Bush with their grandchildren on the rocks at Walker's Point in Kennebunkport, Maine, in 1989. *National Archives*

The George H. W. Bush inauguration on January 20, 1989. *National Archives*

Convention, Reagan brought him aboard as his running mate. Vice President Bush avoided the limelight while handling a variety of special projects for Reagan and attending ceremonial functions. Shortly after being reelected as vice president in 1984, Bush began planning for his next White House bid.

His early preparation, as well as his being vice president, positioned Bush to do well in the state primaries, where he won forty-one out of fifty. Having been nominated, Bush chose James Danforth Quayle as his running mate, and together they faced the Democratic Party ticket headed by Massachusetts Governor Michael Dukakis with his running mate, US Senator Lloyd Bentsen of Texas. The Republicans won handily with 426 electoral votes to 111 for the Democrats, while taking 53.37 percent of the popular vote.

At the Convention, Bush had famously said "read my lips, no new taxes," but a Democratic Congressional majority forced him to compromise, and this cost him credibility. Meanwhile, the strength of the economy that Bush had inherited from Reagan began to wane, and with it, Bush's popularity.

Bush's first major international crisis came in Panama in 1989, when Manuel Noriega, the notorious drug trafficker who had ruled as military dictator since 1983, annulled the Panamanian presidential election, creating widespread unrest. Bush ordered military action to restore order and arrest Noriega on drug charges.

Elsewhere on the international scene, Bush was at the helm as the Berlin Wall finally came down and the Soviet Union imploded. In July 1991, immediately prior to the latter, Bush

VICE PRESIDENT

JAMES D. QUAYLE

Born in Indianapolis, Indiana, on February 4, 1947, James Danforth "Dan" Quayle was the son of newspaper publisher James Cline Quayle and Martha Corinne Pulliam Quayle. He was raised in Arizona, but returned to Indiana to attend DePauw University, from which he graduated in 1969. While attending the Indiana University law school, he worked for the office of the Indiana attorney general as an investigator. After earning his law degree in 1974, he worked as an associate publisher of one of his family's newspapers.

James Danforth Quayle. *National Archives*

Quayle entered politics in 1976 with a successful bid for the US House of Representatives, to which he was reelected by a substantial margin in 1978. In 1980, he became the youngest person ever elected to the US Senate from Indiana. Reelected in 1986, Quayle was invited by George H. W. Bush to join the Republican ticket as the vice presidential candidate in 1988.

As vice president, he was widely ridiculed for his being inarticulate and for having a poor grasp of the facts. His signature gaffe came on June 12, 1992, at a New Jersey elementary school spelling bee. A student correctly spelled the word "potato," but Quayle insisted that it should be spelled "potatoe." Two months later, at the Republican Convention, there was a move to replace the embarrassing Quayle with an alternate candidate, but George Bush remained loyal to his running mate and he remained on the ticket through the unsuccessful reelection bid.

After his defeat in 1992, Quayle considered running for Indiana governor but later relocated permanently to Arizona. He did announce his candidacy for the 2000 Republican presidential nomination, though he withdrew before the primaries. He remained in the private sector, working as an investment banker, while serving on a number of corporate boards.

met with Mikhail Gorbachev in Helsinki to sign the Strategic Arms Reduction Treaty, which had been in negotiation since Reagan was in the White House.

The biggest international event of the Bush presidency was the Gulf War. It began in August 1990, when Iraq's Saddam Hussein sent a large military force to occupy and annex oil-rich Kuwait, while threatening Saudi Arabia. With a substantial proportion of the world's oil reserves suddenly controlled or threatened by the capricious dictator, Bush ordered, with Congressional authorization, a massive American military deployment to protect Saudi Arabia and prepare to liberate Kuwait. A series of United Nations Security Council Resolutions condemned the occupation, imposed sanctions and gave Saddam a deadline of January 15, 1991, to withdraw. This, in turn, allowed for a coalition of more than a dozen countries to be formed for the upcoming military action. When the deadline came and went, the coalition air forces, primarily American, with British and other participation,

launched Operation Desert Storm, a massive air campaign aimed at destroying Iraqi command and control systems within Iraq itself, as well as Iraqi forces in Kuwait. When the ground campaign began on February 24, the coalition ground forces—mainly American—were able to eject Iraqi forces and liberate Kuwait in one hundred hours.

The Gallup Poll reported that Bush's approval rating soared eighteen points with the beginning of Desert Storm and topped out at a historic 89 percent after the successful completion of the Gulf War in March.

With this, it was assumed that Bush would be easily reelected in 1992. However, he faced a stiff challenge in the Republican primaries from conservative columnist Pat Buchanan, a former advisor to President Reagan. Though Bush won all the primaries, he reached the Republican Convention having spent the primary season on the defensive during a period of worsening economic conditions. In turn, the independent candidacy of maverick Texas

President Bush with Gen. H. Norman Schwarzkopf during his visit with troops in Saudi Arabia in November 1990. *National Archives*

billionaire businessman H. Ross Perot diverted many potential Bush votes.

The Democrats, meanwhile, nominated Arkansas Governor William Jefferson "Bill" Clinton, who was twenty-two years younger than Bush, and who was seen as a fresh new face at a time when there was a mood for change. Clinton, like Buchanan, made ample use of the irony of Bush's unkept promise, "read my lips, no new taxes."

In the general election, Clinton won 370 electoral votes and 43.01 percent of the popular vote to 168 and 37.45 percent for Bush. Perot won no electoral votes, but captured 18.91 percent of the popular vote.

Bush and his wife divided their time between Houston, Texas, and the Bush family compound in Kennebunkport, Maine, while remaining active in various charity and Republican Party activities. After his retirement, two of his sons entered politics. His eldest, George Walker Bush, served as governor of Texas from 1995 to 2000 and as president of the United States from 2001 to 2009. Second son John Ellis "Jeb" Bush served as governor of Florida from 1999 to 2007 and was later mentioned as a potential presidential candidate.

George H. W. Bush, who made one of his earliest parachute jumps from a damaged bomber during World War II, made good on a promise to make a parachute jump on June 12, 2014, his ninetieth birthday, as he had on his eightieth and eighty-fifth.

above: President Bush addresses the ceremony for the Fiftieth Commemorative Anniversary of the Pearl Harbor attack at the USS *Arizona* Memorial on December 7, 1991. "I have no rancor in my heart toward Germany or Japan, none at all," said the president, who fought in World War II and was shot down by Japanese gunfire in 1944. "I hope you have none in yours. This is no time for recrimination. . . . World War II is over. It is history. We won. We crushed totalitarianism, and when that was done we helped our enemies give birth to democracies." *National Archives*

below: President Bush walks with his dogs, Millie and Ranger, at Camp David in November 1991. *National Archives*

42

1993–2001

William J. Clinton

DEMOCRATIC PARTY

The first Democrat to be elected to two consecutive terms as president of the United States since Franklin Roosevelt, William Jefferson "Bill" Clinton was also the first president since Roosevelt to make more than fifty international trips. He was the second president to be impeached, and, like Andrew Johnson, he was acquitted in his trial in the US Senate. Clinton was also the first president to embrace the Internet by launching an official website (whitehouse.gov) in 1994 at a time when very few websites existed and a majority of Americans had yet to grasp the concept.

Born William Jefferson Blythe Jr. in Hope, Arkansas, on August 19, 1946, he was the only son of Virginia Dell Cassidy Blythe and traveling salesman William Jefferson Blythe Sr., who was killed in a car wreck three months before his son was born. Billy, as he was known, was initially raised by his grandparents, while his mother lived in New Orleans. She returned in 1950, married Roger Clinton Sr., and the family moved to Hot Springs, Arkansas. William Jefferson Blythe formally became William Jefferson Clinton in 1961, taking on the surname of a hard-drinking stepfather who was brutally violent toward Billy, his mother, and his stepbrother, to the extent that young Clinton was compelled to intervene physically to protect his mother.

Bill Clinton traced his interest in politics to his having met John F. Kennedy at the White House during a high school trip to Washington. As a student at Georgetown University, he clerked for Arkansas Senator William Fulbright. After graduating in 1968, he earned a Rhodes Scholarship to study

above: Arkansas Governor Bill Clinton in 1983 with Dr. Ron Hart of the National Center for Toxicological Research. *FDA*

top: An official portrait of President Bill Clinton. *National Archive*

at University College, Oxford in Britain, but did not earn a degree. He did earn his law degree from Yale University in 1973 and took a job as a law professor at the University of Arkansas in 1974. While at Yale, he met Hillary Rodham, whom he married in 1975. His political career began with an unsuccessful run for the US House of Representatives in 1974, but in 1976, he was elected Arkansas attorney general. Two years later, at age thirty-two, he was elected governor of Arkansas, becoming the youngest governor in the country. He

President Clinton confers with Defense Secretary William Cohen on September 18, 1997, during the celebration of the fiftieth anniversary of the US Air Force. *Defense Department*

lost his reelection bid, but he was elected to a second term in 1982 and remained in the post for a decade. During the 1980s, Bill and Hillary Clinton were investors in the Whitewater Development Corporation, a land company that eventually failed and was investigated by the US Securities and Exchange Commission. Though the Clintons were never charged with wrongdoing, their association with the Whitewater scandal was later used by their political opponents.

Clinton gave the opening speech at the 1988 Democratic Convention and was mentioned as a potential future presidential candidate. In 1992, Clinton made a poor showing in the early Democratic Primaries, but gradually developed momentum and clinched the nomination after winning in New York and California. During his campaign against the once-popular George H. W. Bush, Clinton contrasted his youthfulness with Bush's age and reminded voters of Bush's failed promise not to raise taxes. In the general election, Clinton and his running mate, Senator Albert Gore of Tennessee, won 370 electoral votes and 43.01 percent of the popular vote, compared to 168 and 37.45 percent for Bush and Dan Quayle. Independent candidate H. Ross Perot and his running mate, retired Adm. James Stockdale, won

FIRST LADY
HILLARY RODHAM CLINTON

The first former first lady to later be elected to the US Senate and the first to serve in a presidential cabinet, Hillary Diane Rodham Clinton is also the first former first lady to actively campaign for the presidency in her own right. She was born in Chicago on October 26, 1947, the oldest child and only daughter of Dorothy Emma Howell Rodham and successful businessman Hugh Ellsworth Rodham. Hillary entered Wellesley College in Massachusetts in 1965, and became politically active in presidential politics, first as a supporter of liberal Republican Nelson Rockefeller, and later of liberal Democratic Senator Eugene McCarthy.

After graduating from Wellesley in 1969, she entered the Yale Law School, where she met Bill Clinton. They both campaigned for Democratic presidential candidate George McGovern in 1972, and both graduated from Yale Law School in 1973. After failing the District of Columbia Bar Exam, a fact that she did not reveal for three decades, she decided to follow Bill Clinton to Arkansas in 1974, where they both taught at the University of Arkansas Law School in Fayetteville. They were married on October 11, 1975, and their daughter, Chelsea, was born in 1980.

They maintained separate professional careers, he as Arkansas attorney general and later as governor, and she in the private sector with the well-connected Rose Law Firm, where she became a full partner in 1979. She also served on the board of the New World Foundation, a funding source for various liberal organizations, and as the first female member of the Wal-Mart board of directors.

During the 1992 presidential campaign, she worked actively for her husband's candidacy and garnered national attention by standing by him as he denied accusations of his having had an affair with actress and performer Gennifer Flowers, an affair which he much later confirmed. As first lady, she took the non-traditional role as an active advisor to the president and chaired the Task Force on National Health Care Reform.

As her husband's second term was coming to a close, Hillary Clinton was urged by Democratic Party leaders to run for an open US Senate seat in New York in the 2000 election, which she did. Widely criticized for never having lived in the state before moving there to run, she was nevertheless elected. As a Senator, she supported President George W. Bush's military initiatives in Afghanistan and Iraq, but opposed his tax cut proposals. In 2006, she was reelected to a second term.

In 2007, Hillary Clinton announced that she was a candidate for the Democratic nomination for president in the 2008 election. Though she led in the polls prior to the primary season, she showed poorly in the early primaries. She remained a close second to Barack Obama in delegate count until he reached a sufficient number to be considered the presumptive nominee, whereupon she dropped out and endorsed him. After he was elected, she left the US Senate to serve as secretary of state through Obama's entire first term. During this time, she visited 112 countries, making her the most widely traveled secretary of state in history. In 2015, she announced that she was a candidate for the Democratic nomination in the 2016 presidential election.

The Daughter of Bill Clinton and Hillary Rodham Clinton
Chelsea Victoria Clinton Mezvinsky (1980–)

above: The official 2009 portrait of Hillary Rodham Clinton as US Secretary of State. *Department of State*

below: The official photo of President Clinton and Hillary Rodham Clinton with the 1996 White House Christmas tree. *White House photo from the Clinton Digital Library*

above: Bill Clinton takes the oath of office from Chief Justice William Rehnquist during his presidential inauguration on January 20, 1993. His daughter, Chelsea, is on his right, and his wife, Hillary Rodham Clinton (wearing a hat), is on his left. *Official White House photograph*

a substantial 18.91 percent of the popular vote, possibly tipping the outcome to Clinton.

Though Clinton had run on a promise of reducing taxes on the middle class, he instead chose to raise taxes, considering deficit reduction a higher priority. Another major initiative of Clinton's first year in office was a health care reform plan that was drafted by a panel chaired by Hillary Clinton. Despite a Democratic majority in both houses of Congress, there was little enthusiasm for the plan.

One of Clinton's biggest first-term successes was the passage of the North American Free Trade Agreement (NAFTA), which he strongly supported, and which created a continental free trade zone, lowering tariffs among Canada, Mexico, and the United States. With its having narrowly passed in Congress, Clinton signed it into law in January 1994.

In 1993, troops assigned to an American peacekeeping mission in the failed state of Somalia came under fire during a mission to capture a renegade warlord. Two US Army Black hawk helicopters were downed and a number of troops killed in an extended firefight. Video of American bodies being dragged through the streets provided a graphic illustration of the growing threat. Clinton responded by pulling the American presence out of Somalia.

Clinton suffered a setback in the 1994 midterm elections when the Republicans took control of the US Senate for the

VICE PRESIDENT

ALBERT A. GORE

Albert Arnold "Al" Gore was born in Washington, DC, on March 31, 1948, the son of longtime Tennessee Democratic political icon Albert Arnold "Al" Gore Sr. and Pauline LaFon Gore. The elder Gore served in the US House of Representatives for fourteen years and in the US Senate for eighteen. His son served for eight years in each of the two houses, and for eight years as vice president of the United States. The younger Albert Gore grew up in Washington, spending his summers on the family farm in Tennessee. He graduated from Harvard University

Vice President Al Gore. *National Archives*

in 1969 and, though he and his father both opposed the Vietnam War, he enlisted in the US Army. He spent several months in an engineering brigade in Vietnam prior to his discharge in 1971. He enrolled at Vanderbilt University in Nashville, first in the divinity school and later in the law school. In 1976, without having finished law school, he ran for and was elected to his father's former Congressional seat. In turn, he was elected to the US Senate in 1984.

Gore's first bid for the Democratic nomination for the presidency came in 1988, during which he won seven primaries before dropping out. In 1992, he chose not to run for the nomination but was asked by Bill Clinton to join the ticket as the vice presidential nominee. As vice president, Gore was a leading proponent of the broad development of information technology and its integration into public and private life. However, he is widely criticized for going so far as to tell Wolf Blitzer of CNN in 1999 that "I took the initiative in creating the Internet," a clumsy misstatement that made it sound as though he was claiming the creation of something which he clearly had not created.

In 2000, Gore ran for the Democratic presidential nomination for a second time, this time winning all of the primaries. He chose Connecticut Senator Joseph Isadore "Joe" Lieberman as his running mate, and together they faced Republicans George W. Bush and Richard "Dick" Cheney in one of the closest and most controversial presidential elections in history. The election was so close that neither party had sufficient electoral votes until a recount of votes in Florida gave the win to Bush.

After leaving office, Gore remained active in Democratic Party affairs, but declined to run again for the party's presidential nomination. Instead, he became active in environmental issues and in 2007, he shared the Nobel Peace Prize with the United Nations Intergovernmental Panel on Climate Change for "their efforts to build up and disseminate greater knowledge about man-made climate change, and to lay the foundations for the measures that are needed to counteract such change."

top: President William Clinton enjoys a school lunch at Patrick Henry Elementary School in Alexandria, Virginia, on March 9, 1995, in celebration of the National School Lunch Program. *US Department of Agriculture*

right: William Clinton greets people at a Democratic "Get out the vote" rally in Los Angeles on November 2, 2000. *National Archives*

first time since 1984 and of the US House of Representatives for the first time since 1952. With the opposition in control of both houses for the remainder of his presidency, Clinton found himself having to compromise with Republican leaders, especially Georgia Congressman Newt Gingrich, the new Speaker of the House.

In 1996, Clinton and Gore were challenged for reelection by Kansas Senator Robert Dole, running with former New York Congressman Jack Kemp. The Democrats won 379 to 159 in the Electoral College and 49.24 to 40.71 percent in the popular vote. H. Ross Perot ran again, but took only 8.4 percent of the popular vote.

Throughout his second term, as Clinton moved to the center to compromise with the Republicans, the economy gradually improved and both sides were able to take credit. The Bureau of Labor Statistics reports that during the years that Clinton worked with a Republican Congress, the Gross Domestic Product grew steadily and unemployment fell from 6.6 percent to 4.2 percent.

Internationally, serious challenges arose. Throughout the 1990s, as Yugoslavia disintegrated and the grisly phrase

"ethnic cleansing" entered the vernacular, the United States attempted to broker a peace between factions. NATO air strikes led to a fragile peace deal brokered by the Clinton Administration in Dayton, Ohio, in 1995, but war broke out again in 1999 as Serbia attempted to prevent the creation of Kosovo as a state. This required a further American-led NATO military intervention to defeat the Serbian armed forces and stabilize the region.

In the meantime, Clinton began to experience the rise of new terrorist threats that would eventually torment his successors. In August 1998, Americans first became aware of Osama bin Laden and al-Qaeda when they launched deadly and coordinated bombing attacks on the American embassies in Kenya and Tanzania. Clinton responded with cruise missile attacks at suspected al-Qaeda facilities in Afghanistan and Sudan, though the latter proved to be unrelated to the terrorist group.

Clinton's most perplexing second term personal predicament came as a result of his extramarital affair with Monica Lewinsky, a White House aide in her early twenties. When the news broke in 1998, it was treated as another in a long series of liaisons of which he had been accused through the years and which he routinely denied. In this case, Clinton's public denial under oath was contradicted by admissions he made about the Lewinsky affair in a deposition in the case of another woman who had accused Clinton of similar behavior. The Republican-controlled House of Representatives voted articles of impeachment, accusing Clinton of perjury and obstruction,

but the Senate voted to acquit him. Clinton later called the matter a "terrible moral error" on his part and a generally sympathetic media let the matter fade to a mere footnote in the institutional memory of his presidency.

After leaving office in 2001, Clinton assumed the role of a popular elder statesman. President George W. Bush named Clinton and his father, former President George H. W. Bush, to lead the American relief effort in the wake of the devastating Asia tsunami of 2004, a role that they reprised in 2005 in the wake of Hurricane Katrina on the American Gulf Coast. Acting as a philanthropist, Clinton started his William J. Clinton Foundation and the Clinton Global Initiative to collect money from wealthy donors for distribution to the needy around the world.

After leaving the White House, both William and Hillary Clinton became wealthy through book deals and speaking fees. When Hillary Clinton ran successfully for the US Senate from New York in 2000 and unsuccessfully for the 2008 Democratic presidential nomination, William Clinton was an active and energetic campaigner on her behalf.

President Clinton, with Mrs. Clinton, Chelsea Clinton, and Buddy the dog, in the Marine One presidential helicopter. *National Archives*

43

2001–2009

George W. Bush

REPUBLICAN PARTY

The second son of a president of the United States to be elected to the office, George Walker Bush was the fourth winner of a presidential election to have come in second in the national popular vote. Born on July 6, 1946, in New Haven, Connecticut, he was the eldest son of Barbara Pierce Bush and George Herbert Walker Bush, then a student at Yale, and later the forty-first president of the United States. The younger Bush grew up in Texas, but like his father, he attended Yale. After his graduation in 1968, he joined the Texas Air National Guard and served as a reconnaissance pilot. He was honorably discharged from the Air Force Reserve in 1974. In the meantime, he enrolled in the Harvard Business School, and became the only future president to earn an MBA. Bush met and married Laura Lane Welsh in Texas in 1977, and their twin daughters were born in 1981.

After running unsuccessfully for the US House of Representatives in 1978, Bush entered the oil business, starting a series of small exploration firms. In 1988, he worked on the staff of his father's successful presidential campaign, and in 1989, he became an investor in and managing general partner of the Texas Rangers, the American League baseball franchise in the Dallas–Fort Worth metroplex. In 1994, Bush was elected as governor of Texas. Four years later, he won a landslide reelection by the largest margin in Texas history.

In 2000, he ran for the Republican presidential nomination, losing only seven primaries to Senator John McCain of Arizona. At the Republican Convention, Bush chose Richard

top: An official portrait of President George W. Bush. *National Archives*

above: Standing atop the ruins of the World Trade Center with retired New York City fire-fighter Bob Beckwith, President Bush makes an impromptu speech on September 14, 2001. *National Archives*

"Dick" Cheney, former secretary of defense under his father, as his running mate. The night of the general election ended with the Democratic ticket headed by Albert Gore ahead, but with three states too close to call and with neither ticket having enough electoral votes to claim victory. Ultimately, a recount in Florida, the certification of which was held up by court challenges, gave the state to Bush by a razor-thin margin. Bush won in the Electoral College 271 to 266, though

President George W. Bush delivers his address to the nation from the Oval Office on September. 11, 2001. *National Archives*

FIRST LADY
LAURA LANE WELCH BUSH

Born in Midland, Texas, on November 4, 1946, Laura Welch was the only child of home builder Harold Welch and Jenna Louise Hawkins Bush. She graduated from Southern Methodist University in 1968 and became an elementary school teacher in Dallas, and later in Houston. In 1973, she earned a degree in library science from the University of Texas and was working as a librarian in Austin when she met George W. Bush in 1977. They were married on November 5, 1977, and their twin daughters were born on November 25, 1981.

Claiming little interest, she hosted no formal events during the six years that her husband was governor of Texas, though this changed when the Bushes moved to the White House. As first lady, she made it her mission to be an advocate for breast cancer awareness, for education, and for literacy. She traveled widely, with and without her husband, making several goodwill trips to Africa in connection with the Bush Administration initiative toward AIDS relief.

After her husband left office, she remained a popular public speaker, and active in a variety of non-profits such as the Laura Bush Foundation for America's Libraries, and the Laura W. Bush Institute for Women's Health at the Texas Tech University Health Sciences Center.

The Daughters of George W. Bush and Laura Welch Bush
Barbara Pierce Bush Coyne (1981–)
Jenna Welch Bush Hager (1981–)

above: First Lady Laura Bush calls on a young member of the audience to speak after she finished reading the book *The Spider and the Fly* by Mary Howitt at an October 2006 visit to the West Palm Beach Public Library in Florida. *White House via National Archives*

left: Laura Bush at the First Ladies Conference hosted by the LBJ Library in Austin, Texas, on November 15 , 2012. The one-day event was in partnership with American University, the White House Historical Association, the George Bush Presidential Library and Museum, and the George W. Bush Presidential Library and Museum. *National Archives*

above: The president walking through the White House Colonnade *National Archives*

Gore took 48.38 percent of the popular vote to 47.87 percent for Bush.

Having inherited a sagging economy, Bush planned an ambitious domestic agenda, including tax cuts and stimulus measures. However, the aftermath of the al-Qaeda terrorist attacks of September 11, 2001, against New York and Washington, DC, which killed nearly three thousand people, usurped much of the attention of the Bush Administration during its first term. Under what was termed the Global War on Terror, the initial response included a military intervention in Afghanistan, which had provided a sanctuary to al-Qaeda. Next came the 2003 invasion of Iraq under the belief that Saddam Hussein's regime possessed weapons of mass destruction, including nuclear weapons,

RICHARD B. CHENEY

Born in Lincoln, Nebraska, on January 30, 1941, Richard Bruce "Dick" Cheney was the son of Marjorie Lorraine Dickey Cheney and Richard Herbert Cheney. He grew up in Nebraska and Wyoming, attended Yale University, but dropped out. He graduated from the University of Wyoming in 1965 and earned a master's degree at the school a year later. He married Lynne Vincent in 1964, and they had two daughters.

He went to Washington, DC, as a congressional intern, joined the Nixon Administration as a staff assistant, and became chief of staff to President Gerald Ford. In 1978, Cheney was first elected to the US House of Representatives, where he served five terms. In 1989, President George H. W. Bush named Cheney to serve as secretary of defense, where he presided over the execution of Operation Desert Storm in 1991. With the Cold War over, Cheney advocated numerous cost-saving measures, downsizing, and the elimination of many high-priced weapons systems from the Defense Department budget.

In 1993, Cheney moved to the private sector as a director of the Council on Foreign Relations, and he served as chairman and CEO of Halliburton Company from 1995 to 2000.

In 2000, Cheney headed George W. Bush's vice presidential search committee, but wound up being invited onto the ticket in that capacity. As vice president of the United States, Cheney helped define the Bush Administration's goals in the Global War on Terror, and promoted the preemptive invasion of Iraq. Cheney's active role in helping to design policy was clearly more assertive than that taken by previous vice presidents, leading to suggestions that he was the real power center of the Bush Administration.

After leaving office, Cheney remained active in Republican Party affairs, and an outspoken advocate of conservative positions on many issues, despite serious health issues.

Dick Cheney. *National Archives*

above: President George W. Bush huddles with the enthusiastic cheerleaders of the US Naval Academy on the sidelines during opening ceremonies for the 105th Army-Navy football game on December 4, 2004. *US Navy*

below: President Bush during a visit to Brazil in November 2005. *White House*

which might fall into the hands of terrorists. After Hussein had been deposed, it was determined that he had not possessed such weapons, a revelation which led to extensive criticism of the invasion. The Bush Administration was also castigated for the use of "enhanced interrogation," described by critics as torture, in its dealings with captured terrorists and suspected terrorists.

Domestically, the Bush Administration added prescription drug benefits to Medicare, increased funding for the National Institutes of Health and National Science Foundation, and promoted—with bipartisan Congressional support—its No Child Left Behind Act of 2001, designed to establish educational standards with measurable goals to improve education. One of Bush's most far-reaching international initiatives was the President's Emergency Plan For AIDS Relief which reached millions in Africa and continued after his presidency.

In 2004, Bush and Cheney won reelection with 50.73 percent of the popular vote, and by a margin of 286 to 251 in the Electoral College, defeating a Democratic ticket headed by Massachusetts Senator John Kerry, with North Carolina Senator John Edwards as his running mate.

At the end of 2007, the United States and the world entered the so-called Great Recession, the worst economic downturn since World War II. Triggered by excessive debt and an epidemic of defaults on massive numbers of risky investments and questionable low-interest "sub-prime" loans, the sudden collapse brought down a large number of commercial and investment banks, sent stock markets and gross domestic product into decline, and resulted in a large increase in unemployment. The Bush Administration responded with the Emergency Economic Stabilization Act of 2008, which authorized $700 billion to purchase mortgage-backed securities and pump money into the United States financial system.

Bush maintained an approval rating of around 50 percent for most of his presidency, reaching highs and lows because of circumstances beyond his control. The terrorist attacks sent his ratings to 90 percent, while the Great Recession sent them below 20. After leaving office, Bush retired to Texas, wrote his memoirs, and became a popular public speaker in conservative circles.

above: George W. Bush with his father, former President George H. W. Bush, during a visit to the aircraft carrier USS *George H. W. Bush* on June 10, 2012. *US Navy*

below: President Bush confers with Vice President Cheney in the Oval Office. *National Archives*

Barack H. Obama

DEMOCRATIC PARTY

The first president from Hawaii, Barack Hussein Obama was born in Honolulu on August 4, 1961, the son of University of Hawaii anthropology student Stanley Ann Dunham Obama and Barack Hussein Obama Sr., a foreign scholarship student from Kenya. Married a short time, they separated shortly after the birth of the younger Barack Obama when Stanley Ann moved to Seattle to enroll at the University of Washington. In 1964, they divorced and the elder Obama returned to Kenya. In 1965, Stanley Ann married Lolo Soetoro, an Indonesian graduate student. She and her son moved with him to Jakarta, where the younger Barack Obama lived until 1971. Thereafter, they returned to Hawaii. Though his mother remained in Hawaii until 1975, he lived mainly with his grandparents, Stanley and Madelyn Dunham, until he graduated from high school in 1979.

Obama attended Occidental College in Los Angeles, and transferred to Columbia University, from which he graduated in 1983. After two years working in New York for firms including the New York Public Interest Research Group, he relocated to Chicago,

above: A button from Barack Obama's first campaign for the White House in 2008, showing his distinctive logo. *Author's collection*

top: President Barack Obama during a ceremony for recipients of the National Medal of Science at the White House on November 17, 2010. *NASA photo by Bill Ingalls*

where he worked as a community organizer before enrolling in Harvard Law School in 1988. He graduated in 1991, having served as editor of the prestigious *Harvard Law Review*, and returned to Chicago. Here, until 2004, he divided his time between a post on the faculty at the University of Chicago Law School and working as an attorney with the Sidley Austin law firm, where he specialized in civil rights litigation. It was at the firm that he met Michelle Robinson, a fellow attorney, whom he married in 1992. In the meantime, between 1997 and 2004, he also held a seat in the Illinois legislature.

In 2004, Obama entered the race for an open US Senate seat from Illinois, to which he was elected. Early in 2007, he announced his candidacy for the Democratic presidential nomination for president. During the 2008 primary season, he faced a close race with his principal opponent, former First Lady Hillary Clinton. She won in twenty-one states, including New York and California, while he won in twenty-nine. By June, Obama had secured the number of delegates necessary for nomination, and Clinton had dropped out to endorse him. At the Democratic Convention,

above: President Barack Obama signing a document at his desk in the Oval Office. *Official White House Photo by Pete Souza*

below: President Barack Obama talks with former President William Clinton in the Roosevelt Room of the White House on July 14, 2010. *Official White House Photo by Pete Souza*

he chose US Senator Joseph Biden of Delaware as his running mate. In the general election, Obama and Biden defeated the Republican challengers, US Senator John McCain of Arizona and his running mate, Alaska Governor Sarah Palin, by a margin of 365 to 173 in the Electoral College, and with 52.93 percent of the popular vote.

On the foreign policy front, Obama made good on his campaign promise to withdraw American troops from Iraq, which was completed in 2011. The timeline for a similar withdrawal from Afghanistan was extended several times. In 2014, a terrorist extremist movement calling itself the Islamic State of Iraq and the Levant (alternatively the Islamic State of Iraq and Syria) surprised the world by seizing large parts of Syria and Iraq, including Iraq's second largest city. Obama responded with limited air strikes and a small number of advisors, stating that he preferred Arab nations on the front lines to shoulder the responsibility of confronting the Islamic State. Obama was criticized for his limited and largely ineffective

FIRST LADY
MICHELLE ROBINSON OBAMA

The first African-American first lady, Michelle LaVaughn Robinson Obama was born on January 17, 1964, in Chicago, Illinois, the second child and first daughter of Fraser Robinson III and Marian Shields Robinson. Like her older brother, Craig Robinson, Michelle attended Princeton University, from which she graduated in 1985. In turn, she graduated from Harvard Law School in 1988, becoming the third first lady after her two immediate predecessors with a postgraduate degree. She returned to Chicago to work as an attorney at the Sidley Austin law firm, where she was assigned to mentor a new associate named Barack Obama. They were married on October 3, 1992, and their two daughters were born in 1998 and 2001. During the 1990s, Michelle Obama worked for various non-profit organizations and served as an associate dean at the University of Chicago. She was also active in her husband's political campaigns.

As first lady, she traveled widely, with and without the president, including a 2014 visit to China, accompanied by her daughters, and her mother—who is the first presidential mother-in-law since Elivera Doud, Mamie Eisenhower's mother, to live at the White House.

Michelle Obama spoke at both the 2008 and 2012 Democratic Conventions and became active on the lecture circuit, promoting such initiatives as the Childhood Obesity Task Force and advocacy on behalf of military families and working women.

The Daughters of Barack Obama and Michelle Obama

Malia Ann Obama (1998–)
Natasha "Sasha" Obama (2001–)

Michelle Obama's first-term official portrait. *White House*

President Obama goes over notes in the Red Room prior to a live prime-time press conference in March 2009. *Official White House Photo by Pete Souza*

response, as he had been for having not intervened in the 2011 Syrian Civil War when moderate factions were attempting to dislodge Syrian dictator Bashar al-Assad. Obama's critics maintained that non-intervention in support of the moderates early in that conflict had allowed an opportunity for the Islamic State to emerge and grow into a serious regional threat. Obama's non-interventionist foreign policy was also criticized in the context of the Russian occupation of Crimea and its military intervention on eastern Ukraine.

On the positive side, it was on Obama's watch that the ongoing efforts to kill al-Qaeda mastermind Osama bin Laden finally bore fruit in 2011 as members of the US Navy's elite SEAL Team Six caught up with the terrorist leader in Abbottabad, Pakistan.

During his first term, Obama made two appointments to the United States Supreme Court, naming Sonia Sotomayor in 2009, and Elena Kagan in 2010.

Domestically, Obama's largest and most controversial initiative was the Patient Protection and Affordable Care Act of 2010, referred to informally as "Obamacare." It was intended as a measure to extend health care coverage to uninsured Americans, which it did, though it fell short of its original goals. Passed with no Republican support, it was the largest regulatory measure in the field of health care since the passage of Medicare in 1965. Among its controversial provisions were mandates, enforced by the Internal Revenue Service, requiring individuals to purchase health insurance

VICE PRESIDENT

JOSEPH R. BIDEN

Twice an unsuccessful candidate for the Democratic presidential nomination in elections two decades apart, Joseph Robinette "Joe" Biden Jr. spent his early years in Pennsylvania, but later represented Delaware in the US Senate for thirty-six years. He was born on November 20, 1942, in Harrisburg, Pennsylvania, the eldest child of Catherine Eugenia "Jean" Finnegan Biden and car salesman Joseph Robinette Biden Sr. He attended the University of Delaware, but transferred to Syracuse University to be near Neilia Hunter, whom he married in 1966 one year after graduating from Syracuse. Biden earned his law degree from the Syracuse University College of Law in 1968 and became a member of the Delaware Bar in 1969.

Running as a Democrat, he was elected as a county councilman in 1969 and to the US Senate in 1972. Shortly after his election Biden was not present when his wife and daughter were killed in a car crash that injured his two sons. Deeply depressed, he considered resigning but did not. In 1977, he remarried to Jill Tracy Jacobs, with whom he had one daughter.

In 1988, Biden launched his first bid for the Democratic presidential nomination, entering a crowded field that ultimately narrowed down to the nomination of Michael Dukakis, who lost to George H. W. Bush in the general election.

Elected to the US Senate six times, Biden served on the Senate Foreign Relations Committee, and for many years as chairman or ranking member of the Judiciary Committee. He was popular with his Delaware constituency in part because he commuted into Washington, DC, from his Delaware home, rather that living full time in the nation's capital. In 2007, Biden once again announced that he was a candidate for the Democratic nomination, but he dropped out early in 2008 to endorse Barack Obama, who picked him as his vice presidential running mate.

Biden became known for his gaffes, which some people found endearing. Others used them to impugn Biden's intelligence or situational awareness. During the 2008 campaign, Biden famously told Katie Couric of CBS that "When the stock market crashed, Franklin D. Roosevelt got on the television and didn't just talk about the, you know, the princes of greed. He said, 'Look, here's what happened.'" Unfortunately, Roosevelt was not yet president in 1929, and television was still an experimental medium unavailable to the general public.

Obama tended not to use Biden as a serious policy advisor as George W. Bush had with Richard Cheney but utilized his connection with grass roots "retail" politics and labor unions to make public appearances at informal events.

In the 2012 campaign, when Obama's popularity was ebbing, there was talk of replacing Biden on the ticket, but the president remained loyal to his vice president and together, they won the election.

Jill Biden, Vice President-elect Joseph Biden, President-elect Barack Obama, and Michelle Obama at the Lincoln Memorial on January 18, 2009, during the inaugural opening ceremonies. *US Navy*

Pete Souza's famous photograph of the real-time monitoring of Operation Neptune Spear, which led to the killing of Osama bin Laden on May 1, 2011. The venue is a small conference room that is part of the Situation Room complex of rooms in the basement of the West Wing of the White House. Seated, from left to right, are Vice President Joseph Biden; President Obama; Brig. Gen. Marshall B. "Brad" Webb, Assistant Commanding General of the Joint Special Operations Command; Deputy National Security Advisor Denis McDonough; Secretary of State Hillary Clinton; and Secretary of Defense Robert Gates. Standing, from left to right are Chairman of the Joint Chiefs of Staff Admiral Mike Mullen; Assistant to the President for National Security Affairs Tom Donilon; White House Chief of Staff William M. Daley; National Security Advisor to the Vice President Tony Blinken; Director for Counterterrorism for the National Security Council Audrey Tomason; Assistant to the President for Homeland Security and Counterterrorism John O. Brennan; and Director of National Intelligence James Clapper. *Official White House Photo by Pete Souza*

and businesses to provide health insurance under penalty of fines. Adding to the controversy was Obama's own promise, made in numerous speeches in 2009 and 2010 that "if you like your health care plan, you'll be able to keep your health care plan, period." In fact, when the Affordable Care Act was rolled out in 2013, millions of people lost their existing health care plans, and found themselves scrambling for new plans that were much less affordable, causing the president's approval rating to sink to 39 percent.

Obama and Biden won reelection in 2012 with 51.06 percent of the popular vote, defeating former Massachusetts Governor Mitt Romney and his running mate, Wisconsin Congressman Paul Ryan, 332 to 206 in the Electoral College. Obama countered

Romney's experience as a businessman by pointing out to an audience in Roanoke, Virginia, on July 13, 2012, that "if you've been successful, you didn't get there on your own. . . . Somebody helped to create this unbelievable American system that we have that allowed you to thrive. Somebody invested in roads and bridges. If you've got a business—you didn't build that. Somebody else made that happen."

Though many provisions of the Affordable Care Act were postponed until after the 2014 midterm election, dissatisfaction with the law contributed to the Republicans gaining their largest majority in US Congress, in governorships, and in state legislatures since 1928. Many of the law's mandates and other provisions were unpopular with employers, as well as with trade unions, an important basis of Democratic Party electoral support.

During his second term, a major effort by Barack Obama involved negotiations with Iran aimed at limiting its ability to develop nuclear weapons. From the beginning of his presidency, Obama had expressed a desire to deal diplomatically with America's longtime antagonist. Even after international sanctions were imposed because of a potential Iranian nuclear weapons program, Obama continued these efforts. He favored a relaxing of sanctions to induce Iran to channel its nuclear program solely toward peaceful purposes. A comprehensive nuclear agreement was signed in Vienna on July 14, 2015, by Iran and the five permanent members of the United Nations Security Council plus Germany and the European Union. The agreement called for phasing out sanctions on Iran while allowing that country to continue to develop and modernize its nuclear infrastructure, while limiting for ten years the number of centrifuges that could be used for potential weapons-grade material. The agreement met opposition in Congress from those who felt that it did not go far enough in limiting Iran's weapons program. Prominent US Senator Charles Schumer led opposition within the president's own party, citing Iran's continued threats against Israel and the absence of limitations on Iran's nuclear program after ten years.

After the 2014 midterm election, another major initiative undertaken by the Obama administration was the use of executive orders to address environmental issues. In August 2015, the administration and the Environmental Protection Agency established the Clean Power Plan, described as "the first-ever carbon pollution standards for existing power plants, which will protect the health of our children and put us on a path toward a 32 percent reduction in carbon pollution by 2030." The plan called for increased restrictions on coal-fired power plants and a renewed effort toward solar power development.

Among other honors that he has received, Barack Obama was the 2009 recipient of the Nobel Peace Prize, awarded for "his efforts to strengthen international diplomacy and cooperation between peoples."

The President and King Abdullah II of Jordan meet the press in the Oval Office in 2013. *Official White House Photo by Pete Souza*

45

Donald J. Trump

REPUBLICAN PARTY

Businessman and real estate mogul Donald John Trump is the first American president since Dwight Eisenhower to have not previously held elective office, and the first president with no previous government or active duty military experience. He is also the oldest person to assume the office, and the first billionaire president.

Trump was born on June 14, 1946, in New York City's borough of Queens, the son of Frederick Trump and Mary Anne MacLeod Trump. Having graduated from the University of Pennsylvania's Wharton School, he joined the family construction and real estate business in 1968 and took control in 1971.

Having started with a multimillion-dollar loan from his father, Trump became a billionaire in his own right. Based in New York, he has also maintained business interests elsewhere in the United States and around the world. His real estate development activities have included residential and office skyscrapers, as well as hotels and casinos. His businesses were not always successful, and his hotel and casino holdings experienced six bankruptcies between 1991 and 2009. Other interests have seen him as the owner of an airline, a US Football League franchise, several beauty pageants, and other holdings. He is the author of several books, including the best-selling *The Art of the Deal* (1987).

A Republican for most of his adult life, Trump has also identified himself as a member of the Reform Party and as a Democrat at various times. In 2016, he entered the crowded field vying for the Republican presidential nomination. Running against opponents with elective experience, Trump

above: President Trump delivers his State of the Union address on February 28, 2017, with Vice President Mike Pence and House Speaker Paul Ryan behind. *Official White House Photo by Shealah Craighead*

top: Donald Trump on the phone aboard Air Force One on January 26, 2017. *Official White House Photo by Shealah Craighead*

was not taken seriously until he started winning primaries. He won 46 of 56 state and territorial primaries. Texas Senator Ted Cruz was second with seven.

In the November 8, 2016, general election, Trump ran against former first lady Hillary Rodham Clinton (see page 234), the Democratic Party nominee. Neither candidate won a majority of the popular vote, with Clinton garnering 65.9 million (48 percent), while Trump took 63 million (46 percent). However, Trump won in 30 states, netting 304

President Trump and North Korea's Kim Jong-un shaking hands during their Singapore Summit on June 11, 2018. *Official White House Photo*

electoral votes to Clinton's 227. As president, Trump adopted many pro-business, pro-growth measures, including regulatory reform and tax cuts, especially the Tax Cuts and Jobs Act of 2017, which cut the corporate tax rate to 21 percent and increased personal tax exemptions. According to the Bureau of Labor Statistics, unemployment, a key economic indicator, remained below 5 percent from 2017 to 2019. In 2019, it averaged 3.7 percent, the lowest rate since 1970.

Within his domestic policy agenda, Trump opposed the Affordable Care Act of 2010, and successfully advocated for the repeal of the ACA's controversial individual health care mandate. Meanwhile, Trump made lowering drug prices a priority and, in October 2018, signed legislation to accomplish this.

Among Trump's most controversial domestic initiatives were border security and immigration enforcement. His campaign promise to build a wall on the US-Mexico border was largely unfulfilled, but he did take measures to restrict immigration.

President Trump with UN Secretary-General António Guterres at the United Nations General Assembly on October 2, 2017. *Official White House Photo by Shealah Craighead*

IVANA ZELNÍCKOVÁ

Born on February 20, 1949, in Czechoslovakia, Ivana Zelnícková was Donald Trump's first wife. She was the daughter of Miloš Zelnícek and Marie Francová Zelnícková. An accomplished skier, she married Austrian ski instructor Alfred Winklmayr, but divorced him in 1973. She worked as a model in Canada before moving to New York in 1976.

She married Donald Trump in 1977 and soon became a prominent New York socialite. They had three children between 1977 and 1984. She became an executive in the Trump Organization, but the couple went through a bitter divorce in 1992.

FIRST LADY
MELANIA KNAUSS TRUMP

The second first lady after Louisa Adams (see page 36) to have been born outside the United States, Melanija Knavs (in German, Melania Knauss) was born on April 26, 1970, in Novo Mesto, Slovenia, when that country was part of Yugoslavia. She was the daughter of motorcycle dealer Viktor

MARLA ANN MAPLES

Donald Trump's second wife was born on October 27, 1963, in Cohutta, Georgia, the daughter of real estate developer Stanley Edward Maples and Laura Ann Locklear. A contestant in beauty pageants in her early years, she later became an actress on Broadway and in film.

She married Trump in 1993 and they had one child. In 1996 and 1997, she was the cohost of the Miss Universe pageant, which was owned by her husband. After their divorce in 1999, she worked as an actress and motivational speaker.

Knavs and Amalija Ulcnik Knavs. Having worked as a fashion model in Paris and Milan, she moved to New York in 1996. She met Donald Trump in 1998 and they were married in 2005.

A citizen since 2006, she was often criticized as first lady for supporting her husband's strict policies on immigration when she herself was an immigrant and a naturalized citizen. As a former model, the first lady's choices of apparel were widely and extensively scrutinized by the fashion press. First ladies typically adopt causes in the social arena, and the one undertaken by Melania Trump was the Be Best public awareness campaign, which opposes cyberbullying. She accompanied her husband on numerous overseas trips, including a 2017 audience with Pope Francis at the Vatican, and 2019 state visits to Emperor Naruhito in Tokyo and Queen Elizabeth II at Buckingham Palace.

**The Daughters of Donald Trump
and Ivana Zelnícková**
Donald Trump Jr. (1977–)
Ivanka Trump (1981–)
Eric Trump (1984–)

The Daughter of Donald Trump and Marla Maples
Tiffany Trump (1993–)

The Son of Donald Trump and Melania Knauss Trump
Barron William Trump (2006–)

The official White House portrait of Melania Trump. *National Archives*

President Trump delivers his State of the Union address on February 5, 2019, with Vice President Mike Pence and House Speaker Nancy Pelosi in the background. *Official White House Photo by Shealah Craighead*

Trump also drew condemnation for his campaign promise of a temporary restriction of travel into the United States from seven majority-Muslim countries.

In 2017 and 2018, Trump nominated two US Court of Appeals judges, Neil Gorsuch and Brett Kavanaugh, to fill vacancies as justices on the US Supreme Court. Both were approved by the US Senate on party line votes.

A major challenge faced by the Trump Administration involved speculation of Russian interference in the 2016 election, and the suggestion that the Trump campaign may have colluded with Russian agents. In 2017, a Special Counsel investigation led by former FBI Director Robert Mueller began. Known as the "Russia investigation" or the "Mueller probe," this inquiry examined links between the Trump campaign and individuals with ties to the Russian government, but concluded in its final report in 2019 that the campaign had not "coordinated or conspired with the Russian government in its election-interference activities." On the issue of the obstruction of justice, the report deferred further action to Congress.

President Trump and Ambassador Woody Johnson at the window of Winfield House, the official residence of the US Ambassador to the United Kingdom in June 2019. *Official White House Photo by Shealah Craighead*

Donald and Melania Trump with Britain's Queen Elizabeth II at Buckingham Palace in London on June 3, 2019. *Official White House Photo by Shealah Craighead*

Donald Trump golfing with Japan's prime minister Shinzo Abe on May 26, 2019, at the Mobara Country Club in Chiba, Japan. *Official White House Photo by Shealah Craighead*

In 2019, Congress began an impeachment inquiry in response to reports that Trump had used the threat of withholding foreign aid money to pressure Ukraine to investigate business dealings inside the country by the son of former US Vice President Joe Biden.

On international trade policy, Trump opposed multinational agreements, which he viewed as unfavorable to American businesses and workers. He withdrew the United States from the controversial Trans-Pacific Partnership, and moved to replace the 1994 North American Free Trade Agreement (NAFTA). With respect to trade with China, Trump sought to curb the widespread theft of American intellectual property by Chinese firms and reduce the steep and long-standing US-China trade deficit through the use of targeted tariffs.

President Donald Trump on the south portico balcony of the White House.
Official White House Photo by Andrea Hanks

Elsewhere on the international scene, Trump withdrew from the Joint Comprehensive Plan of Action aimed at preventing Iran's nuclear armament (aka the "Iran Nuclear Deal") and reimposed US sanctions against Iran.

In 2017, Trump ramped up American military actions against the Islamic State. By 2018, the contiguous "empire" in parts of Iraq and Syria controlled by this terrorist organization was reduced from around 81,000 square miles to practically nothing. The group itself, while badly mauled, was not defeated, and Trump was heavily criticized at home and abroad for his decision to withdraw American forces from Syria in 2019.

In an effort to curb North Korea's nuclear expansion, Trump became the first American president to meet face to face with a North Korean leader when he sat down with Chairman Kim Jong-un in 2018. No firm agreement has been reached, but to date Kim has curtailed nuclear tests.

In August of 2019, a whistleblower complaint was filed alleging that in July 2019, President Trump had abused his office by pressuring the president of Ukraine, Volodymyr Zelensky to investigate potential 2020 rival presidential candidate Joe Biden and his son Hunter Biden with the assistance

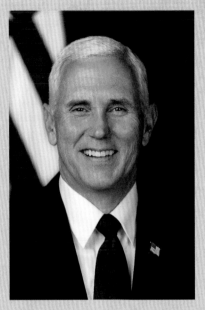
of Trump's personal lawyer Rudy Giuliani, associates of Giuliani, and even potentially Attorney General William Barr. If Ukraine did not cooperate, Trump would withhold military aid to the country. Additionally, the whistleblower alleged that the White House attempted to cover-up these discussions. In September 2019, the House of Representatives began an impeachment inquiry based on the whistleblower complaint.

On December 18, 2019, Trump became the third president in American history to be impeached by the House of Representatives, and the first to be impeached in the first term of his presidency. Two articles of impeachment were brought forth—abuse of power and obstruction of Congress.

Index

Presidents Jimmy Carter, Bill Clinton, Barack Obama, and George W. Bush enjoy a laugh on April 25, 2013, as they wait backstage to be introduced at the dedication of the George W. Bush Presidential Library and Museum on the campus of Southern Methodist University in Dallas. *Official White House Photo by Pete Souza*